APM

Teaching Christian Mission in an Age of World Christianity

First Fruits Press
The Academic Open Press of Asbury Theological Seminary
204 N. Lexington Ave., Wilmore, KY 40390
859-858-2236
first.fruits@asburyseminary.edu
asbury.to/firstfruits

APM

Teaching Christian Mission in an Age of World Christianity

The 2016 proceedings of
The Association of Professors of Missions

Edited by
Robert A. Danielson
&
Linda F. Whitmer

2016 APM Annual Meeting
St. Paul, Minnesota
June 16 - 17, 2016

Teaching Christian Mission in an Age of World Christianity
The 2016 Proceedings of the Association of Professors of Missions.

Published by First Fruits Press, © 2017
Digital version at http://place.asburyseminary.edu/academicbooks/18/

ISBN: 9781621716402 (print), 9781621716754 (digital), 9781621716761 (kindle)

For all other uses, contact
Association of Professors of Missions
108 W. High St.
Lexington, KY 40507
http://www.asmweb.org/content/apm

Teaching Christian Mission in an Age of World Christianity
The 2016 Proceedings of the Association of Professors of Missions.
    1 online resource (v, 247 pages) : digital
    Wilmore, Ky. : First Fruits Press, ©2017.
    ISBN: 9781621716402 (pbk.)
    1. Missions – Study and teaching – Congresses. 2. Missions – Theory – Congresses.
    3. Education – Philosophy – Congresses. 4. Teaching – Methodology – Congresses.
    I. Title. II. Danielson, Robert A. (Robert Alden), 1969- III. Hartley, Benjamin L.
    (Benjamin Loren) IV. Association of Professors of Mission annual meeting (2016: St.
    Paul, Minn.) V. Association of Professors of Mission. VI. The 2016 proceedings of
    the Association of Professors of Missions.
    BV2020 .A876 2016eb

Cover design by Jon Ramsey

About the Association of Professors of Mission

ROBERT DANIELSON, ADVISORY COMMITTEE MEMBER

The Association of Professors of Mission (APM) was formed in 1952 at Louisville, Kentucky and was developed as an organization to focus on the needs of people involved in the classroom teaching of mission studies. However, the organization also challenged members to be professionally involved in scholarly research and share this research through regular meetings. In the 1960's Roman Catholic scholars and scholars from conservative Evangelical schools joined the conciliar Protestants who initially founded the organization.

With the discussion to broaden membership to include other scholars from areas like anthropology, sociology, and linguistics who were actively engaged in mission beyond the teaching profession, the decision was made to found the American Society of Missiology (ASM) in 1972. Since the importance of working with mission educators was still vital, the APM continued as a separate organization, but always met in conjunction with the ASM at their annual meetings.

The APM continues as a professional society of those interested in the teaching of mission from as wide an ecumenical spectrum as possible. As an organization it works to help and support those who teach mission, especially those who often lack a professional network to help mentor and guide them in this task. Through its influence, the APM has also helped establish the prominence and scholarly importance of the academic discipline of missiology throughout theological education.

Table of Contents

Plenary Papers

Conference Papers

Conference Proceedings

Foreword

ANGEL SANTIAGO-VENDRELL

Teaching Christian Mission in an Age of World Christianity

The June 2016 Annual Meeting of the Association of Professor of Mission examined how the concept of World Christianity has impacted the teaching of mission. Mission and World Christianity are terms that seem to exclude each other. If Christianity is already a world religion, what is the need for mission? By the late 1970s, Andrew Walls drew attention to the fact that Christianity in the twentieth century was spreading and gaining converts mostly in the areas of Africa, Asia, and Latin America, while at the same time Europe and North America were experiencing stagnation and decline in numbers and fervor.

This recognition of Christianity as a world religion, spread over all six continents has given way to conceiving the study of mission, ecumenics, and interreligious studies under the new nomenclature of World Christianity. This new field of World Christianity studies the Christian faith as expressed in all six continents placing emphasis on the experiences of the poor, women of color, and marginalized communities in the Majority World. These churches at one time were known in missionary circles as "receiving" or "younger" churches.

Given that the majority of Christians now live in Africa, Asia, Latin America, the Caribbean and the Pacific, and that the gospel was spread mostly through indigenous Christians, how are we supposed to teach mission in North American colleges, universities, and theological seminaries? What role do the European and

North American churches play today? Are the experiences of Christians in the Majority World at the center of our teaching of mission in North America? What are the new resources for teaching mission in an age of world Christianity?

Papers were brought forward exploring theological metaphors or models for excellent teaching and thinking about teaching mission studies in an age of world Christianity. Historical, biblical, and theological factors continue to contribute to the changes one observes in modern mission studies.

It also becomes clear that changes in one's own teaching or in an institution's curriculum itself are necessary for promoting gender equality in mission studies. Case studies and other instructional methods focused on women can help put the study of Christianity in Africa, Asia, and Latin America into new forms of learning about the global nature of Christianity. As North American professors we must find ways to put the experiences of majority world women at the center of our research agendas.

We must also learn to deal with different cultural contexts and related constructs (e.g. conceptions of the self, face, power-distance, etc.) and how they affect teaching and learning for mission. We need new effective strategies to work with such differences in any given teaching context or in the multicultural classroom. As professors, we need to find new ways to communicate the spiritual experiences of Christians in the majority world to our students in North America. It is in this dynamic that we will find how mission interrelates with the new field of World Christianity.

Angel Santiago-Vendrell

2016 APM President

Conference Theme

Association of Professors of Mission
Annual Meeting
16-17 June 2016

Teaching Christian Mission in an Age of World Christianity

The 2016 Annual Meeting of the APM will examine the theme, "Teaching Christian Mission in an Age of World Christianity." Mission and world Christianity are terms that seem to exclude each other. If Christianity is already a world religion, what is the need for mission? By the late 1970s, Andrew Walls drew attention to the fact that Christianity in the twentieth century was spreading and gaining most converts in Africa, Asia, and Latin America while at the same time Europe and North America were experiencing stagnation and decline in numbers and fervor. This demographic shift and the recognition of seeing Christianity as a world religion spread in all six continents has given way to conceiving the study of mission, ecumenics, and interreligious studies under the new nomenclature of world Christianity. The new field of world Christianity studies the Christian faith as expressed in all six continents placing emphasis on the experiences of the poor, women of color, and marginalized communities in the Majority World. These churches were called at one time in missionary circles the 'receiving' or 'younger' churches. Given that the majority of Christians now live in Africa, Asia, Latin

America, the Caribbean and the Pacific, and that the gospel was spread mostly through indigenous Christians, how are we teaching mission in North American colleges, universities, and theological seminaries? If the explosion of Christianity in the Majority World was possible because Christianity was already being contextualized by local agency, what role do the European and North American churches play today? Are the experiences of Christians in the Majority World at the center of our teaching of mission in North America? What are the new resources for teaching mission in an age of world Christianity?

Theological and Historical Perspectives on Teaching Mission in an Age of World Christianity. What theological metaphors or models for excellent teaching and learning are most generative for thinking about teaching mission studies in an age of world Christianity? What historical, biblical, or theological factors seem to be contributing to the changes one observes in mission studies in an age of world Christianity?

Gender, Mission, and World Christianity. What changes in one's own teaching or in an institution's curriculum are necessary for promoting gender equality in mission studies? What case studies or other instructional methods best promote gender specific mission practices? What would the study of Christianity in Africa, Asia, and Latin America look like if scholars put women into the center of their research? What does putting the experiences of majority world women at the center of our research agendas means for professors in North America? How could this process be achieve?

Anthropological Considerations for Teaching Mission in an Age of World Christianity. How do different cultural contexts and related constructs (e.g. conceptions of the self, face, power-distance, etc.) affect teaching and learning for mission in an age of world Christianity? What strategies are most effective in working with such differences in any given teaching context or in a multicultural classroom? What are the ways for professors to mediate the spiritual experiences of Christians in the majority world to their students in North America?

Other subjects. Topics of particular interest to APM contributors but not directly related to the conference theme may still be submitted and will be considered by the conference organizers.

Persons interested in presenting papers may submit a proposed title with a 150-200 word abstract and a 30 word bio to APM president Angel Santiago-Vendrell at _angel.santiago-vendrell@asburyseminary.edu_ by February 15, 2016.

APM

Plenary Papers

Teaching Missiology in and for World Christianity Content and Method

Peter C. Phan
Georgetown University

Allow me first of all to extend my sincere thanks to Professor Angel Santiago-Vendrell for his kind invitation to address the Association of Professors of Mission at its annual convention on June 16, 2016. Not being a missiologist by academic training and by professional guild, it was with fear and trembling that I accepted to speak on the assigned topic of "Teaching Mission in an Age of World Christianity."

With a clear awareness of my scholarly limitations in the field of missiology, and from the etic perspective as it were, I will organize my reflections around three theses. The first will, I suspect, please you enormously as professors of mission. By contrast, the second will most likely raise a few eyebrows. The third attempts to resolve the apparent antinomy between the first and the second theses by proposing a way of understanding mission, and correlatively, the teaching of mission in and for World Christianity.

Briefly, my three theses run as follows: First, in World Christianity without missiology there can be no adequate theology. Secondly, the recent method of teaching missiology is ineffective for World Christianity. Thirdly, the future of theological education, including the teaching of mission, lies in the happy marriage between missiology and history of Christianity. However, before expounding these three theses, since their validity depends on the concept of World Christianity, I will begin with a brief exposition of what is meant by it as the context for our reflections on the teaching of missiology, with respect to both method and content. Throughout my paper my perspective is that of a Roman Catholic, but I hope that it is not provincial---though it certainly *is* that---but sufficiently open so that it may find resonances in other church traditions.

What Is "World Christianity"?

In the last couple of decades the expression "World Christianity," first used by Francis John McDonnell in his 1929 book *Human Needs and World Christianity*, together with its lexical cousin "Global Christianity," has appeared in the titles of a plethora of publications and study centers, especially in the fields of church history and missiology. Whether the expression is merely a trendy buzzword manufactured by clever publishers to peddle their books with a catchy title, or by desperate academic administrators to attract new enrollments to their dying institutions, or on the contrary, whether it signals a methodological and substantive shift in the study of Christianity as such, the answer depends on what is meant by "world" and "Christianity," taken separately or in conjunction, with "world" used adjectivally to qualify "Christianity."

If by "world" is meant that Christianity is by nature "global" or "catholic" (with the lower-case c), then the expression "World Christianity" is theologically trite, since Christianity, by intent and design, and from its very beginning, has been open to the whole world, whether by "world" is meant the created order (*kosmos*), or the inhabited earth (*oikumene*), or the present age (*aion*). Again, if "Christianity" refers to the religion or church that has its origins in Jesus of Nazareth and is professed to be one, holy, catholic, and apostolic as a transcendent reality apart from its manifold historical embodiments, the expression would not acquire any significantly new and earth-shaking meaning, even if qualified by "world."

What then is the new meaning of the expression "World Christianity" when "world" and "Christianity" are conjoined together? Wherein lies its novelty? As Dale Irvin has argued, the current concept of "World Christianity" emerged in the confluence of three disciplines, namely, missiology, ecumenical theology, and the study of world religions: "It continues to pursue a threefold conversation, across borders of culture (historically the domain of mission studies), across borders of confession or communion (the domain of ecumenics), and across borders with other religious faiths (historically the domain of world religions."[1] To these three fields I would add church history. How these four academic disciplines have conspired to produce the concept of "World Christianity," with the notion of "border" as its operative key, will be made clear in the course of my essay.

Out of the wide-ranging and profound permutations in the methods and subject-matters of these four fields, especially under the pressure of postmodern thought and postcolonial studies, both "world" and "Christianity" as historical and theological concepts, have acquired radically new connotations. First of all, "world" in "World Christianity" denotes much more than the so-called First World, namely, the West or the Global North, comprised of Europe and North America. From the geopolitical, economic and military perspectives, worldwide globalization has produced an ineluctable network of interlocking interdependence and reciprocal influence between the dominant First World and the so-called Third World, or Majority World that is comprised of Asia, Africa, and Latin America. Our contemporary world has become polycentric, with no one center, not even the United States as the remaining sole superpower, able to control and dominate, and not for lack of trying, the politics, economies and cultures of the other states. It goes without saying that this polycentricity has a deep impact on Christianity whose day-to-day existence is intimately interwoven with its host countries, especially on churches, such as the Roman Catholic Church, that have a strong central organization and therefore feel a heavy pressure for total decentralization. A transnational, transcultural, polycentric, and centrifugal Christianity has been rapidly emerging as a result.

---

1   Jonathan Y. Tan & Anh Q. Tran (eds), *World Christianity: Perspectives and Insights: Essays in Honor of Peter C. Phan* (Maryknoll, N.Y.: Orbis Books, 2016), 4.

As for "Christianity," the changes that have occurred within it since the end of the fifteenth century are even more radical. Demographically, there has been a steady movement of the Christian population, and with it the shift in the ecclesiastical center of gravity, from the Global North to the Global South. It is projected that by the middle of the 21st century four out of five Christians will live in the Global South. Of course, this shift in the ecclesiastical center of gravity does not necessarily bring about an immediate reduction in the power of Christianity of the Global North. But there is no doubt that Christianity of the Global South, with its vastly different and diverse doctrinal, liturgical, ethical, and organizational traditions, is radically changing the face and nature of Christianity itself, producing what is now called "World Christianity." This fact has been highlighted by mission studies which examine in detail the "younger churches" or churches in "mission lands"---to use the highly problematic nomenclature of the recent past---and call for a new methodological approach that rejects the old imperialistic dichotomy between "Christian lands/mission lands" and "historic churches/younger churches."

On its part, church history has undergone a thorough overhaul. Shedding colonialist and Western-centric blinders, church historians have come to recognize that there is not, nor has there ever been, *one* Christianity (read: Western); rather there exist Christianities (in the plural!), all over the world and all the time. As a result, a radically different methodology is advocated for church history; now even the nomenclature is changed from "church history" to "history of Christianity" to mark this paradigm shift.

Finally, two more aspects of World Christianity should be mentioned. Firstly, as the number of Independent Christians (such as Evangelicals, Pentecostals, and Charismatics) and the so-called Marginal Christians explodes in the Global South, the question of ecumenical unity becomes much more complex, challenging the model of church unity long advocated by the World Council of Churches and the Roman Catholic Church. Which model for ecumenical unity is appropriate for this new ecclesial reality is too soon to say, but no doubt it will be determined by the new features of World Christianity. Secondly, as Christianity is still a minority religion in Asia, Christians will live cheek by jowl with believers of other religions, and the nature and purpose of Christian mission, especially the question of conversion, will come in for close scrutiny.

In sum, then, by "World Christianity" is meant the kind of Christianity as a word religion that has always been but is becoming more than ever diverse, multiple, transnational, transcultural, and polycentric in all aspects of its life, due to demographic shifts, globalization, and migration. Thomas Thangaraj has drawn out three corollaries from this conception of World Christianity. First, it recognizes all local forms of Christianity as forms of the Christian faith, however limited and partial they might be. Second, it relativizes all local expressions of Christianity, ruling out the use of any of them as the benchmark of Christianity. Third, it enables the revitalization of Christianity through the interaction among the diverse local Christianities.[2]

Outside Missiology There Is No Theology

In this World Christianity, does missiology still have a role to play? Not so long ago Christian theologians, especially Roman Catholic, used to proclaim with great confidence the axiom: "Outside the church there is no salvation" (in the crisp Latin formula: *Extra ecclesiam nulla salus*). My deep admiration for missiology notwithstanding, I am not, at least not yet, prepared to pronounce: "Outside missiology there is no salvation" (*Extra missiologiam nulla salus*). However, I can affirm with self-assurance my conviction: "Outside missiology there is no theology" (*Extra missiologiam nulla theologia*). Since I am preaching to the choir, there is no need to mount an extensive defense for my quasi-infallible pronouncement. But there are at least three reasons to substantiate it, especially in light of World Christianity.

First, missiology keeps theology honest to its raison d'être and purpose. A classical definition of theology that goes back to Anselm of Canterbury, and further back, to Augustine, asserts that it is faith in search of understanding (*fides quaerens intellectum*). Informative as this characterization of theology is, it runs the risk of obscuring the real nature and *telos* of theology, which is not merely understanding but love, love that overflows and is shared with others. This joyful-sharing-of-love, which is brought forth by the Good News, is what Christian mission is all about. Pope Francis's two recent writings express well this intimate connection between faith and theology on the one hand and mission-in-joy on the other: *The Joy of the Gospel* (*Evangelii Gaudium*) and *The Joy of Love* (*Amoris Laetitia*). Without this innate orientation to mission-in-love, theology is often nothing more than a system of thought ("systematic theology"), not rarely formulated in complex philosophical categories and couched in impenetrable neologisms---preferably in German---but having little relevance for Christian living. In short, theology exists for mission.

The second reason why without mission theology is ineffective is that mission opens new vistas and perspectives for theology. Without mission, theology is bound to become a tribal, provincial, sclerotic in-house shop talk, often in air-conditioned university and seminary smart classrooms. By contrast, mission operates on the open and unfamiliar borders of countries, classes, ethnicities, genders, cultures, Christian denominations, and religions. Missionaries, as the etymology implies, are people-being-sent-out. By vocation they are border-crossers, and border-crossers

---

2   See Thomas. Thangaraj, "An Overview: Asian and Oceanic Christianity in an Age of World Christianity," in: Heup Young Kim, Fumitaka, and Anri Morimoto, eds., *Asian and Oceanic Christianities in Conversation* (Amsterdam: Rodopi, 2011), 15-17.

have the best opportunities to discover new and strange things. Without mission, contemporary would not have developed such trends as liberation, contextualization (inculturation), interreligious, and feminist, theologies, just to cite a few. In fact, it is missionaries who alerted theologians of the emergence of World Christianity occurring under their very own noses.

Thirdly, mission introduces theology to new partners-in-dialogue. The traditional conversation partner of theology is philosophy. Important as this discipline is, a theology that is limited to it is bound to be abstract, highbrow, and elitist. Again, it is mission that broke up the philosophy-theology exclusive club and brought to the dialogue table new disciplines such as literature, history, social psychology, cultural anthropology, sociology, ethnography, gender studies, cartography, linguistics, art and architecture, and even statistics, again only to cite a few. No systematic theology, theological ethics, and pastoral theology worthy of their names, can afford ignoring the contributions of mission in these fields today. In brief, *extra missiologiam nulla theologia.*

But Which Missiology?

I have been singing a full-throated hymn to missiology in the company of missiologists, which is not a hard thing to do. But which missiology? That is the million-dollar question. Since, I am not, as I have confessed earlier, a professional missiologist, the following observations are little more than impressions gathered from a reading of some textbooks on missiology written before "World Christianity" became a popular concept. If my critique is beside the point and does not apply to how you yourself teach missiology, more power to you, and my apologies. My following remarks then can be taken as simply a cautionary tale about the changes that must be made to the discipline of missiology and the teaching of mission in light of the new reality of World Christianity.

The first pitfall I would like to draw your attention to is the well-entrenched division in the seminary curriculum and academic scholarship between church history and missiology. While a division of labor and scholarly specialization are unavoidable, the division, and eventual separation, between church history and missiology is not dictated by merely practical considerations and jealous defense of disciplinary turf but is deeply ideological. In fact it can be traced back to the very missionary enterprise, first in the Roman Catholic Church in the sixteenth century, and then among the Protestant Churches, especially since the nineteenth century. There is no need to belabor the point about the intimate and intricate connections between Christian mission and the imperialistic, capitalistic, and colonialist activities of the West in Latin America, Asia, and Africa. Of course, I am referring to the institutional ties and official arrangements between the Cross and the Sword, and not to individual missionaries, among whom we find a cloud of heroic and saintly witnesses to the Gospel. While eternally grateful to the missionaries for their self-sacrificing work to bring the Good News to these continents and in the process uplifting the standards of education, healthcare, and social services, and in some cases, even contributing to the struggle for national independence against colonial powers, still we must in all truth and humility acknowledge and repent of the past alliance between church and empire.

Implicit in the subsequent separation between church history and missiology is the colonialist understanding of Christianity/Church as the West and mission as the Rest. Church history then deals with the Western churches, dubbed "historic churches," and missiology with "mission lands" with their presumably immature "younger churches," beholden in every way, not least financially, to the "historic churches." As a consequence, mission is understood exclusively as the activities of the Western "historic churches" *overseas* to plant churches in their own images. Thus the ideological divide between "modern" and "colonial" in secular history is replicated in the divide between the churches in the West ("modern") and the churches in the Rest ("Colonial").

Unfortunately, in this ecclesiological framework, both church history and missiology have paid a dear price. If you look at the older textbooks on church history, this is what you most probably find. The bulk of the historical narrative in church history deals with the West, and the lion's share of attention is given to the doctrinal, mainly Trinitarian and Christological, disputes and their settlement by various councils in the early church, then to the rise of the medieval church with the tug of war between the papacy and the Holy Roman Empire, next to the Reformation and its aftermath, and finally to the church's struggle against modernity. Little attention is given to the church's mission, and when it is, the focus is on the achievements of Western missionaries, especially church leaders, in founding churches, with nary a word about how local Christians, especially lay, contributed to the formation of local communities. Fortunately, more recent church history books have attempted, as I have alluded to above, a new approach by taking "World History" into consideration, but old patterns of thought die hard.

Not only is this version of church history Eurocentric but it also gives short shrift to mission, and as a result, skews the picture of Western Christianity. For example, the most momentous event in the modern life of Western Christianity is not the Enlightenment and the rise of deism and atheism and the consequent separation of Church and State but the extensive and lively missionary enterprise in the Roman Catholic Church, the Anglican Church, and the Protestant Churches. Without this missionary movement Western Christianity would have remained tribal and provincial and would have experienced a much worse decline that it is now.

The second pitfall in missiology is its inadvertent adoption of the narrow approach and tendentious narrative of "church history." Missionary practice has not yet caught up with the perspective of World Christianity. To put it briefly, it has not yet made the paradigm shift from "Church History" to "History of Christianity." Take, for instance, the Reformation. For fully understandable reasons, post-Reformation missionaries took the Catholic-Protestant divide for granted and carried out their evangelistic activities along denominational line. It was not until the 1910 World Missionary Conference at Edinburgh that church unity was made an imperative for the success of mission. As a result, many Protestant missionary societies were founded along interdenominational or nondenominational lines. Unfortunately, Christian mission in Asia was and is still being performed at best in comity but not in unity, especially between the Roman Catholic Church and the Protestant Churches. This division is being exacerbated by the presence of Pentecostals and Pentecostal-like church groups with their aggressive evangelistic style, often against Catholics and mainline Protestants. This has given rise to the strange but historically justified classification by the secular governments of several Asian countries of Roman Catholicism and Protestantism as two distinct "religions." (So far there is no legal classification of Pentecostalism as a separate religion, though when Pentecostal Churches have accepted to register with the State, they did so separately.) The Christian churches in Asia have de facto accepted this legal categorization without protest and without taking the initiative to clarify the theological issue. Mission history, and missionary practice, by and large still organize its narrative and organization along the denominational demarcation, thus making the Reformation, which was at bottom a family quarrel among the Western churches, into a dividing issue for World Christianity. This is all the more unfortunate as many recent bilateral ecumenical statements have declared that the key issues that divided the Reformation and the Roman Catholic Church are no longer church-dividing.

The third pitfall of missiology is, at least in some circles, its narrow focus on conversion/baptism and church-planting as the twofold goal of Christian mission. While it is possible to defend this view on the basis of selected biblical texts such as Matthew 28:18-20, dubbed the "Great Commission," a full-scale study of the *missio Dei* as narrated in the Old and New Testament would commend a more comprehensive conception of mission. The Federation of Asian Bishops' Conferences speaks of a threefold dialogue constituting Christian mission in Asia, namely, dialogue with the poor and marginalized Asians (liberation), with Asian cultures (inculturation or contextualization), and dialogue with Asian religions (interreligious dialogue). Mission in Asia is not only mission done *to* the pagan or unreached people (*missio ad gentes*) but also mission *among* the people (*missio inter gentes*) and mission *with* the people (*missio cum gentibus*). Thus, the church in mission is the People of God working for, among, and with the Peoples of God, not for the church itself, but for the Kingdom of God. Teaching missiology in this way responds to the challenges of World Christianity, in which all churches are local churches, with none at the center and the others at the periphery, with none as the historic church and the rest younger churches, with no part of the world as Christian territory and the rest mission lands. The modern/colonial divide does not run between the West and the Rest, but cuts through every single church, East West North South, in all the six continents, because the church as a whole and as such is by nature missionary.

Missiology *in* and *for* World Christianity

Where do we go from here in World Christianity? In his account of Christianity in South-central Asia, 1910-2010 Paul Josua Bhakiaraj begins with two vignettes. The first tells the story of a group of people, mostly men, from poor backgrounds in Dhaka, Bangladesh, who gather on Friday in a small room for worship. They are called the "Fellowship of the Ones Faithful to Jesus" (*Jama'at Isa imandars*). They begin their worship with enthusiastic singing of *bau gan* or folk songs, followed by the reading of Bengali scriptures and by the preaching of their leader who urges them to live devoutly in a society that is predominantly Islamic. They are not Christians but Muslims, but they maintain that they are Muslims who follow Jesus the Son of God because Jesus is a "Muslim," in the sense of one who surrenders to God.

The second vignette depicts the scene of thousands of people in Allahabad, Uttar Pradesh, India on a Sunday morning, who travel to *Yesu Mandir* [Temple of Jesus] in the *Yesu Darbar* [Court of Jesus]. At about half past eight, the service begins with a thunderous congregational shout: *Yesu Masih ki Jai* [Hail Jesus Christ!]. For about four hours the crowd of thousands sit listening in rapt attention to the gospel of *Yesu Masih* and singing hymns. The vast majority of the crowd are non-Christians and are poor. They are the new breed of *Yesu Bhaktas* [Jesus devotees] who come to the Court of Jesus to experience the power of Jesus to liberate them from their poverty, oppression, and battles against evil spirits, and to share with others how the peace, healing, and freedom that *Yesu Masih* gives them have transformed their lives.[3]

Let's travel from India eastward into China and meet a large group of new and bewilderingly varied religious movements that are inspired by or connected to Protestantism, especially of the Pentecostal type, and which are usually categorized as "Marginal Christians." These movements, with colorful and biblical-sounding names, can pop up anywhere with charismatic founders, quickly attract a large following, and are not officially registered. These include the Local Church (also known as the Shouters), the Established King Sect, the Lightning from the East,

---

3   See Paul Joshua Bhakiaraj, "Christianity in South-central Asia, 1910-2010," in Todd M. Johnson and Kenneth R. Ross, eds., *Atlas of Global Christianity* (Edinburgh: Edinburgh University Press, 2009), 142.

the Lord God Sect, the All Scope Church, the South China Church, the Disciples Sect (also known the Narrow Gate in the Wilderness), the Three Ranks of Servants, the Cold Water Sect, the Commune Sect, the New Testament Church (also known as the Apostolic Faith Sect), the Resurrection Sect, the Dami Evangelization Association, and the World Elijah Evangelism Association.[4]

The Chinese government criminalizes these as "evil cults" and arrests, fines, and imprisons their leaders and followers, especially those of the Local Church and its offshoot, the Lightning from the East. Ostensible reasons for this suppression are their heterodox beliefs (end-time predictions and deification of leaders), superstitious practices (derived from folk religion and Pentecostal healing practices) and threat to public order (large-scale activities and meetings), but their large size, rapid growth, and avoidance of government control also play a key role. The Chinese "house-churches" assiduously distinguish themselves from these groups, which they themselves condemn as heretical, partly because they do not want to be lumped with them as "evil cults," a deadly legal categorization, partly because these groups try to recruit members from them. India and China are but two examples that offer a dazzling variety of churches constituting World Christianity. To these may be added a long, dizzying list of no less perplexing and confusing independent or indigenous churches in other Asian countries, Africa, and Latin America.

How can missiology deal with these new ecclesial phenomena, which are part and parcel of World Christianity, alongside with other more traditional, so-called mainline churches? In no way do I claim to offer a solution to this missiological conundrum; nor do I think that a satisfactory proposal able to command a universal consensus is in the offing, given the fact that, as pointed out above, there is, nor has there ever been, one Christianity but rather that there exists a diversity and multiplicity of Christianities, and dramatically so in World Christianity. In light of this, I suggest that a happy marriage between missiology and history of Christianity (note: not church history!) is a good place to start.[5]

1. The church historian Justo González has suggested a new way of reading and writing the history of Christianity in and for World Christianity. For this purpose he suggests that we need a new cartography and a new topography. First, a new map. The demographic shift of the Christian population from the Global North to the Global South spoken of earlier requires a radical redrawing of the map of Christianity. A new cartography is needed to reflect this shift of the center of gravity of Christianity. There have been of course shifts of the centers of Christianity in the

---

4   See Fenggeng Yang, *Religion in China: Survival and Revival under Communist Rule* (New York: Oxford University Press, 2012).

5   The one analogous phenomenon is found in some early Jewish-Christian communities where a number of Jews accepted Jesus' teaching and even followed some Christian practices and still remained within Judaism. See Oskar Skarsaune and Reidar Hvalvik, eds., *The Jewish Believers in Jesus Peabody*, MA: Hendrickson, 2007). Unfortunately, soon the two faith communities parted their ways and became mutually exclusive.

past---from Jerusalem to Antioch, to Constantinople, to Western Europe, and to the North Atlantic---each time the map of Christianity got bigger. But this time the shift is radically different. In the previous shifts, one center was largely replaced, politically, economically, and ecclesiastically by the next; by contrast, today, world Christianity is *polycentric*, that is, it has many concurrent centers, so that there are Christiani*ties*, each being a local/regional/national Christianity, with none capable of claiming superiority over and normative for the others. In other words, it is not simply a geographically larger Christianity but a qualitatively *different* Christianity.

In addition to a new cartography, Justo González suggests, World Christianity requires a new topography. Maps are flat and do not represent the terrain accurately. Hence, the saying: "The map is not the territory." However, what is badly needed is not the familiar church topography, but a new topography, one that represents the systemic changes brought about by World Christianity. The old topography of church history is basically orography; it focuses on mountains and mountain chains. To shift the metaphor, the old topography of church history gives prominence almost exclusively to ecclesiastical leaders such as popes, bishops, and ecumenical councils. It is the ecclesiastical counterpart of the ancient secular historical genre *De viris illustribus* [note *viris*---males], as practiced by the Father of church history Eusebius of Caesarea in his *Church History*. In this genre, church history is the narrative of the achievements of ecclesiastical elites and intellectual virtuosi; it is the equivalent of the contemporary idol and celebrity talk and television shows. It is from these church elites and virtuosi---popes, bishops, councils, the Roman Curia, academic theologians---that systematic theology and missiology are constructed.[6]

While such a narrative can be informative and useful, it tends to lead to distortions and misrepresentations, as if these people were the only ones that constitute the church and the magisterium. By contrast, what is needed today in world Christianities is a new topography that highlights the valleys out of which mountains arise, a *koiladology* ---to coin a new word---which shows the beliefs and practices of ordinary Christians. Without them, church leaders could not have achieved the feats celebrated in past church history textbooks. Without their contributions, theology could not have been produced and transmitted. Consequently, the new *koiladology* will privilege the voices of the poor and the marginalized, including women, the colonized, the dalits, the people of color, the migrants and refugees, the young, and the people of the so-called Third World, where nearly four out of five Christians will live in 2050.

---

6   See Justo González, *The Changing Shape of Church History* (St. Louis: Chalice Press, 2002).

2. With this new approach and methodology for the history of Christianity in mind, how would one write a textbook on missiology? Where should we begin the history of Christian mission? Orthodox missiologists would begin perhaps with Constantine's moving the center of the Roman Empire from Rome to Byzantium in the fourth century; Roman Catholic missiologists with the so-called discovery of the New World in 1492 and the missions of the religious orders in the sixteenth century; and Protestant missiologists with the Pietists' mission in the eighteenth century.

But why not begin at the beginning, and more specifically, with the mission of the Apostle Thomas to India in 57 AD, when there was not yet even a Roman Christianity? Historical purists may object that there is no solid historical evidence that Thomas ever went to Kerala, and that the stories about his mission there belong to the genre of legend. It may be retorted that the number of historical references to Thomas' presence in India is greater than that of references to Peter's presence in Rome.[7] Be that as it may, beginning the history of mission with Thomas's evangelization of India has at least the virtue of adding another narrative to the hallowed Eurocentric history of mission, of introducing students to an unfamiliar culture, of acquainting them to another church tradition, namely. the Syriac, in addition to the Greek and Latin traditions, and thus inviting them to rethink Christianity in terms of World Christianity?

If one is reluctant to anchor the history of mission in an allegedly improbable event, then start with something that is incontrovertibly historical, as testified by the Xian Stele erected in 781, namely, the missionaries of the Church of the East, misnamed Nestorian, led by the monk Alopen, (Aluōbên), who came to Chang-an (modern Xi'an) in 635 during the Tang dynasty. Again, this alternative history of mission, like the one that begins with St. Thomas's mission to India, has the advantage of introducing our often historically and culturally challenged students to a different non-Western land, language, culture, people, and church tradition. This will disabuse them of the common notion that Christian mission began from Rome, or Canterbury, or Geneva, or the United States. Furthermore, the text inscribed on the Xi'an Stele offers an unparalleled example of contextualizing the Christian faith into a non-Semitic and non-Western context, with an extraordinarily bold employment of Buddhist, Confucian, and Daoist concepts and terms to express the Christian beliefs.[8]

In summary: We have seen how the rise of World Christianity, which highlights the diverse and multiple forms of Christianities, especially in the Global South, and their polycentricity, has vast implications for the study of the history

---

7   On St. Thomas in India, see George Menachery, ed., *The Thomapedia* (Ollur, Kerala: St. Joseph's Press, 2000).

8   For an introduction to the early Chinese Church, see Martin Palmer, *The Jesus Sutras: Rediscovering the Lost Scrolls of Taoist Christianity* (New York: Ballatine Wellspring, 2001).

of Christianity and missiology. But what about the future of World Christianity itself? Will it survive and prosper? More importantly, what are the tasks it should carry out in order to survive? And how should it do so?

Prognosticating the future of religions, especially of Christianity, is an extremely hazardous business. Their obituaries, like that of Mark Twain, have been vastly premature, and the intrepid forecasters of the death of God—and of religion—from Nietzsche to Marx to the "New Atheists," have been buried if not by God, certainly by religion, whose "return" has been loudly rumored in recent decades. But if out of modesty we should refrain from prognosticating the future of World Christianity, we can at least reflect on what Christians must do—and how well—to respond to the new challenges facing World Christianity.

In concluding their book *World Christianity in the 20th Century*, Noel Davies and Martin Conway suggest six ways to ensure the health and flourishing of World Christianity. First, to emphasize less quantity of growth and more quality of witness, to increase not number but Christian commitment and discipleship. Second, to practice mission not as sending missionaries from North to South, West to East but as mutual witnessing for the transformation of the whole person and the whole of society, each in one's own location. Third, to be Christian in a locally rooted and globally aware way. To use a neologism, to be Christian "glocally." Fourth, to be firmly rooted in the Christian Tradition and to be open to creative change; in other words, to be dynamically faithful. Fifth, to promote worship in a way that is both contextual (or local) and universal; its vibrancy derives from the combination of both of these elements. Sixth, to build up the church and to act for justice and peace. These two activities do not exclude each other, rather the efficacy of one depends on that of the other.[9]

It is not difficult to add another list of tasks to these. But the important thing for Christians to remember is that the future of World Christianity is not in Christians' hands, though of course they do have a part to play. Rather its future lies in the faithfulness and loving mercy of God—God's *emet* and *hesed*—to use two descriptions of God in the Hebrew Bible, which Jesus himself embodies in his promise: "I am with you always, to the end of the age" (Matthew 28:20).[10]

---

9   See Noel Davies and Martin Conway, *World Christianity in the 20th Century* London: SCM Press, 2008), 288-293.

10 Some of the ideas in this essay can be found in an earlier piece, "World Christianity: Its Implications for History, Religious Studies, and Theology," *Horizons* 39/2 (2012), 171-188, which contains a large bibliography pertinent to the theme of "World Christianity," not listed here for lack of space.

The Bodies We Teach By: (En)Gendering Mission for Global Christianities

MAI-ANH LE TRAN

Association of Professors of Mission (APM) Annual Meeting
June 16-17, 2016
University of Northwestern
St. Paul, MN

On October 22, 2010, a fire broke out and destroyed the 129-year old Immanuel Chapel at Virginia Theological Seminary in Alexandria, Virginia.[1] Among the terrible losses were the chapel's beloved stained glass windows illumined by the iconic words, "Go ye into all the world and preach the gospel." In her book, *Rethinking Mission in the Postcolony* (2011), constructive theologian Marion Grau of Oslo recounts the incident and a "postcolonial" quip that proves postmoderns' occasional affinity for supernatural signs: "There are not a few who have wondered whether this 'Great Commission' did not go up in flames some time ago, and what might be left in the smoldering embers of its claims."

As a 4th-generation Vietnamese by-product of missionary-driven Christian nurture forged in early-20th-C Vietnam, I am delighted to be invited to face your field of Christian mission studies (or "world Christianity") at a moment of profound reflexivity and flux. One can see why this necessary introspection, done in correspondence with an intensifying inversion of an academic field of study, could result in no less than what some have called a "conversion of the missionary self"[2]—an epistemological reckoning with historically polydoxic and embattled "techniques and technologies"[3] of missiology, now that the "mission field" is closing in, Christianity has permutated explosively in the "Majority World," and formerly "receiving" churches are talking back to their dominant centers of origin in Europe and North America.

As the Call for Papers for this annual meeting suggests, your field has had to retrace its disciplinary itineraries (to borrow Grau's language) to rediscover the ways in which the study (and the teaching) of "mission" has been done with what Grau calls "Great Omissions." Among them are two thematic strands explored by you this weekend—and also the focus of this plenary:

1) "[the] absence and erasure of the theological and linguistic contributions of local interlocutors in the consideration of mission history, interfaith and intercultural encounter"; and

---

1   http://www.episcopalchurch.org/library/article/virginia-fire-destroys-vts-chapel (accessed June 5, 2016)

2   Grau, *Rethinking Mission*, 21. Citing Joerg Rieger, "Theology and Mission," 222.

3   Grau, 17.

2) "the absence in dominant accounts of mission history of the contribution of women, as missionaries and as local interlocutors and the implied limitations of what is considered "mission."[4]

It is a terrible yet exciting hermeneutic quagmire for contemporary scholars of any theological discipline to reconcile: the "great omissions" of our long-standing study of the "Great Commission." It is exciting because now, the field of "Christian mission studies" must also mean critical inquiry into what many have described as porous, polydoxic, and polycentric engendering of "good news" in so-called "zones of symbiotic, translational interaction" between peoples and cultures (that's a nod to postcolonial theorist Homi Bhabha), across times and spaces, and buttressed by the infrastructures of "empire and divinity."[5]

Our excitement veils a more embarrassing aspect of internal field examination, because we know by now that our great omissions are no mere accidental academic "oops." As has been argued in theology writ large, we are looking at the enduring struggles of "canon wars" and the enduring politics of production and erasure of presence and contribution. Here, the piercing laments of second-wave feminists of various discursive communities are helpful in re-orienting what is at stake for us all. These boundary transgressors were *not* just asking the question, "why am I excluded?"— knowing from experience that the response may very well be strategies of paternalistic, tokenistic, supplemental addition. Rather, they queried the concerted intellectual effort it takes to sustain an exclusionary canon as it is. Literary giant Toni Morrison spoke to the heart of this in an emblematic question: What intellectual feats had to be performed by the author or his critic to erase me from a society seething with my presence, and what effect has that performance had on the work?[6] At this acute angle, we realize that the task is not simply to figure out "what to include" in our teaching of a field, but to more fundamentally interrogate and refigure the hermeneutic assumptions that facilitate the very framing of the field.

In doing this, we are asking questions that are native to educational theory and philosophy, and I am delighted that you have welcomed me as a "pedagogy junkie" in your midst for this cross-disciplinary conversation. Allow me, if you will, to speak from a knowledge base that is closer to my wheelhouse—that of critical pedagogy—to invite us all to ponder the possibilities of a critical *intersectional pedagogical stance* that may be fitting for the teaching of "Christian mission" in an age in which Christianity remains dominant, albeit not in numbers. At this

---

4　Grau, 18.

5　Grau, sic passim.

6　Toni Morrison, "Unspeakable Things Unspoken: The Afro-American Presence in American Literature," *Michigan Quarterly Review 18*, no. 1 (1989): 11-12. Cited in Ruth Behar, "Introduction: Out of Exile," in *Women Writing Culture*, ed. Ruth Behar and Deborah A. Gordon (Berkeley: University of California Press, 1995), 10.

intersectional location, the missiologist is a "teaching body" inasmuch as they are an "interpreting body." Thus, to explore who we are as "teachers of mission" with attention to great commissions and omissions, we ask two guiding questions:

1. What does it mean to take seriously *our* teaching bodies?

2. What does it mean to take seriously the bodies *with* and *about* whom we teach?

(Marion Grau asked these same questions of hermeneutics: "What does it mean for bodies to interpret? What happens when we interpret bodies?"[7])

Let's take the first question.

What does it mean to take seriously *our* teaching bodies?

I begin with the following striking words by education theorist Freema Elbaz-Luwisch:

> There is a body in the room. We ignore it . . . . Usually, of course, we ignore the body by ignoring it—we don't speak about it, we don't look directly at it, we change the subject quickly if there's a risk of noticing it. Sometimes, however, we have to ignore it by speaking about it—by saying the right things and then carrying on with our assigned topic.[8]

The ignored "body in the room" in the quotation refers to an educator's lament over the body dilemmas of those teaching in lands ravaged by conflict and violence in Israel and Palestine, where "Xs" mark the spots on the ground where bodies lay lifeless due to unceasing, brutal transnational identity politics. Few US (theological) educators could fathom their teaching/learning environments to be so deadly--unless you are teaching on the "wrong" side of town in some parts of this country ... or you are practitioners and professors whose "subject matter" is typically conceived to be an open, unknown, perhaps even perilous "mission field" that is somewhere out there.

Just as missiology has relied upon anthropology and ethnography for instincts about positional reflexivity, critical pedagogists remind us that every teaching/learning location is an "ever-changing confluence of culture, environment, politics,

---

7   Grau, 7.

8   Greenwood, "Education in a Culture of Violence," 351. Citing Elbaz-Luwisch, "How Is Education Possible When There's a Body in the Middle of the Room?," 9.

and power," and that the teacher must inevitably respond to the tides of their social location.[9] This conviction follows the liberationist educational philosophy of Brazilian education reformer Paulo Freire.

". . .[E]ducation is by nature social, historical, and political," Freire famously declared. "[T]here is no way we can talk about some universal, unchanging role [or identity] for the teacher."[10] Thus, just as theology cannot be spoken from a position of nowhere, the contemporary teacher of mission must reckon with the *intersectionality* of their social location—the ways in which their teaching bodies are particularly raced, classed, nationalized, and sexualized not only out there in the (mission) field, but also in the academy ... and even in the pages of their writings.[11]

Here, the existential crises of academics "minoritized" by gender and race—particularly academics of the empirical sciences—are poignant and illuminating. I stress empirical studies because, arguably more than scholars of other disciplines, these scholars must immerse their bodies in "the field" both figuratively and literally. What does it mean to teach with bodies that are constantly configured by the political markings of the multiple socio-cultural fields which we must navigate? (A more direct translation for the field of missiology could be: How do men's and women's *bodies* appear in the discourses of mission studies?)

REFLECTIVE MOMENT [2 min]

Would you take 2 minutes to chat with a neighbor about
what comes to mind as you free-associate with the notions
of "visibility, vulnerability, and viability" of the teaching
body?

Visibility, Vulnerability, Viability

In recent years, women academics of color have broken tough ground in bearing witness to the struggle to be taken seriously within majority institutions of higher learning. Anthologies such as *Still Searching for Our Mothers' Gardens*[12] invoke the rallying cry of earlier generations of feminist/womanist scholars to continue the tradition of narrating counter-stories of the multiple jeopardy of scholar-teachers whose positionality is minoritized by the intersections of race,

---

9   Greenwood, 356.

10   Freire, "Letter to North-American Teachers," 211.

11   This hermeneutic strategy follows postcolonial feminist cues, as modeled by Mohanty, *Feminism without Borders*, 5.

12   Niles and Gordon, eds., *Still Searching for Our Mothers' Gardens*. Cf. Alice Walker 1983 classic. Early respected anthologies of Asian feminist voices include Making Waves, edited by Asian Women United of California, and *Dragon Ladies,* edited by Sonia Shah. A more recent contribution edited by Gabriella Gutiérrez y Muhs, *Presumed Incompetent: The Intersections of Race and Class for Women in Academia,* is garnering much attention.

faith, gender, sexuality, and nationality. With anecdotal honesty, empirical details, painstaking research, and analytic sharpness, these educators testify to inscrutable academic dilemmas imbedded in familiar taxonomies of struggle: the problem of diversity, (in)difference, sex- and color-"blindness"; the complications with voice, power, agency, and "otherness"; the constricting normative gazes of dominant audiences; the fragmenting territorialization of identity politics; the insufferable practices of profiling, prejudice, and structural discrimination; the vexing curricular tensions and classroom power dynamics; the tenuousness of collegial ally-ship, institutional negotiations, and disciplinary politics (e.g., the feminization of a field). Three generative themes illustrate this web of complexity: the themes of "visibility, vulnerability, and viability."[13]

FIRST, the problem of VISIBILITY.

Visibility—being seen—already means to be judged by what one looks like. This enfleshment of teaching bodies is not freeing, but rather fear-ridden for minoritized teachers due to the knowledge that one is constantly under the shadows of scrutinizing gaze. It is a form of psycho-political exposure which turns teachers into what educator Ana Maria Freire calls "interdicted bodies"—"forbidden to be," inhibited through self-monitoring.[14] At the intra- psychic level, the demands of physical, mental, and emotional health beckon prudent attention to care of self, but such concern is often difficult to negotiate within the *habitus* of institutional and academic life. Physiologically, female teaching bodies are inevitably sexualized by mere appearance, even as we are supposed to assume an androgynous identity performance. Who cares when the teacher is only supposed to be a disembodied "talking head"—mentally objective, emotionally persuasive, physically virulent?

With biology being culturally and politically charged, we recall Audre Lorde's description of the "mythical norm" which haunts marginalized female consciousness: "white, thin, male, young, heterosexual, christian, and financially secure."[15] "Somatophobia" ensues as academics contend over which "-ism" is more malignant (sexism or racism), forgetting that "flesh-loathing" attitudes arise out of "interlocking" or "intersectional," not additive, type- casting—the entwining of misogynistic, racist, heteronormative, classist, ageist, imperialistic, colonialist, jingoistic, capitalistic, and even militant type-casting of "difference."[16]

Taking seriously the standpoint feminist concepts of *positionality* (identity is placed- based, situational and contextual) and *intersectionality* (identity is constructed and performed within a matrix of dynamic, intersecting social identity

---

13 Foss-Snowden, 83. Citing Mitchell, "Visible, Vulnerable, and Viable."

14 Freire, *Teachers as Cultural Workers*, 9.

15 Lorde, *Sister Outsider*, 116.

16 Spelman, *Inessential Woman*, 26, 126.

markers),[17] it is important to take account of the very particular ways in which oppressive body (stereo)types serve as identity straight-jackets. This entails rejection of essentializing tropes of identity—especially "victimhood" identity, as third-wave feminist scholars have long argued. Instead, we scrutinize "visibility"— being seen—along the intersecting "historical, geographical, cultural, [and] psychic" dimensions.[18] Visibility often functions as a source of *de*-authorization. One must look the part, and it is a white-water rafting adventure to figure out which part is desired at which moment. Desperate attempts could result in "cultural impersonation," or the mimicry of projected identity (stereo)types in order to fit in or blend in at all cost.[19]

Here lies a Catch-22: is it better to be *in*visible? That is a converse dilemma for the teaching body. It is the problem of the second "V"—VULNERABILITY.

Whether visible or invisible, the marked teaching body is *vulnerable* when it comes to various levels of performance evaluations. The cooperative of women faculty of color in the aforementioned anthology reports higher external and self-imposed expectations when it comes to identity and performance evaluations. Entrenched within the institution of academic disciplines are implicit, covert standards by which scholars are assessed, and according to which vulnerable teachers may be found wanting. As the evaluative criteria for the "holy trinity" of the academia (research, teaching, and service) constantly shift, our approval ratings wax and wane based on what is deemed "valuable" at various moments.

This vulnerability of having to "write [oneself]" into the mainstream of one's discipline and guild is portrayed with analytic lyricism in the ground-breaking anthology for anthropology and ethnography, *Women Writing Culture*, edited by Ruth Behar and Deborah Gordon. Reflecting on the quest for legitimacy among distinguished *men* who deem their work lacking of disciplinary rigor and innovation, these women writers must reckon with the fact that the competition for legitimacy requires them to write each other *off*, even as they endeavor to reclaim the trail-blazing paths of the "foremothers" of their field.[20] It is akin some variation of contemporary television reality shows, in which one calculates and connives one's way toward the winner circle. Space is limited, after all. There is usually only room for one or two.

---

17 See Harding, "Gendered Ways of Knowing and the 'Epistemological Crisis' of the West."
18 Mohanty, 106.
19 Mohanty, 102. Floyd-Thomas and Floyd-Thomas, "Emancipatory Historiography as Pedagogical Praxis," 127. The "superwoman-villain dichotomy" is attributed to womanist scholar Katie G. Cannon.
20 Behar & Gordon, 11.

The minoritized scholar bears the weight of representation in what Willie James Jennings calls an "economy of display"[21]: they must prove that their presence serves the discipline's best interest; they must fight to make context-specific perspectives and concerns *central* rather than peripheral to the "mainstream" curriculum—and they must not offend in doing so; they must demonstrate credibility and integrity in their craft, all the while mastering the art of ventriloquism; in other words, they must be fluent with the dominant "discursive currency."[22]

The paranoia over tokenism, "not living up to standard," or impostership often results in self-censoring. Minority bodies suspected of having an "agenda" are subjected to surveillance and regulation.[23] When there pervades within the cultural climate the bigotry of post-racial or post-feminist blindness, one often hears hammed-up cries of "reverse racism" or "reverse sexism": "It sure is rotten to be a straight White male these days!" someone would declare. The racial-ethnic minority female teacher suddenly realizes the vulnerability of her teaching task: on the one hand, she desires to expose a variety of "invisible" privileges at work such a statement and worldview; on the other hand, she is aware of the potential risks of being dismissed wholesale for alleged political bias.

One could charge that majority academic institutions operate by the principle of *unnatural* selection. It is not so much "survival of the fittest," because Darwinian natural selection assumes that species that can adapt to their immediate environment will survive. In this case, no matter how hard they try to "fit in," some teaching bodies remain vulnerable to (r)ejections from their host environments. The *viability* of the teacher as "outsider within"[24] is dependent upon their ability to cultivate coping mechanisms for both **pluri-cultural** and *fringe* existence.

This takes us to the third "V"—VIABILITY.

What would it take for the teacher to remain *viable* in a constant state of insecurity, isolation, or alienation? Minoritized teachers have called for a variety of "fringe" practices for institutional maneuvering, some of which will be highlighted later on.[25] But meta-reflections by Willie James Jennings on the "architecture of intellectual desire" are evocative for our thinking about viability.

---

21 Willie James Jennings, "What Shall We Teach? The Content of Theological Education," in *Teaching for a Culturally Diverse and Racially Just World*, ed. Eleazar S. Fernandez (Eugene, Oregon: Cascade Books, 2014), 117.

22 Ibid., passim.

23 Foss-Snowden.

24 Gordon, "Watching My B/lack," 47.

25 See Gatison, "Playing the Game."

In a recent anthology edited by Eleazar Fernandez, titled *Teaching for a Culturally Diverse and Racially Just World*, Willie Jennings laments: "[a]t heart, we ["otherly marked" academic Subjects] are still confronted with living in a house we did not build."[26] Describing theological curricular design as analogous to "an architectural structuring of intellectual desire," propelled by particularly configured white, male, heteronormative "historical inertia," Jennings describes a "love/hate psychical condition"[27] suffered by "otherly marked" academics who are acutely aware that they are "resident aliens" in an ivory tower not designed for them. Jennings puts it bluntly: women and racial/ethnic faculty of color live in a house/empire built by the Master[28] for his sons, and we have been trained to employ—with skill and artistry— disciplinary tools created within historic moments in which we were never imagined as likely inheritors. More disconcerting is the reminder from scholars of fields such as the natural and social sciences that a number of academic disciplines, of which missiologists are contemporary borrowers, were "from their inception" used to master us—e.g., geology, tropical medicine, anthropology were born "in service of Europe's colonial enterprise."[29] Following Jennings- speak, within this *habitus*, the academic navigates "conceptual fetishes" that undergird the "desired structures" of the discursive space, which in turn structure their very own intellectual desires.[30] A viable teacher is one who is able to assess these embedded "logics of habitation," and is able to re-create the space through their own realized imaginative *desire*, rather through inherited structured design.

We will think about what this means for teaching tactics later on. For now, all of this said, a generative question that has *not* been answered pertains to the bodies that enjoy the "mythical normal" status: What does it mean to take seriously that ideal "white, thin, male, young, heterosexual, christian, and financially secure" teaching body? How must those bodies reckon with their intersectional privilege?

REFLECTIVE MOMENT:

Would you take 2 minutes to share brief thoughts with a neighbor on this?

---

26 Jennings, "What Shall We Teach?," 110.

27 Ibid., 111.

28 A reference to Audre Lorde's ground-breaking metaphoric essay in *Sister Outsider : Essays and Speeches*, Crossing Press Feminist Series (Freedom, CA: Crossing Press, 1984).

29 Angela P. Harris and Carmen G. González, "Introduction," in *Presumed Incompetent : The Intersections of Race and Class for Women in Academia*, ed. Gabriella Gutiérrez y Muhs, et al. (Boulder, Colo.: University Press of Colorado, 2012), 5.

30 Jennings, "What Shall We Teach?."

What does it mean to take seriously the bodies *with* and *about* whom we teach?

We have asked what it means to take our teaching bodies seriously. Next comes the question, what does it mean to take the bodies that we teach seriously? What does it mean for "ex-centric," "interdicted" bodies to *occupy* a central place in the canon of your field?

Here we go back to the issue of "canon wars" mentioned earlier. Here we probe more deeply what it means to correct the omissions of our academic "canons." Contrary to many academics' instincts, the solution to this curricular dilemma is *not* one of arithmetic. That is to say, you cannot solve this by doing addition—add to the great intellectual mansion an extra room here for this group, a room there for that group ... so that those who want "inclusion" can have their place around the center, too. I've also heard of yet another equally problematic solution: Just move out of the house! If the Master's house is cramping your style, just move out. Build yourself another home; establish your own canon; write your own textbook!

While in some measure legitimately and strategically pragmatic, these solutions come with challenges. We can enumerate a few here:

First, the problem of "omission" is *not* a problem of those being omitted; rather, as was referenced earlier in Toni Morrison's quotation, it is a problem of those who are fighting hard to maintain their intellectual center and mono-centrism. Thus, the question for the discipline of Christian mission studies is *not* what to do with those whom we've excluded, but rather what to do with those who continue to engage in exclusionary strategies. It is time to examine: how has your own work been impacted by this long-standing practice of omitting women's contributions to the history of missions? How has the field been impacted by this insidious technology of exclusion?

Second, the problem of omission cannot be remedied by appendices. Additive inclusion operates on convenience, essentialism, and repressive tolerance. German philosopher Herbert Marcuse wrote an essay on the notion of "repressive tolerance" in 1965. In it, Marcuse argued that what masquerades as democratic tolerance of multiple views and contributions "always ends up legitimizing an unfair status quo."[31] Resting on the metanarratives of liberalism and democracy (the product of which includes meritocracy based on sex-blindness and color- blindness), repressive

---

31 Brookfield & Holst, 191.

tolerance assumes an already equalized playing field in the sharing and valuation of sources and traditions of ideas. In reality, due to pervasive ideological conditioning, minority/minoritized repertoires are typically considered "alternative" and therefore supplemental to dominant ones—overshadowed, co-opted, or exoticized, but not "normalized."

The effect of placing heretofore excluded traditions next to the existing mainstream is that the "radical" qualities of the newly introduced ideas are inevitably "diluted." They are subject to unfair, uneven comparisons. Learners are told that they have the so-called "freedom" to evaluate the relative worth of the newly introduced traditions however they may choose, when in fact, few learners are equipped for such comparison and contrast. We forget that the "mainstream" is able to remain dominant due to enduring undergirding "ideological conditioning." Thus, without ideological "detoxification," "[r]epressive tolerance ... neutralizes dissenting [or alternative] views ... while appearing to support them."[32]

Third, if our desire is simply not only to expand the Master's canon, but to dismantle the Master's tools, as Audre Lorde once called for, then we must reckon with the fact that the Master's tools have shape-shifting effect, as biblical scholar R.S. Sugirtharajah has warned. The Master may have once been the Bible-and-bullwhip-wielding master, or the missionary-explorer- translator-civilizer of foreign lands and cultures. However, in today's transnational theological scene, the Master may very well be the globalized Market, with its lexicon of "success, expediency, performance, profit."[33] (In this market-driven force field, academic questions such as "who will read this material?" is code for "who will buy this?") Perhaps another Master is the repressive tolerance of neoliberalism in academic discourse, which claims that statistical diversity is proof of equality of rights, power, and opportunity. Perhaps there are mini-Masters to be found in the methodological paucity and rigidity of our fields, or implicit tensions among disciplinary hierarchies, resulting in the siloed existence of hyper-specializations. Perhaps even the once-cutting-edge vocabulary of the discipline—such concepts as border-crossing, liminality, polycentrism, inter-contextuality, multilogicality, etc.—has become too comfortable and safe within the Master's house. Like Elbaz-Luwisch's metaphoric "body in the room," we acknowledge these notions, and then move on with the familiar "conceptual fetishes" of our disciplines.

Finally, perhaps the most dangerous problem for benign inclusion is if our inclusive practices are deployed to prove our magnanimity as earnest scholars who lift up the voices of the "marginalized and oppressed." Argentinian theologian Marcella Althaus-Reid cautioned scholars against the use of what she calls "body parts"—especially women's body parts—as theological currency. Arguing that

32 Brookfield & Holst, 192-193.
33 R.S. Sugirtharajah, *Postcolonial Configurations: An Alternative Way of Reading the Bible and Doing Theology* (London: SCM Press, 2003), 32.

theological (and scholarly) praxis is political, economic, and sexual, Althaus-Reid insisted that theologizing about liberation/salvation only in terms of the spiritual or figurative "shackled self" without regard for the physically, sexually, and politically "shackled body" is to ignore la mala vida ("bad living") of fleshly subjects—like the women lemon vendors of the streets of Buenos Aires, who may or may not follow dominant rules of decency.[34] For scholars like Althaus-Reid, the sexualized body should serve as the locus of interpretation for theological discourse. However, we need to move beyond touristic or voyeuristic gazing, which "expropriate[s]" local knowledges and commodifies them as "intellectual property of the owner of the intellectual system of production, the [scholar-]theologian."[35] How do we ensure that the "marginalized and oppressed" not become a profit margin for missiological discourse?[***]

Taking Althaus-Reid's cues, the teacher of mission who attends to women's bodies as "locus" of interpretation must not take their eyes off of the day-to-day conditions of women's life, love, and labor, as inscribed by rules of (sexual and economic) decency, productivity, and marketability. They will realize that the study and teaching of mission is necessarily an interdisciplinary task. It might entail re-examination of "women's work" alongside re-examination of what constitutes "mission." It might entail a feminist, materialist approach to understanding women's roles as "carriers" and "performers" of religion across cultures, spaces, and time. The list of themes and issues for analysis seems inexhaustible.

REFLECTIVE MOMENT:

Would you take 2 minutes to free-respond with a neighbor about possible themes, issues, and/or questions?

We have spent some time thinking about the two questions: How to take seriously our teaching bodies, and how to take the bodies that we teach (*with* and *about*) seriously? In typical pedagogic fashion, after you've wrestled with the "who" and the "what" (and "what for?"), you then consider the "how." How shall we teach? I appreciate the question in your Call for Papers: "What changes in [our] own teaching or in an institution's curriculum are necessary for promoting gender [and racial] equality in mission studies?"

---

34 Althaus-Reid, 21.

35 Ibid., 27.

*** In a follow-up conversation, Dana Robert offered an insightful comment about the prevalence of academic co- optation of missiologists' fieldwork. Missiology as a field is dismissed as hegemonic in some (typically liberal- leaning) academic circles; however, the raw data gathered from missiologists' scholarly labor in the field continue to be utilized for abstract theological construction.

How shall we teach?

In a letter penned for North American educators, the late Brazilian education reformer Paulo Freire wrote: "[A] teacher must be fully cognizant of the political nature of his/her practice and assume responsibility for this rather than denying it."[36] Freire was not alone in articulating the *political* nature of teaching. It is at base persuasive, if not directive; to varying degrees, it is an intentional effort to exert influence upon knowledge (what we know), affect (what we value), behavior (how we act). As such, scholars of critical pedagogy push the recognition that "knowledge is power" toward closer scrutiny of how power is configured by the boundaries of knowledge systems, and how the boundary coordinates of such systems can be "remapped, reterritorialized, and decentered" for multiplied reference points in our "reading of the world."[37] This epistemological disposition of what many have labeled as "border pedagogy" assumes that learners are crossers of borders that are "historically constructed and socially organized within maps of rules and regulations that limit and enable particular identities, individual capacities, and social forms."[38] Teachers, therefore, are also border-crossers who might do well if they learn and apply certain practices which sociologist Aihwa Ong describes of the contemporary global "flexible citizen": "*trans*versal," "*trans*actional," "*trans*lational," and "*trans*gressive" practices that are "incited, enabled, and regulated by the logics" of our academic disciplines.[39] These alliterative abstractions can be broken down into a few components of "practical wisdom" for the teacher, following the cues of those who employ critical race theory (CRT) for education aimed at gender and racial EQUITY.

For educational theory and praxis, CRT informs the examination of deep structural roots of institutional policies and everyday practices which contribute to racialization—and for our purposes here, gender omission. CRT scrutinizes the function of power/differentials in race (and gender) relations, especially the power of White male privilege ("whitestream" and "menstream"). In principle, CRT posits three central tenets. First, it highlights counter-narratives of marginal, subordinated voices as a strategy to de-centralize and de-normalize dominant grand narratives. Second, it takes advantage of "interest convergence" as leverage for championing

---

36 Freire, "Letter to North-American Teachers," 211.
37 Giroux, *Pedagogy and the Politics of Hope*, 147. In his "Letter to North-American Teachers," Freire wrote that the skill to read the *word* generates the capacity to read the *world*. Also in Freire, *Teachers as Cultural Workers*, 18.
38 Giroux, 147.
39 Ong, *Flexible Citizenship*, 4.

equity, since the majority would be more prone to accommodate minority interest if there is overlapping benefit. Third, it targets systemic, structural change (social justice), informed by inter-disciplinary and multi-issue analyses.[40]

Together, CRT's tenets and Aihwa Ong's "*trans*versal," "*trans*actional," "*trans*lational," and "*trans*gressive" techniques might provide some clues for how we may forge what I propose as a *critical intersectional pedagogic stance* for our study and teaching of mission.

FIRST TENET:

Following CRT's first tenet, the teacher of mission may learn to become a "border-crosser" who wields the *trans*gressive power of counter-stories that subtly offer "oppositional" definitions of reality.[41] Some call this a "pedagogy of dissent."[42] This means we submit our own teaching bodies as "oppositional text," just as we strive to interject otherly-marked interpreting bodies as counter-texts to the teaching canon.

Reckoning with their social location, minoritized teachers might open up to the possibility that their own "teaching body" may serve as a living enactment of *trans*versed norms: a "non-standard" subject asserting credibility and authenticity in ways that are slightly slanted, off-kilter, zigzagging, but enough to render problematic so-called normative coordinates of identity. Meanwhile, mythically "normative" teaching bodies might query their own privileged locations, and ask, What difference would it make if my gender and race were to become the "explicit curriculum"—open and subject to analysis of their impact upon the disciplinary status quo? In these differing ways, the identity work of these teachers would serve as counter- normative "curriculum," juxtaposed against the written curriculum of academic disciplines which are in themselves racialized and genderized texts.[43]

Oppositional narratives need not be mild, as womanist scholars have long insisted. What Audre Lorde called *symphonic anger*, "loaded with information and energy," may very well be the emotive response in the face of "exclusion . . . of racial distortions, of silence, ill-use, stereotyping, defensiveness, misnaming, betrayal, and co-optation."[44] Similarly, bell hooks found her confidence through risky "back talk," or presumptive speaking as an equal to an authority figure. Preferred over silent protest (which are in themselves no less potent), and more directive than

---

40 Gillborn, "Critical Race Theory and Education," 26-7; Zamudio, *Critical Race Theory Matters*, 16, 22-3; Museus, *Conducting Research on Asian Americans*, 59; Brookfield and Holst, *Radicalizing Learning*, 193. See also Delgado, *Critical Race Theory*.

41 Zamudio, *Critical Race Theory Matters*, 16.

42 Chandra Talpade Mohanty, *Feminism without Borders: Decolonizing Theory, Practicing Solidarity* (Durham: Duke University Press, 2003).

43 Kong, "Immigration, Racial Identity, and Adult Education," 240. Cites Pinar, "Notes on Understanding Curriculum as Racial Text."

44 Lorde, *Sister Outsider*, 124.

informal women speech, "sharp-tongued" talking back is, for hooks, "a gesture of defiance."[45] Taking a cue from this, perhaps teachers of mission could lift up the "great omissions" as "counterdiscourse," and equip learners with strategies to "talk back" against the normative narratives of the tradition.[46]

THIRD TENET:

Constructing or resurrecting counter-narratives is *not* to be confused with the facile celebration of difference typically found in "repressive tolerance."[47] Therefore, following CRT's third tenet (I am going out of order here), the teacher as border intellectual passes over banal tolerance in favor of educational practices that examine power and privilege in the macro- structures and micro-realities of their academic discipline.

Education theorists Stephen Brookfield and Stephen Holst suggest three concrete practices:

1. "ideological detoxification," or deconstruction of implicit ideological values undergirding definitions of institutional "normal";

2. intentional disruption of privilege of all forms (viz., racial, sexual, class, citizenship status), especially those enjoyed in daily routines and institutional configurations; and

3. deep, sustained immersion in "alternative conceptions of normality," a pedagogy of contrast which seeks opportunities for serious confrontation with difference rather than dismissing it as inessential.[48]

This last practice suggests epistemological re-wiring—something akin to moving from a conception of "Christian mission around the world" to "engendering mission in global Christianities" (the plural form being argued for by Peter Phan). This alternative conception of "normality" requires sustained inquiry and a shift of what education theorist Jack Mezirow calls "meaning-perspective" (worldview).

SECOND TENET:

CRT's 2nd tenet regarding "interest convergence" is perhaps most elusive for minoritized teachers, for they must seek ways to *trans*late their talents and interests to academic cultures "incited and regulated" by fluctuating bottom-lines. In this act of negotiation, the teacher as "flexible citizen" knows that minority interests are more

---

45   Hooks, "Talking Back," 337-40.

46   Mohanty, *Feminism without Borders*, chapter 8.

47   Brookfield and Holst, *Radicalizing Learning*, 190-7. The notion of "repressive tolerance" is attributed to the work of philosopher Herbert Marcuse.

48   Brookfield and Holt, 201-9.

readily considered if and when they align with dominant interests. Put differently, majority-serving educational, pedagogical, and curricular norms are unlikely to change as long as they continue to serve majority students (and teachers) who happen to be predominant and by all standards excelling.[49] Thus, viability (survival) depends on vigilance with useful cues for continuous *trans*lational work. It also relies on forms of "horizontal comradeship"[50] forged out of affinities or strategic alliances. More directly, we could ask, What kinds of ally-ship may be forged among teachers of mission to alter the vision, so that the problem of "gender" is *not just* a "woman's issue"; and the problem of "race" is not one with which only scholars of color must address?

Reflective Moment: (Quick Minute)

What think you about these pedagogic strategies?

Conclusion

In the late 1990s, feminist theorist Zillah Eisenstein wrote:

> Women's and girls' bodies determine democracy: free from violence and sexual abuse, free from malnutrition and environmental degradation, free to plan their families, free to not have families, free to choose their sexual lives and preferences.[51]

More recently, postcolonial feminist theorist Chandra Talpade Mohanty recasts the ideological conviction through the following question:

> What are the concrete effects of global restructuring on the 'real' raced, classed, national, sexual bodies of women in the academy, in workplaces, streets, households, cyberspaces, neighborhoods, prisons, and in social [and religious] movements?[52]

There is a version of that question for the field of Christian mission studies. This inductive, bottom-up hermeneutic avoids sterilized explorations of the "other" and their experience, and shifts the locus of our description and interpretation of "Christian mission" to lived practices and struggles in particular, intersectional spaces of everyday life. It is what postcolonial biblical scholar Sugirtharajah calls a "praxiological deconstruction"—an *unlearning* of dominant ideological settings of

---

49 Zamudio, 47-8.
50 Mohanty, 46. Citing Anderson, *Imagined Communities*, 11-6.
51 *Global Obscenities: Patriarchy, Capitalism, and the Lure of Cyberfantasy* (New York: New York University Press, 1998), 161. Cited in Chandra Talpade Mohanty, *Feminism Without Borders: Decolonizing Theory, Practicing Solidarity* (Durham & London: Duke University Press, 2003), 245.
52 *Feminism Without Borders*, 245.

"Christian praxis" in local and global communities, so that we can be "converted" to "the other" in new ways. It is dissatisfied with benign toleration of so-called "emerging new perspectives," and interrogates the persistent disciplinary inertia and intransigence. It pushes the limits of our pedagogic imagination, such that we might entertain the question, what happens if we were to dismantle the "mission field" as we have *learned to know* it? What happens if the disciplinary world *as we have always known it*...would actually come to an end?

After all, are these not questions of "salvation"—one of the original driving forces of the study of mission? I submit that if we truly desire to seek and teach mission differently in the 21ˢᵗ century, then we start there.

Bibliography (incomplete)

Behar, Ruth.
"Introduction: Out of Exile." In *Women Writing Culture*, edited by Ruth Behar and Deborah A. Gordon, 1-29. Berkeley: University of California Press, 1995.

Harris, Angela P., and Carmen G. González.
"Introduction." In *Presumed Incompetent: The Intersections of Race and Class for Women in Academia,* edited by Gabriella Gutiérrez y Muhs, Yolanda Flores Niemann, Carmen G. González and Angela P. Harris, 1-14. Boulder, Colo.: University Press of Colorado, 2012.

Jennings, Willie James.
"What Shall We Teach? The Content of Theological Education." In *Teaching for a Culturally Diverse and Racially Just World*, edited by Eleazar S. Fernandez, 109-25. Eugene, Oregon: Cascade Books, 2014.

Lorde, Audre.
Sister Outsider: Essays and Speeches. Crossing Press Feminist Series Freedom, CA: Crossing Press, 1984.

Mohanty, Chandra Talpade.
Feminism without Borders: Decolonizing Theory, Practicing Solidarity. Durham: Duke University Press, 2003.

Morrison, Toni.
"Unspeakable Things Unspoken: The Afro-American Presence in American Literature." *Michigan Quarterly Review* 18, no. 1 (1989): 11-12.

Sugirtharajah, R.S.
Postcolonial Configurations: An Alternative Way of Reading the Bible and Doing Theology. London: SCM Press, 2003.

Teaching Christian Mission in an Age of World Christianity:

A Reflection on the Centenary of the 1916 Panama Congress

PHILIP WINGEIER-RAYO, PH.D.

Introductions

I would like to thank Dr. Angel Santiago-Vendrell and the Association of Professors of Mission (APM) leadership team for the invitation to share today on the topic "Teaching Mission in an Era of World Christianity." This is a provocative topic that brings to mind such questions as: What does it mean to teach mission today? What did it mean to teach mission in the past? What is it in relationship to world Christianity? What is teaching mission like today relative to itself, for example 100 years ago? Any of these questions would be worthy pursuits, however I do not have the time or space to address all these questions today, and so I will focus on the last two, namely: What is mission in relation to world Christianity, specifically Latin American Christianity, and how does teaching mission today compare to 100 years ago? I say 100 years ago even though the APM was only founded 64 years ago and the teaching of mission goes back further. I will begin with my experience teaching mission and world Christianity in higher education. The bulk of the paper, however, will be on Christian Mission a hundred years ago and the transition to World Christianity—primarily reflecting on the 100th anniversary of the 1916 Panama Congress as an example of mission at the time. In this paper I will posit that over the last 100 years since the Panama Congress, teaching mission has shifted in its understanding of ecumenism, seen the contribution of indigenous churches and placed more emphasis on what God is doing through the Holy Spirit.

Before I begin I would like to say a word about ecumenism and how I will use certain terms. The Association of Professors of Mission is one of the few spaces where missiologists can gather outside our individual tribes and discuss the big picture. Having worked and studied Roman Catholic, conciliar and evangelical churches, I have come to respect the contributions that each make to the reign of God, but there are too few spaces where we can all be in the same place to dialogue. I will never forget the 2014 gathering of the European Missiological Conference held in the Sofia Conference Center of the Russian Orthodox Church in Helsinki, Finland. As you know, the Nordic countries are famous for their nude saunas followed by a plunge into an icy cold pool. If you go to a conference in the UK you have afternoon tea. If you go to the Middle East you have Turkish coffee. At the Panama Congress they had a siesta break in the schedule. Well, in Finland, every afternoon in the schedule was a sauna break. After a full day of tense ecumenical discussions about evangelical incursions into Eastern Orthodox lands, nothing seemed to place our doctrinal and missiological differences into perspective like having Orthodox, intentionality of rotating positions between Roman Catholic, conciliar and evangelical candidates. Nevertheless I acknowledge that I am Protestant and this inevitably will inform my interpretation of the following events.

In keeping of the APM/ASM tradition I will use the term "conciliar" to refer to historical Protestant denominations with one caveat. In Spanish, the generic term "*evangélico*" is inclusive of mainline Protestants, evangelicals and Pentecostals. And although it is beyond the scope of this paper, I argue in other places that Pentecostals are deserving of their own category aside from evangelical.[1]

Teaching Christian Mission in an Age of World Christianity: Personal Experience and Reflections

I am fortunate in my career to have served as a practitioner first and subsequently as a missiologist—as have many of you. In 2003 I returned from 15 years of missionary service in Latin America and the Caribbean and joined academia. In my academic career I have taught at a small church-related university, a large divinity school connected to a university, and now a conciliar seminary in the United States, giving me a broad variety of experiences and perspectives with which I approach this topic. At my first academic post in the States, much to my surprise, my dean invited me to develop an undergraduate and graduate program in missions. Up to this time I was a practitioner and not privy to the latest higher education trends or jargon in academia. So I consulted with some mission leaders and searched school websites. I would name some and I'm sure most are represented in this room, but my memory is sketchy and I would probably leave someone out. I would, however, like to take a moment of privilege and lift up the name of John Nuessle, who was very generous with his time and knowledge during my research. John was a mission executive with Global Ministries in New York and was one of the first executives to accept the invitation to join and regularly attend ASM. John passed away June 8th at the age of 63. He will be missed, but his passion for missions will be carried on.

As I had these conversations and studied the various programs in the field, I noticed a shift away from the term "Christian Missions" toward more neutral terms such as "intercultural studies" at Asbury Theological Seminary and Biola University, for example. Pfeiffer ultimate decided to name its undergraduate major the more traditional name of "Christian Mission" even as other schools were going the opposite direction. For example, in 2002-2003 Fuller was in the process of changing the name of the School of World Mission to the School of Intercultural Studies. In her 2015 APM plenary presentation Elizabeth Glainville identified the impetus for Fuller's name-change as coming from its graduates who were serving in no access countries and needed a less "religious" sounding degree on their

1   See "A Third Phase of Christianity: Reflections on 100 Years of Pentecostalism in Mexico," chapter in Vinson Synan, Amos Yong, and Miguel Alvarez, eds., *Global Renewal Christianity: Latin American Spirit-Empowered Movements: Past, Present, and Future, vol. II: Latin America*, Lake Mary, Fla.: Charisma House Publishers, 2016.

diplomas.[2] Resistance to Fuller's name change came from older faculty and some trustees who felt that it would take the school away from its "initial and primary purpose."[3] "What's in a name?" was the topic for last year's gathering, so for those of you who were unable to attend I refer you to the proceedings in *First Fruit* for a fuller review (no pun intended). My purpose here is not to duplicate Glainville's paper or last year's topic, rather I refer to this name-change only as it transitions smoothly to this year's theme (kudos to the organizers). I believe that Fuller's name change was not random, rather that is was representative of a trend. There was/is something bigger happening in the study of religion, namely a move from the sacred to the secular, from the biblical to the scientific, from the Euro-centric to the global, from modernity to the post-modern and post-colonial, and from Christian Mission to global Christianity.

Still very new to the field I joined the AAR began attending the AAR/SBL annual meeting. My first annual meeting was in 2002. No sooner had I joined that I learned of plans to de-couple the two guilds annual meetings. The initiative came from Professor of Religious Studies at Harvard University and AAR president in, 2003, Robert Orsi, who acted upon sentiments within the AAR that the SBL was too dominated by Christian practitioners and therefore lacked the objectivity of social scientists. Orsi argued in his 2004 presidential address: "We need to engage the history of the study of religion in the United States more critically than we have done, at the same time recognizing how deeply we are in the debt of earlier scholars."[4] The AAR began as an off-shoot of the then National Association of Biblical Instructors in 1963 and this split was the latest move toward objectivity. This sentiment was also present in the trend to re-name university religion departments to religious studies. This trend sped up considerably after 9/11 with greater interest in non-Western religions and Islam in particular. Nevertheless practical and economic concerns from the individual members and institutions that make up the two organizations pushed the AAR and SBL to reconsider the split. Publishing houses, philanthropic organizations, and hiring institutions were forced to either choose or attend two conferences to meet their constituencies. In 2010 the leadership of the AAR and SBL signed a letter of intent to "enhance cooperation, not competition, between the organizations" and they both agreed to have concurrent annual meetings in the same city and began this practice in November 2011 in San Francisco.[5] The underlying differences between the two guilds still exist, however the practical and economic concerns forced them to have overlapping meetings.

2   Elizabeth Glainville, "Name Change at Fuller's School of World Mission to School of Intercultural Studies," Association of Professors of Mission, *First Fruits*, June 18-19, 2015, 14.

3   *Ibid*, 19.

4   Robert Orsi, "A New Beginning, Again," presidential address to the 2003 AAR annual meeting, Religious Studies, Oxford University Press, Vol. 74, No. 3, September 2006, 589.

5   American Academy of Religion, https://www.aarweb.org/annual-meeting/aar-sbl-annualmeetings-letter-of-intent (accessed May 30, 2016)

In 2009 I was asked by the president of Garrett-Evangelical Theological Seminary, Phil Amerson, to form part of a task force to re-design their mission program. Garrett had received a large Luce grant that allowed them to explore this field and hire a professor. For years Garrett had maintained a professor of mission, however the position was not filled after the last occupant, Walter Cason, who was my professor and retired in 1994. Given the considerable 15 year vacancy, the task force was given the responsibility of studying the field and competing institutions and recommending to the president the title and direction of the new position.[6] After a year of study, the task force came to the conclusion that language of "Christian Mission" was passé and terms such as global or world Christianity were more appropriate for the position and the discipline. The Luce grant allowed Garrett to hire a professor, Henk Pieterse, who joined the faculty full-time in 2010 and has been promoted to Associate Professor.

Also in 2009 Pfeiffer hired a new provost and began preparing for its SACS 10-year reaccreditation visit. The provost called for all the majors to have a program review to see how many students had graduated and what were the costs involved. Our religion department had multiple overlapping majors of youth ministry, Christian education and missions—along with a religion major for preseminary students. The mission major had been in existence for 5 years and was only graduating one, two or three students a year but was trending upward. Under pressure from the provost our department streamlined the major into a more general Bible and Intercultural Studies major with two internal tracks for age appropriate ministries or intercultural studies. The intent from an administrative perspective was to lessen the number of course offerings and thus the cost per student by also utilizing course offerings in other fields such as sociology and communications. However this was also another domino in the movement from the sacred to the secular and the biblical to the scientific.

Now this is only anecdotal evidence and I admit not conducting a general survey across the discipline with representative institutions. In fact, there are many schools that retain the traditional nomenclature. Even if I had been able to conduct a broad survey, there would still be other variables such as the complexity of namechange among the stakeholders, such as faculty, administrators, trustees, donors, current and former students. Moreover, when a chair has been endowed then the name is restricted by the intent of the donors, as is the case of my current position.

Presently I am professor of Evangelism, Mission and Methodist Studies at Austin Presbyterian Theological Seminary, which is an endowed position. It would be very difficult to alter the position title because there is a binding memorandum of understanding that was signed by the advancement office. I suspect that many

6   Garrett-Evangelical's decision to apply for this grant and reinstate the position was due, in part, to the urging of the Dana Robert and United Methodist Professors of Mission, whom wrote a prophetic call in the early 2000s to the denominational seminaries to reverse the trend and fill the vacant mission positions.

schools with an endowed position in mission would have great difficulty changing the name, in spite of the trend toward terms like world or global Christianity. Perhaps there are some development officers here who can clarify this.

In the first section, I have outlined three shifts in our field in the last few years: 1) the trend to change school or program names away from Christian Mission, 2) the decision of the AAR to split from the SBL reflecting the name change of religion departments to religious studies, and 3) the movement in college, universities, and seminaries from teaching Christian Mission to Global or World Christianity.

Panama Congress of 1916: from Christian Mission to World Christianity

Now I will move to the body of my presentation, which is a reflection on the 1916 Panama Congress as a case study of mission on this, its centenary. I lift up this congress, and the early 20th century conciliar mission efforts in Latin America, as an example of the transition from teaching Christian Mission to World Christianity. Being well-documented with three volumes of proceedings, the congress is an excellent time-capsule to compare the nature of Christian Mission then and now. I will make three principal observations in the difference of Christian Mission in 2016. The first observation is the changes in the ecumenical spirit, the second is the agency of autonomous church leadership in the global south, and the third is greater dependence on the Holy Spirit between then and now.

Regarding ecumenical relations, the 1916 Panama Congress had 481 attendees including 299 church workers (230 of whom were official delegates) from 22 nations representing 50 ecclesial bodies and mission organizations.[7] It was the first conference of its kind in Latin America. The conciliar movement had been building since William Carey's 1792 "Inquiry" and the call for unity intensified with the 1854 Union Missionary Conference in New York and ensuing conferences.[8] The idea for a meeting about Latin American work was ironically birthed at the 1910 World Missionary Conference in Edinburgh even though the region was excluded as a mission field. The purpose of Edinburgh was "to consider missionary problems in relation to the non-Christian world" and therefore, as a predominantly

---

7   Homer Stuntz, *South American Neighbors*, Methodist Book Concern, New York, 1916, 173.
8   Norman E. Thomas, *Mission and Unity: Lessons from History, 1792-2010*, Cascade Books, New York, 2010, 31.

Roman Catholic region, the international committee considered Latin America to already be Christian.[9] Presbyterian mission executive Robert Speer challenged this decision and the criteria for additional mission work:

> The first test of religious conditions is to be found in the facts of social life. No land can be conceded to have a satisfactory religion where the moral conditions are as they have been shown to be in South America. If it can be proved that the conditions of any European or North American land are as they are in South America, then it will be proved also that that land needs a religious reformation.[10]

Rather than precluding the need for Protestant missions based on religious affiliation, Speer assessed the need based on moral conditions. His rationale for doing missionary work in South America is not based on denominational affiliation, rather on quality of life. Writing his book *South American Problems* in 1913 after Edinburgh to advocate for Protestant mission work in the region, Speer is making two important contributions to missiology. On one hand he is challenging the understanding of Christendom--the idea that a geographical place can be Christian. This is an important challenge, which is revolutionary for its time, or to use the words of David Bosch "a paradigm shift," which challenged the basis on which whole continents were included or not in the Edinburgh conference. The second major contribution that Speer is making is the connection between Christianity and a just society. This is a precursor to Latin American liberation theology that some 60 years later would introduce the concept of social sin. This concept articulated by Gustavo Gutierrez and others argued that private sins that violate personal piety such as drinking, smoking or using foul language are relatively minor sins compared to participating in systematic evil and economic systems that impoverish people and deny they basic human living conditions such as food, potable water, employment and shelter. This understanding of systemic injustice moves beyond petty concepts of church membership or religious affiliation to a deeper understanding of justice as a criteria for mission work. For Speer, what matters most is not whether a society or people are called Roman Catholic or Protestant. What matters is whether the society is organized according to Christian understandings of social justice. This is a profound ecumenical spirit to which many of us can still aspire.

Mexican layperson Gonzalo Baez Camargo not only disagreed with Edinburgh's decision to exclude Latin America, he challenged Edinburgh's bifurcation of the world between "civilized" Christian countries that "sent" missionaries and "uncivilized" non-Christian countries of Africa, Asia and the pacific

---

9   Missionary Education Movement of the United States and Canada, "Christian Work in Latin America," 1917.

10   Robert E. Speer, South American Problems, Student Volunteer Movement for Foreign Missions (New York: Lanham, 1913), 145.

rim that "received" missionaries. Of course he took exception to placing Latin America in the former category.[11]

In spite of being excluded from Edinburgh the pre-reports from mission work in Latin America were included in the proceedings, especially in Commission I: "Carrying the Gospel to all the non-Christian World."[12] While in Edinburgh a group of delegates who disagreed with Latin America's exclusion gathered for an informal lunch. They decided to hold a follow-up meeting and invite some leading mission executives.[13] At the conclusion of the second meeting they issued the following statement:

> The undersigned delegates to the World Missionary Conference, rejoicing over the success of that great gathering and the impulse it must give to the evangelization of the non-Christian world, feel constrained to say a word for those missions in countries nominally Christian that were not embraced in the scope of the Edinburgh Conference, we do not stop to inquire whether the dominant Churches in these lands are or are not Christian Churches, or whether they are or are not faithful to their duty; we only affirm that millions and millions of people are practically without the Word of God and do not really know what the Gospel is.

This group commended the systematic approach of the World Missionary Conference and wanted the same attention for Latin America. This statement is careful to avoid falling into the Roman Catholic-Protestant polemic and rather places the emphasis on sharing the Gospel to the unreached. Before departing Edinburgh the Foreign Missions Conference of North America appointed a committee to make plans for a congress with Robert Speer as the chair, known as the committee of five.

Formation of the Committee on Cooperation in Latin America

These plans came to fruition with an ensuing meeting in New York City on March 12-13, 1913 that was attended by executives of 30 different mission organizations and missionaries home on furlough. The conference picked right up

---

11 Gonzalo Baez Camargo, "Mexico: a Long Stretch from Edinburgh," *Ecumenical Review*, vol. XVI, Oct. 1963-July 1964, 267.

12 Missionary Research Library Archives: Section 12, World Missionary Conference Records, Edinburgh, 1910.

13 Missionary Education Movement of the United States and Canada, "Christian Work in Latin America," 1917.

where Edinburgh left off in the theme of Christian unity and a country-by-country analysis of mission work. Representatives gave a total of 15 reports on topics such as: "The Present Extent and Condition of Mission Work in Latin American Lands," "Unoccupied Fields and the Unreached Populations in Latin America," "The Bible in Latin America," and "Religious Liberty and the Problem of Church and State in Latin America" to name a few. In these reports contained the most recent statistical data on the status of mission efforts in Latin America.

Near the end of the 2-day meeting, Rev. Ed Cook D.D. gave his report about the conciliar work in Mexico. By this time the revolution had broken out in Mexico, and as a result, Cook advocated seizing this opportunity to implement unification of Protestant mission efforts:

> In Mexico there is a situation demanding our immediate study and our closest and most careful cooperation in the handling. The problems involved in this situation relate first to Christian education; second to Christian literature; third, to self-support on the part of the native congregations.[14]

Regarding his third and final point about autonomy, Cook concluded:

> In the matter of 'self-support' the cause of Protestantism in Mexico has suffered most on accord of the lack of cooperation between the denominations. After sixty years of Christian work in Mexico we are almost as far from the establishment of the native church as we were at the end of the first ten or fifteen years of continuous effort.[15]

Yet Cook's report did not seem to comprehend a social analysis of what was happening in the larger Mexican society as an extension of Protestant mission work. His report looked very narrowly at church institutions and instead referred to the instability in Mexico as the ideal time to carry out sweeping changes. Since Cook's presentation came near the end of the conference, there was little time for discussion or questions. The final task of the 1913 meeting was creating the Committee on Cooperation in Latin America (CCLA), known as the committee of 18, to continue the work.

The first meeting of the newly formed CCLA was convened in Garden City, Long Island in January 1914 with the task of planning the Panama Congress, however the news from Mexico grabbed everyone's attention. The words of Ed Cook's report on Mexico the previous year were still relevant: "We have talked much in recent years about fraternity, comity, cooperation, and union." The CCLA

---

14 *Ibid.*
15 *Ibid*, 153.

considered the chaos in Mexico to be an opportunity to realign the overlapping of territories and increase cooperation in educational work and publishing. So the CCLA concluded their meet in Long Island then called for a meeting in Cincinnati on June 30-July 1, 1914 and invited representatives from mission agencies and missionaries working in Mexico, many of whom were back in the U.S. for their own safety.[16]

U.S.-Mexico Diplomatic Relations

In the interim between the meeting in January in Long Island and the meeting in Cincinnati, U.S.-Mexican diplomatic relations took a turn for the worst. In the spring of the same year some U.S. sailors were arrested for entering a fuel loading station in Tampico and President Woodrow Wilson commanded the U.S. Navy to invade and occupy the Port of Veracruz on April 9, 1914. In the years leading up to the revolution, the U.S. enjoyed great influence in the government of Porfirio Diaz, president from 1876 to 1880 and 1884 until he was overthrown in 1911. This was a period of growing U.S. investments when Jay Gould built the Mexican Southern Railroad, J.P. Morgan established banks and Rockefeller's Standard Oil began acquiring sub-soil mineral rights and extracting oil.[17] When the Committee on Cooperation in Latin America met in Panama in 1916, reports on Mexico's economy estimated the U.S. total investment at $1 billion, which was 51% of Mexico's commerce.[18]

So when the sixty representatives from eleven different mission agencies gathered on June 30, 1914 in Cincinnati, U.S.-Mexican diplomatic relations were tense. Given the situation in Mexico, it would have been difficult to hold the meeting there—even if this were a consideration, nor were Mexicans able to travel had they been invited.

The Cincinnati Plan

While the CCLA meeting earlier in 1914 received general reports about the Protestant work throughout Latin America, the meeting in Cincinnati was completed focused on Mexico. There had been a lot of talk about Christian unity coming out of Edinburgh, but the unique situation in Mexico made it a pressing

---

16 Christian Work in Latin America, Reports of Commissions I, II, & III, February 2016, The Missionary Education Movement, New York, 1917.
https://archive.org/stream/christianworkinl01cong/christianworkinl01cong_djvu.txt

17 John Ross, *The Annexation of Mexico*, Common Courage Press, 1998, 53.

18 Missionary Education Movement, Committee on Co-operation on Latin America, New York, 1917, vol.1, 57.

matter. Cincinnati was the first meeting to actually implement the sweeping changes and unification recommended at Edinburgh. Cook's report and specific recommendations at the CCLA's founding meeting in 1913 were the impetus for the Cincinnati Plan. Namely, he called for cooperation in three areas: Christian education, publications and decrease competition among mission agencies in order to increase self-support for native congregations. Present in Cincinnati were representatives from the Congregationalists, United Presbyterian Church (UPCUSA), Disciples of Christ, Methodist Episcopal Church, Disciples of Christ, Episcopalians, Friends, and Northern Baptists, the YMCA, among other denominations and organizations.

The ultimate goal of the meeting in Cincinnati was to unify all the Protestant mission efforts under one umbrella that would be called "The Evangelical Church of Mexico."[19] In order to accomplish this larger goal, the plan called for much smaller and more concrete steps. The Cincinnati Plan called upon the denominations to consolidate their evangelization efforts across Mexico to avoid competition and enhance efficiency.

When news of the Cincinnati Plan reached the leadership of the Mexican churches, the response was less than positive. Pastors and leaders had given their lives to certainly ministries and certain regions of the country, and did not want to leave them.[20] When missionaries met with leaders of the Presbyterian mission in the spring of 1919 to implement the plan, Mexican leaders demonstrated their clear differences. Leandro Garza Mora articulated this frustration when he stood up an exclaimed: "The Plan of Cincinnati [which is what the Mexican churches called the outcome of the Cincinnati Conference--sic] is nothing other than the plan to assassinate the Presbyterian Church in Mexico."[21] The word for assassinate in Spanish is "*asesinato*," so the Plan of Cincinnati was dubbed "*el Plan de Asesinato.*"

Historian Daniel J. Young, wrote in regarding the Cincinnati Plan: "The specific actions on the part of the foreign mission boards working in Mexico caused hurt among Mexican church members and in many cases strained the relationship between Mexican and American Protestants in an already charged atmosphere, heightened by American interventions in Mexico during the Mexican Revolution."[22] In many ways the expedited Cincinnati Plan was unfortunate, however the preparations for the Panama Congress were much more intentional

---

19 Daniel J. Young, "The Cincinnati Plan and the National Presbyterian Church of Mexico: A Brief Study of Relations Between American Mission Boards and Mexican Protestant Churches During the Mexican Revolution," Master's Thesis. UTEP, 2006, 33.

20 Young, 33.

21 Quote from Charles Petran, "Cincinnati Plan," unpublished paper, p. 9. Cited in Young, 33.

22 Daniel J. Young, 33.

and sensitive to local concerns. The U.S. government called upon "ABC Diplomacy" (Argentina, Brazil and Chile) to resolve the immediate stand-off with Mexico, although the Revolution and U.S. intervention was not over with.[23]

1916 Panama Congress

The Panama Congress was held February 10-20, 1916 in the canal zone in Panama City, the same city that hosted the 1826 meeting of newly independent Latin American nations. The CCLA had ruled out hosting the congress in the US "because it was a gathering for Latin America,"[24] as well as Rio de Janeiro and Buenos Aires and settled on Panama. Another attraction was the newly opened Panama Canal inaugurated just two years prior. John R. Mott, chairman of Edinburgh conference responded to the welcome from Panamanian Minister of Foreign Affairs of Jose E. Lefevre: "We have delegates from virtually every one of the republics of North and South America. We likewise have representatives from Europe and the distant parts of the world."[25] Mott continued in his usual grandiose and optimistic tone in spite of the ongoing Mexican Revolution and the start of World War I in Europe, "I fancy that not in the history of the Western Hemisphere has there been assembled a gathering so representative of the leaders and the forcesof righteousness of this great sphere of the world's activity."[26]

The congress was an accomplishment, a challenge and a step toward ecumenism. An accomplishment because 145 Latin American representatives, in addition to 159 supporters from the U.S., Canada, Great Britain and Italy attended the Congress and offered details reports on the state of missions and lively discussions about how to best support work in the region. The congress had 22 different denominations and mission societies represented who earnestly attempted to harness the spirit of Edinburgh to reduce competition and duplication, while increasing cooperation.[27]

It was a challenge because this was the first such conciliar Protestant gathering in a region generally recognized to be predominantly Roman Catholic. In fact, some evangelicals objected to the idea of the congress fearing compromise and cooperation with the Catholic Church. They were afraid of any movement toward

---

23 Although later in 1916 after the congress the U.S. invaded Mexican territory with an incursion from the north to chase Poncho Villa. For more see Joseph Smith, *The United States and Latin America: A History of American Diplomacy 1776-2000*, Routledge, 2005, 77.

24 Harlan P. Beach, *Renaissant Latin America: An Outline and Interpretation of the Congress on Christian Work in Latin America*, held at Panama, February 10-19, 1916, Missionary Education Movement of the United States and Canada, New York, 1916, 2.

25 *Ibid*, 1.

26 As chairman of the World Missionary Conference in Edinburgh in 1910 John Mott set a very optimistic tone based on his book entitled *Evangelization of the World in this Generation, Student Volunteer Movement for Foreign Missions*, New York, 1900.

27 Stuntz, 173.

reconciliation with Rome.[28] At the other end of the Protestant camp were those who objected to the meeting out of respect for the Roman Catholic Church. The Episcopal Church was particularly conflicted because they saw themselves between Catholics and Protestants and longed for the eventual unity of the whole church. The Church of England was one of the primary opponents of including Latin America at Edinburgh, and didn't even want to reports to appear in the proceedings. The Mission Board of the Protestant Episcopal Church in the U.S. initially voted not to participate in the Panama Congress but then in May of 1915 decided to allow delegates to attend "provided that whatever invitation is given to every Christian body shall be sent to every Christian church having work in Latin America."[29] The Episcopalians already had work in Mexico and Brazil. At the October meeting of the Mission Board a vote was taken to repeal the decision to send delegates but failed by a 26-13 margin. This action was protested by some board members fearing it moved the church closer to Protestantism and after the vote, five members, included two bishops, resigned their position on the board. Resolutions were subsequently adopted stating that the congress is not about legislation, rather "to recognize all the elements of truth and goodness in any form of religious faith, that its approach to the people will be neither critical nor antagonistic, and that all communions and organizations which accept Jesus Christ as divine Saviour and Lord and the Holy Scriptures ... are invited to the Congress."[30] The Roman Catholic Bishop of Panama was vehemently opposed to the congress and warned his constituents to be aware of false prophets and "wolves in their interior."[31] In spite of this warning five Catholic bishops attended and according to Harlan Beach's interpretation of the proceedings "were most helpful participants in its deliberations."[32]

It was a step toward ecumenism because the congress was successful at its main purpose of collaboration between Protestant mission work in Latin America. As a result of the meeting the denominations standardized educational requirements at training institutions within countries and through these efforts eventually joint conciliar seminaries were established in Buenos Aires, Santiago, Rio de Janeiro, San Jose, Costa Rica and Mexico City to train future church leaders.[33] Ecumenical publishing houses and Bible societies were established to produce Christian literature. Comity agreements were signed marking the territories where denominations would focus their efforts, so as to not compete or duplicate efforts. This specifically meant that mission agencies agreed to not start work in towns where another Protestant denomination was already working. They even focused

---

28 Beach, 10.

29 *The American Year Book: A Record of Events and Progress*, T. Nelson & Sons, Vol.6, 715.

30 *Ibid.*

31 *Ibid.*

32 *Ibid, 11.*

33 Homer Stuntz, *South American Neighbors*, The Methodist Book Concern, New York, 1916, 189-90.

on areas where the Catholic church was not present, such as rural areas and among indigenous populations. This was already underway in Mexico after the Cincinnati Plan and was expanded to other countries as well. Immediately following the Panama Congress six follow-up meetings to disburse and implement plans were conducted in Lima, Santiago, Buenos Aires, Rio de Janeiro, Havana, and San Juan, Puerto Rico and Barranquilla, Colombia. By 1930 the CCLA reported 28 cooperative enterprises in Latin America and donors were more willing to give to these efforts than denominational projects.[34]

The congress also acknowledged that many of the Protestant mission efforts had been among the "humbler" classes and therefore it was proposed to "begin a 'drive' to reach the 'intellectuals'—the influential classes.[35] This was a two-step strategy to reach out to current students and to provide better education and training for candidates for ministry. Bishop William C. Brown of the Protestant Episcopal Church, who agreed to come on his own accord and not as a spokesperson for his denomination, stated: "I believe most fully in the educated native minister. I am convinced that the Anglo-Saxon cannot within one generation fully understand the of the Latin man [and woman]."[36] The congress was conducted primarily in English with some speaches by Spanish and Portuguese delegates. Another fact about the congress is that all the meetings were conducted in English, limiting the local participation, although the proceedings were published in Spanish, Portuguese, in addition to English.[37] Subsequently congresses in Montevideo (1925) and Havana (1929) had increasing percentages of Latin American delegates and more contextualization of the themes generated by regional and local concerns.[38]

With successive meeting there was a growing sense of nationalistic pride and ownership that Latin American leaders were feeling. By reading the proceedings from Panama, Montevideo and Havana, one can notice the growth and expansion of topics becoming more and more contextualized. The 1929 Havana meeting was planned, organized and run by Latinos with an agenda shaped predominantly by the Latin American context. Mature Latin American leaders such as Gonzalo Baez Camargo and Alberto Rembao were instrumental in the Latinization of the conference.[39] For example the issue of ministry among indigenous peoples was barely mentioned at the Panama Congress, however by the Havana meeting in 1929 this was explicit. The topic of women was discussed in Panama, but by the Havana meeting there was deeper reflection on the role of the Latin American

34 "Annual Report of the Committee on Cooperation on Latin America," New York, 1930, p.10.

35 Stuntz, 193-4.

36 *Ibid*, 196.

37 Jean-Pierre Bastian, *Breve Historia de Protestantismo en America Latina*, CUPSA, Mexico,157-163.

38 *Ibid*, 163-165.

39 Alberto Rembao, http://www.bu.edu/missiology/missionary-biography/r-s/ rembao-alberto-1895-1962/ (accessed June 13, 2016)

woman in conciliar Protestant ministry.[40] The contextualization of the themes reflected the emergence of stronger Latin American leadership, but efforts for Latin Americans to gain more authority within Protestant institutions was slow and gradual. The Havana Congress saw the birth of the idea for the Federation of Evangelical Churches in Latin America and appointed a committee that met in August of the following year in San Juan, Puerto Rico. This committee was the forerunner of the *Consejo Latinoamericano de Iglesias* (CLAI).[41] At the closing of the Havana Congress on June 30th, no one could have predicted the major economic challenges caused by the crash of the stock market later that fall that would make fundraising more difficult and hamper mission support.[42]

Another of the factors in the transition from teaching Christian mission to global Christianity is precisely the rise of autonomous local leadership. There was a growing anti-American sentiment in Latin America, generally speaking, as a reaction against U.S. imperialism. Meanwhile the 1823 Monroe Doctrine was a more passive document asking European nations not to increase their involvement or recolonialize Latin America, President Teddy Roosevelt's "Big Stick" policy was more pro-active. Following the invasion of the "rough riders" in Cuba's war of Independence in 1898, known in our history books as the "Spanish American War," President Roosevelt announced in December of 1904 that the U.S. could intervene in Western hemispheric nations to assure that they upheld their obligations to international creditors and avoided "foreign aggression to the detriment of the entire body of American nations."[43] This came to be known as the Roosevelt Corollary to the Monroe Doctrine. As a result, the U.S. conducted 32 military missions in Latin America between the Spanish American War and the Great Depression in countries such as Cuba, Panama, Mexico and Nicaragua. These interventions fomented an anti-American backlash that negatively impacted missionary effectiveness in the region. Responding to U.S. military interventions in Nicaragua, American missionary E.M. Haymaker wrote:

> Our Secretary of State in order to protect the interests of a few Americans
> of doubtful character and to win some advantages without greater sacrifice,
> dispatched some marine infantries in Nicaragua and provoked the rage of

---

40   Guy Inman, *Evangelicals at Havana: being an account of the Hispanic American Evangelical Congress, at Havana, Cuba, June 20-30, 1929*, Committee on Cooperation in Latin America, New York, 1929. Also see *Gonzalo Baez Camargo, Hacia la renovación religiosa en Hispano- América. Resumen e interpretación del Congreso Evangelico Hispano-Americano de la Habana*, CUPSA, Mexico City, 1930.

41   *Consejo Latinoamericano de Iglesias* (CLAI) began with an idea from a meeting in Oaxtepec, Mexico in 1978 and was formally organized in Huampaní, Lima, Peru in 1982. Currently there are 55 denominations from the Latin America and the Caribbean who belong to CLAI. http://www.claiweb.org/index.php/el-clai/que-es-el-clai-2 (accessed June 11, 2016)

42   "Annual Report of the Committee on Cooperation on Latin America," New York, 1930, p.8.

43   "Roosevelt Corollary to the Monroe Doctrine," https://history.state.gov/milestones/1899-1913/roosevelt-and-monroe-doctrine (accessed June 11, 2016)

> Latin Americans from Aunt Juana to Ushia, and also provoked the rage of all
> the Americans who are not friends of imperialism and bullying. All the other
> interests, of whatever nature, have to suffer the consequences of this monumental
> mistake…The anti-American sentiment has been intense. Publications and
> demonstrations have been multiple and viral.[44]

It is very telling that the 1930 Annual Report of the Committee on Cooperation
in Latin America began with these words:

> Any treatment of Latin America for the year 1930, from whatever standpoint,
> seemingly must begin with reference to the widely scattered revolutionary
> movements which are having a profound effect on spiritual as well as
> material conditions. Not since 1810, when a general movement throughout
> Latin America was begun to free the colonies from Spain, have our neighbors
> to the South been so universally convulsed by political agitation as they are
> today.[45]

Also, in 1930 the Methodist Churches in Mexico and Brazil gained their autonomy
from the Methodist Episcopal Church in the U.S. The Methodist Church in
Brazil wanted to elect their own bishops and the church in Mexico needed to
become autonomous to function under the 1917 constitution that emerged from
the Mexican revolution preventing the intervention of foreign-born clergy.[46] The
National Presbyterian Church of Mexico organized its first general assembly in
1947. Mexico had an anti-American sentiment after U.S. interventions during
the revolution and the church also felt it as a result of the Cincinnati Plan. So a
transition to national leadership was a natural occurrence.

Eugene Nida outlined four categories of Latin American churches in his
anthropological assessment from 1961: 1) mission-directed churches that are run
by expatriates and foreign mission agencies, 2) "national-front" churches that have
figureheads of national leaders, but are really directed from abroad, 3) indigenized
churches that have broken away from the "mother" churches abroad and are now
under national leadership, and 4) fully indigenous churches that have developed

---

44 M.E. Haymaker "Ecos de Kellogg," *The Evangelist*, VI:6, 1927, p. 14. Cited in Juan Stam,
    "La Misión Latinoamericana y el Imperialismo Norteamericano, 1926-1928," published
    in Contribuciones para una Historia del Protestantismo en America Latina," Taller de
    Teología, no.9, año 1981. (my translation).

45 "Annual Report of the Committee on Cooperation on Latin America," New York, 1930, p. 1.

46 Katherine Ryan-McIlhon, Los Artículos Anticlericales en la Constitución Federal de 1917
    y sus Consecuencias Históricas en Mexico, *Ave Maria International Law Journal*, Vol. 1:2,
    2012, 489-90.

under Latin American leadership and are self-funded.[47] So far this paper has focused on categories one and two, but now I will turn to models three and four as representatives of the transition from teaching mission to teaching global Christianity. Examples of the third and fourth categories emerged with the arrival of Pentecostalism in Latin America in the early 20th century.

Arrival of Pentecostalism in the Latin America

The Azusa Street revival occurred on April 14, 1906 on Azusa Street in Los Angeles when Seymour and seven others fell to the floor in a religious ecstasy, speaking in tongues.[48] There were blacks, whites, Mexicans, Italians, Chinese, Russians, and Indians involved early in the revival, which was unusual for a segregated American society. People came from all around the world to see and experience the revival. By November of the same year "Spirit filled" workers went out to nine different American cities and also left for India, China, Europe, Palestine and Africa.[49] It arrived in Latin America after Methodist woman missionary and early Pentecostal missiologist, Minnie Abrams, mailed a copy of her book, *The Baptism of the Holy Spirit and Fire*, from India to friend and former classmate at the, Chicago Training School for deaconesses, May Hilton.[50] Hilton was one of the first two graduates of the school and subsequently married Dr. Willis Hoover and became a William Taylor self-supporting missionary in Chile.[51] Having a copy of Abrams book, Hoover sought and experienced baptism of the Holy Spirit in Valparaiso, Chile in 1909 and began a movement within the Methodist Episcopal Church before being expelled to the start of the Methodist Pentecostal Church of Chile.[52]

47 Eugene Nida, "The Indigenous Churches in Latin America," *Practical Anthropology*, 8:3, 1961, 97.
48 Vinson Synan, *The Holiness-Pentecostal Tradition in the United States* (Grand Rapids: William B. Eerdmans Publishing Company, 1971), 96.
49 Allan H. Anderson, *Spreading Fires: The Missionary Nature of Early Pentecostalism* (Maryknoll: Orbis Books, 2007), 51.
50 Minnie Abrams, *The Baptism of the Holy Spirit and Fire*, 2nd edition, Muhkti Mission Press, Kedgaon, 1906, 67.
51 Dana Robert, *American Women in Mission: A Social History of their Thought and Practice*, Mercer University Press, 1997, 247.
52 Philip Wingeier-Rayo, "Hoover C. Willis," in Charles Yrigoyen and Susan Warrick, eds., *Historical Dictionary of Methodism*, 3rd ed. (Scranton: Historical Dictionary of Methodism, 2013), 191-92.

Italian Waldensian Luigi Francescon received the gift of the Spirit in Chicago in 1907 and then had a vision to go to Argentina and Brazil in 1910 to share his faith.[53] Pentecostalism reached Mexico when a couple from Villa Aldama, Chihuahua went to Los Angeles during the Mexican Revolution began attending a Pentecostal church where they experienced revival, were converted and baptized. After a couple years, they were well-established in the Pentecostal congregation when the wife, Romana de Valenzuela, began to miss her family and was concerned about their spiritual well-being. In the fall of 1914 she returned home to Villa Aldama to convert them to her new faith.[54] On November 1, 1914 Romana was leading a time of prayer with 12 people when they received a baptism of the Holy Spirit and spoke in tongues. Romana's vision had been fulfilled and Pentecostalism had arrived in Mexico under the name of *Iglesia Apostolica*.[55]

José Miguez Bonino reflects on the arrival, growth and varieties of Latin American Protestantism in his classic book, *Faces of Latin American Protestantism*. On the arrival of Pentecostalism, Miguez Bonino writes:

> The seed could have started in Los Angeles or Chicago, but it was planted in Latin American soil and was nourished with the vital juices of this land and new Latin American grassroots masses have proven that the flavor of the fruits corresponds to the demands of their pallet.[56]

Míguez Bonino goes on to recognize that Pentecostalism represented both a challenge and a temptation for Protestants, which generated conflicts and some divisions among Baptist, Methodist, Presbyterian and Disciples of Christ congregations.[57] Walter Hollenweger, Cecilia Mariz, and David Martin, among others, analyze the emergence of Pentecostalism from a sociological perspective and interpret it as a coping mechanism easing and preparing people for the transition from a primarily agrarian to an industrialized society.[58] In the process, many more national churches were formed representative of Eugene Nida's fourth category of indigenous churches.

---

53 José Miguez-Bonino, *Rostros del Protestantismo Latinoamericano*, ISEDET, Buenos Aires, 1995, 59.

54 Kenneth D. Gill, *Toward a Contextualized Theology for the Third World: The Emergence and Development of Jesus Name Pentecostalism in Mexico* (Frankfort and Berlin: Peter Lang, 1994), 43.

55 Philip Wingeier-Rayo, "A Third Phase of Christianity: A Reflection on One Hundred Years of Pentecostalism in Mexico," in Amos Yong, Vinson Synan and Miguel Alvarez, (eds.) *Global Renewal Christianity: Latin America Spirit Empowered Movements: Past, Present, and Future*, Charisma House: Lake Mary, FL 2016.

56 José Miguez-Bonino, *Rostros del Protestantismo Latino americano*, ISEDET, Buenos Aires, 1995, 60. (my translation)

57 *Ibid.*

58 See the discussion on Pentecostalism in Latin America in Edward Cleary and Hannah Stewart-Gambino, *Power, Politics and Pentecostals in Latin America*, Westview Press, Boulder, 1998. Also see Philip Wingeier-Rayo, *Where are the Poor?*, Wipf and Stock, 2011, 32-3.

Clayton Berg and Paul Pretiz highlighted a growing phenomenon in the region with their article: "Latin America's Fifth Wave of Protestantism." The authors rightly argue that has been much written about (AICs) African Independence Churches or African Indigenous Churches, but not so much about autochthonous churches in Latin America. The authors define autochthonous as churches that:

> (1) have developed spontaneously, without a history of missionary involvement; or (2) were planted by missionary efforts of other Latin American autochthonous churches; or (3) were formerly mission related but have broken foreign links and reflect the people's culture in the deepest sense.[59]

While doing research a few years back in Mexico I visited the annual convention of *La Iglesia Cristiana Apostolica Pentecostes* (ICAP) at their headquarters in the small rural town Zacapalco, Morelos—about two hours south of Mexico City. The gathering met under a large circus tent and was attended by over a thousand people lasting for three days. This autonomous denomination began in 1986 as a legally registered entity with the Mexican government under the leadership of General Apostle Crescenciano Roa Bueno. The ministry quickly spread to 17 small towns in the State of Morelos, then expanded to six other Mexican states, and more recently has sent missionaries to the United States.[60] This is just one example of a growing sector of indigenous Christianity that David Barrett's *World Christian Encyclopedia* calculated to be 40.6% of all *evangélicos* in Mexico.[61]

Conclusion

So this brings us back full circle to our reflection on teaching Christian mission in an age of world Christianity. Here I would like to highlight certain observations that have emerged from our review of the 1916 Panama Congress and early 20th century mission work in Latin America. The congress reported a Latin American population of 18 million in 1916 and predicted that it would grow to 250 million by the year 2000.[62] Currently the population of Latin America and the Caribbean is more than double that figure at 530 million according to the World Bank.[63] In 1916 the U.S. had about 33% more inhabitants than Latin America and today this trend has reversed. According to a 2014 Pew Research Center poll sixty-nine percent of Latin Americans consider themselves Roman Catholic and 19% *Evangélico*.[64]

59   Clayton Berg and Paul Pretiz, *International Bulletin of Mission Research*, October 1996, 157.

60   *La Iglesia Cristiana Apostolica Internacional* (ICAP) http://www.icap-ar.org/quienessomos/ (accessed June 13, 2016)

61   David B. Barrett, ed., *World Christian Encyclopedia*, Oxford University Press, 1982.

62   Beach, 27.

63   The World Bank, 2015. http://data.worldbank.org/region/LAC (accessed June 1, 2016)

64   Pew Research Center, "Religion in Latin America," November 11, 2014 http://www.pewforum.org/2014/11/13/religion-in-latin-america/ (accessed May 31, 2016)

The 160,000 Protestants in 1916 have grown to around 60 million in 2015, and most of this growth has been unplanned or uncoordinated by mission agencies or congresses.[65] The denominations represented at the Panama Congress are relatively small minorities and 65% of Latin American *evangélicos* identify as Pentecostal.[66] So if we were to measure the growth of those historical denominations present at the 1916 congress as our measure for success, then we would have to state that the efforts of the CCLA were a failure. It is, indeed, the growth of the indigenous churches that provoked David Stoll to ask the question: *Is Latin America Turning Protestant?*[67] However Pope Francis, the first Latin American Pope, has re-energized the Catholic faithful as evidenced through the response to his recent visits to Brazil, Cuba and Mexico.

In spite of Andrew Walls prediction that the greatest issues facing the body of Christ in the 21st century will be ecumenical issues,[68] we have seen a movement away from organized mission congresses, such as Edinburgh, Panama, Montevideo and Havana with their reports, maps, well-planned centrifugal missionary initiative from the center to the margins and sometimes from the North to South. And replacing them have been a trend toward an indigenous, polycentric, empowered indigenous and nationalistic Christianity that starts locally and moves from South to South, and sometimes South to North that marks the transition from teaching of Christian Mission to Global Christianity. In my research I have seen the emergence of indigenous leadership that has inculturated the gospel according to local context, language and culture.

Regarding ecumenism, the controlled spirit of organizing conferences and intentional dialogues between mission agencies has waned and splintered, a new ecumenical spirit of partnerships and impromptu relationships has emerged. *Evangélicos* reluctantly acknowledge that in spite of Catholic-Protestant tensions, most converts come from a deep faith learned in the Roman Catholic Church. Recent studies of Pentecostalism have acknowledged that the two traditions have more in common than originally thought.[69] Todd Hartch in his book, *The Rebirth of Christianity*, calls for better ecumenical relations in the future of Latin American Christianity where Pentecostalism and Catholicism mutually enhance one another.[70] Moreover, the Roman Catholic Church has been strengthened by

65 Samuel Escobar, "It's Your Turn, Young Ones—Make Me Proud! Evangelical Mission in Latin America and Beyond," chapter in *Latin American Mission: Mission Theology for the 21st Century*, Miguel Álvarez, ed., Regnum Books, Oxford, 2016.

66 Pew, "Religion in Latin America," 2014.

67 David Stoll, *Is Latin America Turning Protestant? The Politics of Evangelical Growth*, University of California Press, 1990.

68 Andrew F. Walls, "From Christendom to World Christianity," in *The Cross-Cultural Process in Christian History: Studies in the Transmission and Appropriation of Faith* (Orbis, 2002), 69.

69 Yong, Synan and Alvarez, 15.

70 Todd Hartch, *The Rebirth of Latin American Christianity*, Oxford University Press, Oxford, 2014.

the presence of *Evangélicos*, whose emphasis on the Word of God, passion for evangelism, and music have challenged the Catholic Church. At the same time, *Evangélicos* have learned from the institutional strength, unity, academic rigor and long-standing traditions of Roman Catholics. Finally on the topic of ecumenism, I believe that Robert Speer had a point when the criteria for mission is not whether another religious group is already there, rather on the ethical conditions present. You and I might disagree about doctrines, but no one cannot argue against clean drinking water, food and security for marginalized communities.

Lastly, I also see greater dependence on the Holy Spirit practiced in Latin American Christianity, a trend well documented by Philip Jenkins and Harvey Cox, among others.[71] Gone are the scientific studies and heavy-handed directives from mission agencies. In their place, indigenous leadership has emerged that relies on discernment of the Holy Spirit and empowerment to be nimble within a complex and changing cultural context.

In closing, I would like to share that teaching Christian Mission can no longer be a top-down, "how to" tool box for future practitioners. It needs to be more about cultural sensitivity and listening to emerging and marginal voices. Teaching Christian Mission in an Age of Global Christianity is more about spiritual discernment of where God is already at work, what God is already doing and how we can humbly participate. Perhaps in this age of World Christianity Bishop William C. Brown was right when he stated a hundred years ago in Panama: "I believe most fully in the educated native minister. I am convinced that the Anglo-Saxon cannot within one generation fully understand the view-point of the Latin man [and woman]."[72]

---

71 See Philip Jenkins, *The Next Christendom: The Coming of Global Christianity*, University of Oxford Press, 2002. Also see, *The New Faces of Christianity: Believing the Bible in the GlobalSouth*, Oxford University Press, 2006. Also see Harvey Cox, Fire from Heaven: The Rise of Pentecostal Spirituality and the Reshaping of Religion in the 21st Century, Addison-Wesley, Reading, PA, 1995.

72 Stuntz, 196.

APM

Conference Papers

Theological Metaphors of Teaching Mission in An Age of World Christianity in the North American Context

DAVID THANG MOE, PH.D STUDENT[1]

1   The author is a Ph.D student in Intercultural Theology and World Christianity at Asbury Theological Seminary, 204 Tennent Dr. Wilmore, KY 403209, USA. He came from Myanmar He has published several articles in several peer-reviewed academic journals, including forthcoming articles "The Significance of Karl Barth's Political Theology for the Politics of Myanmar," in *International Journal of Public Theology*, Vol. 10.3. (Leiden: Brill, 2016) and "Postcolonial and Liberation Theology as Partners in Praxis Against Sin and Suffering: A Hermeneutical Approach in Asian Perspective," in *EXCHANGE: Journal of Missiological and Ecumenical Research*, Vol. 45. 4. (Leiden: Brill, 2016).

Abstract

The aim of this paper is to present not WHAT to teach, but HOW to teach mission in an age of World Christianity in the context of North American seminaries/theological institutions. In response to the encounter between North American teachers and Global South students, this paper would like to propose three theological metaphors of teaching mission as the excellent pedagogies in an age of World Christianity. First—a shepherding metaphor of guiding— teachers as the guides should know the needs of their sheep and the models of how to guide them. The second metaphor is a hospitable form of teaching that demands gift exchange between the hosts and the guests. Students have been for many years on the receiving side, but hospitable teachers should reveal their students' gifts and affirm what they have to offer by using their gifts. The third metaphor is a dialogical method of subject-centered teaching where teachers and students are colearners to discern God's voice anew in the process of interaction. Defining mission as a dialogical discipline, teaching must be both mutually informative and transformative.

Introduction

In his seminal book The Next Christendom,[2] Philip Jenkins rightly argues that the "center of gravity in the Christian world has shifted away from the global north, Europe and North America—to the global south—Latin America, Africa and Asia."[3] However, North America in particular remains a center for world theological education. Many students (including the author) from the global south come to the North America, especially the United States of America, for their theological education. At the dawn of World Christianity, we may contend that

---

2   Philip Jenkins, *The Next Christendom: The Coming of Global Christianity*, 3rd edition. (Oxford: Oxford University Press, 2013).

3   Ibid., 1-3. See also Andrew F. Walls, *The Cross-Cultural Process in Christian History: Studies in Transmission and Appropriation of Faith* (Maryknoll, NY: Orbis, 2002), 84.

a theology of mission is what British scholar Christopher Wright rightly calls "A cross-cultural team game playing with the global players. And the Western academy is no longer a referee, but the Bible itself is."[4]

Yet, we still put western professors at the center of the classroom. What Asian, African and Latin American students are thinking and writing seem marginal to the western professors.[5] If Christianity is a World Religion, the way we teach mission and the way we discuss theology must be attentive to global conversations. The point is not whether we like everything we hear in global conversations, but whether we are willing to listen to each other. Related to this, Kosuke Koyama said, "Christianity suffered from a teacher complex."[6] Western missionaries in particular, and theologians in general, are more interested in teaching than in learning. This is teaching mission as a one way traffic. As far as Koyama's word is concerned, a one way traffic of teaching mission comes from a Christian *crusading mind*. What he proposed was a two way communication of a *crucified mind* that comes from the humble mind of a kenotic Christ (Phil. 2:5).[7]

Koyama's four-decades-old word remains true to our contemporary context of World Christianity. Some professors remain more interested in teaching than in learning, more interested in speaking than in listening. In this paper, I propose to re-define teaching mission as reflecting a dialogical God who speaks and listens to humans. This calls for teaching mission as a mutuality of active speaking and listening between teachers and students with both being centers of the classroom or a metaphor of 'little mission field.'

In response to the encounter between North American teachers and global south students in an age of World Christianity, this paper proposes three theological metaphors as excellent pedagogies. First, I will discuss the metaphor of shepherd-sheep communication as the model for teacher-student relationship. Second, I will speak of the host-guest relationship as the metaphor for teacher-student relationship in a hospitable classroom. Third, perhaps most important, I will discuss the subject-centered classroom as the metaphor of the little mission field in which teachers and students treat each other as subjects of dialogical teaching and learning. They enter into the classroom to engage with each other to hear and experience anew God's voice in the process of interaction.

---

4   See Christopher J.H. Wright's forward in Timothy C. Tennent, *Theology in the Context of World Christianity: How the Global Church is Influencing the Way We Think About and Discuss Theology* (Grand Rapids, MI: Zondervan, 2007).

5   Ibid., xviii.

6   Kosuke Koyama, *Three Mile an Hour God: Biblical Reflections* (Maryknoll, NY: Orbis, 1979), 54.

7   Ibid., 51-54.

Shepherding Metaphor of Teaching: Shepherd-Sheep Relationship

In proposing the shepherding metaphor as a pedagogic teaching in an age of World Christianity, I would like to draw on Johanine's use of a shepherd-sheep relationship (Jn. 10:11-18). John's Gospel is the Gospel of metaphors through which we see Jesus as a shepherd and teacher (Jn. 9:1-5; 11; 17, 22, 35-37).[8] The metaphor of Jesus as a teacher is not limited to John's Gospel, it can also be seen in Mark's Gospel. Mark 4:35-41 provides an interpretive lens for Jesus as teacher in Mark's Gospel.[9] Both Gospels reveal that Jesus teaches by engaging and guiding His hearers. By studying a shepherding metaphor of Jesus' teacher of the past, we get a glimpse of how we can do a better job of teaching mission, that is, embodying the life and work of Jesus in the present and future.[10] What are the implications of Jesus' shepherding metaphor for teachers?

First, Parker Palmer argues that "Good teaching comes primarily from knowing the self and others and secondarily from techniques."[11] For him, knowing one's self (identity) as God's appointed-shepherd (teacher) is crucial to knowing others (students). "Without knowing myself, I cannot know who my students are,"[12] he asserted. He went on to say, "When I cannot see my students clearly, I cannot teach them well."[13] Palmer' aim is to know ourselves by connecting to others.[14] His idea of mutual knowing the self and others echoes Jesus' use of mutual knowing between Himself and His sheep. Jesus said, "I know the need of my sheep and my sheep also listen to my voice" (Jn. 10:14-17).

---

8   Craig R. Koester, *Symbolism in the Fourth Gospel: Meaning, Mystery and Community,* 2nd edition. (Minneapolis, MN: Fortress, 2003).

9   Brian K. Blount, "Jesus as Teacher: Boundary Breaking in Mark's Gospel and Today's Church," in *Interpretation: A Journal of Bible and Theology*, Vol. 70. No. 2. (2016): 184-193 (here p. 184).

10 Ibid., 184-185, Koester, *Symbolism in the Fourth Gospel,* 112-113. Jesus as Master Teacher, see also, Robert W. Pazmino, *God Our Teacher: Theological Basics in Christian Education* (Grand Rapids, MI: Baker Academic, 2001), 59-86.

11 Parker J. Palmer, *The Courage to Teach: Exploring the Inner Landscape of a Teacher's Life* (San Francisco, Calif: Jossey-Bass, 1998), 9.

12 Ibid., 2-3.

13 Ibid., 3.

14 Ibid., 117.

Though Jesus does make it plain who the sheep are here, they are not limited to the disciples and hearers of His teaching. We may take sheep and hearers of Jesus as the paradigms of students for our purpose. After having asked Peter three times, "do you love me?" Jesus said, "tend my sheep," (Jn. 21:16-17). Jesus' use of tend my sheep, is applied exclusively to the pastoral metaphor.[15] It should also be applied to the teaching metaphor. In both metaphors, guidance is crucial. As a shepherd, Jesus guides His hearers or sheep by knowing their needs (Jn. 10:14). Knowing the need of sheep shapes the ways of how He guides them well. Similarly, what teachers should do is to take heed to knowing one's self and students (their identities and needs). In his book, *Tell Us Our Names*, Asian theologian C.S Song argues that God does not give us the name-giving power, but the name-knowing power: the power to identify the names of people with whom we interact, the power to pronounce them correctly, and the power to understand their contexts.[16]

Second, knowing one's self and knowing students is not enough, what the matter is to know the methods of seeking how to guide them on the right path. This requires the intellectual skills and methods of teachers. As a shepherd, Jesus is a skillful guide. Skillfulness is the primary characteristic of a shepherding metaphor of the teachers. As the proverb states; "it is not enough to give hungry people fish, but you have to teach them how to fish." By the same token, the shepherding role of teachers is not simply to transfer knowledge to their students, but to provide them with informative skills.

In order to teach students from different contexts, it is imperative that teachers have multiple skills, such as "linguistic skills, interpersonal skills, and knowledge of global worldviews,"[17] of which the latter two are necessary. Without having these skills, it would be hard for teachers to guide students forward a level of growth. In my own experience, it is difficult to study with teachers those who do not know or reject our contexts. The challenge happens especially when talking about contextualization. For example, spirit-worship[18] is crucial to an Asian worldview, but this does not make sense to some western teachers those who do not accept or believe the spiritual existence.[19]

---

15   Quentin P. Kinnison, "Shepherd Or One of the Sheep: Revisiting the Biblical Metaphor of the Pastorate," in *Journal of Religious Leadership*, Vol. 9, no. 1 (Spring 2010): 59-91.

16   C.S. Song, *Tell US Our Names: Story Theology From An Asian Perspective* (Maryknoll, NY: Orbis, 1984), 93-96.

17   David Kolb, *Experiential Learning: Experience as the Source of Learning and Development* (Upper Saddle River, NJ: Prentice Hall, 1983). The other two types of students are convergent and accommodative learners.

18   For a full discussion, see my article, David Thang Moe, "Nat-Worship and Paul Tillich: Contextualizing a Correlational Theology of Religion and Culture in Myanmar," in *Toronto Journal of Theology*, Vol. 31. No. 1 (Spring 2015): 123-136.

19   For the Western rejection of the existence of the spirits, see Philip H. Wiebie, *God and Other Spirits: Imitation of Transcendence in Christian Experience* (Oxford University Press, 2004), 1-2.

When teachers do not understand the local contexts of their students, not that we serves methods, but that methods serve us as our tour guides. Received knowledge happens when teachers are knowledgeable and skillful.[20] To argue that skillfulness is an important character of a shepherd, let me compare the shepherding metaphor of skillful teachers with the metaphor of skillful midwives. The role of midwives is not simply to tell the pregnant woman all she needs to know about the birth process, but to help the woman make the birth possible by using the intellectual skills. Similarly, good teaching is not simply telling the students what to do, but it is guiding them how to do things.[21]

Third, generosity is another important character of a good shepherd. Jesus said, "I lay down my life for my sheep," (Jn. 10:15). Jesus' generosity is the model for the teachers' love toward their students. True we are not Jesus and, we cannot lay our lives down exactly like Jesus does for His sheep, but in our limited way, we should strive for Jesus' generosity by being generous to our students. By generosity, I do not necessarily mean being generous in giving undeservingly high grades to students, but rather by guiding them with patient love. It is natural that some students less talented in the subject matters than others, which require that the generous act of patience is crucial to a teacher's shepherding ministry. Palmer rightly notes that "Good teaching is a gift and a generous act of commitment and it comes from the inner heart of a patient teacher."[22]

Finally, a shepherding metaphor of guidance is not from above, but from beside and before. By a shepherding metaphor of guidance from above, I mean the teachers' guidance of students with power. The teacher's role in reference to the shepherding 'metaphors of before and beside is to lead students and to walk the same speed with them. As Koyama noted in his book *Three Mile an Hour God*, our God of patient love is in no hurry, but walks the same speed of three miles as finite creatures do. In the desert, God took 40 years to teach a lesson to Israel (Deut. 8:1-4). How slow and patient![23] If God the patient shepherd is the model for us, teachers should also walk beside with their students. Patient shepherds never leave the sheep behind, but also guide them forward.

---

20   Mary F. Belenky et al, *Women's Way of Knowing: The Development of the Self, Voice and Mind*, 10th anniversary (Basic Books, 1997), chapter 10.

21   Ibid.

22   Ibid., 1-5.

23   Koyama, *Three Mile an Hour God*, 3-7.

Hospitable Metaphor of Teaching: Host-Guest Relationship

In our metaphor of host-guest relationship, we will regard North American teachers as hosts and global south students as guests. This is the reality. Students coming to North America see themselves or are seen by teachers as guests. They even feel themselves or are made felt by teachers as strangers or aliens (*xenos*). It is painful to be strangers in the land where local people do not welcome you as neighbors. Especially painful is the experience when people laugh at your English with different accent and when your hidden gifts are unnoticed. Equally painful is the reciprocal experience when hosts and guest built the wall of hostility instead of extending hospitality to each other (Rom. 12:3).[24] What I want to propose is to see hosts and guests as 'bread' for each other.

In making my case that hosts and guests are to be seen as "bread for each other," I would like to define the true meaning of hospitality as reciprocal. Hospitality has been defined in some contexts, especially in Asia, as a one way relation. By "one way relation," I mean hosts are seen as bread for guests. Hosts are the givers, while guests are the passive revivers or consumers. From the perspective of Christian education, such is what one may call a 'banking model' thereby students or the metaphors of guests are often seen as the mere receivers of knowledge or the metaphor of bread from teachers. This is not the model of hospitality of which I speak. Instead, we need to re-define the meaning of hospitality. Who do we mean by hospitality in an age of World Christianity?

According to French philosopher Jacques Derrida, hospitality comes from a combination of two Latin words—*hostis* (stranger) and *hospes* (host and guest). The meaning of hospitality is to be defined as the exchange of hostility for hospitality and mutual acceptance between two groups.[25] The New Testament word for hospitality is *philoxenia*, to make the stranger become the guest by way of making friendship.[26] In this sense, we contend that host-guest relationship nothing more

---

24 Kosuke Koyama, "Extend Hospitality to Strangers: A Missiology of Theologia Crucis," in *Currents in Theology and Mission*, Vol. 20. No. 3 (June 1993): 165-176. I drew the idea of painful experience as "difference" by Lalsangkima Pachuau, "Engaging the Other in a Pluralistic World: Toward a Subaltern Hermeneutics of Christian Mission, in *Studies in World Christianity*, Vol. 8, No. 1 (2002): 63-80.

25 Jacques Derrida, *De L'hospitalite* (Paris: Calman-Levy, 1997).

26 Koyama, "Extend Hospitality to Strangers," 165.

or less making friendship. If this is so, the classroom should not be perceived as a stranger-centered environment. It must be a hospitable classroom. But who would create the latter type of classroom?

In all contexts the hosts are responsible for creating a hospitable environment. A good host is the one who not only receives his or her guests with goodwill, but also makes them feel comfortable at home. First of all, this asks for North American teachers as the metaphors of hosts not only to welcome their foreign students as guests with goodwill, but also to make them feel comfortable in the classroom dominated by the local white students. In describing classroom as a hospitable environment, I do not necessarily mean that teachers have to provide food, snacks and coffee. Instead what I propose is that the teacher should create a hospitable classroom. The hospitable classroom can be defined as a space where teachers and students enter with the generous attitude of exchanging blessing and bread of insights to be primary sources of mutual nourishment.

It follows from this hospitable space that the hospitable teachers have two additional tasks. They are what Henri Nouwen convincingly calls: "revelation and affirmation."[27] First, revealing involves teachers' exposing the hidden gifts and insights of students. Reveling task of teachers is relevant to the context where students, especially foreign students keep silent in the class. In my own experience, many Asian students keep silent in the classroom, not because they know nothing or have nothing insights or talents to offer in the classroom, but mainly because they feel shy. Their shyness stems from two places. First, they feel shy about their spoken English. Second, they are afraid the questions they ask might be wrong. In this context, the task of teachers is not only to reveal and help students see their hidden talents, but also to empower and aid them.

Without revealing their hidden gifts and empowering them, the shy students would remain silent in the classroom. As a result, they would remain the metaphors of the passive guests who simply receive food from their hosts. Thus in this sense, we may say that a good guest or student is the one who not only honors the house of his or her host with a joyful sense of presence, but also honors the host with a generous sense of contribution. Likewise, a good host or teacher is the one who not only exposes the hidden talents of students as sources worth serious attention for their own sakes as well for their fellow students and teachers,[28] but also empowers them with all the care they need.[29]

---

27 Henri J.M. Nouwen, *Reaching Out to Our Fellow Humans: The Three Moments of the Spiritual Life* (New York: Doubleday, 1966), 87-88.

28 Ibid.,

29 Ibid., 84.

Second, the teachers have to affirm their students' voices of questions or discussions.[30] If the revealing task of teachers is to expose the invisible talents of students and to empower their ability, the affirming task of teachers is to confirm what students discuss or contribute. Metaphorically, a good host not only accepts all the food a guest brings, but also appreciates what the guest contributes. Regardless of being delicious or not, a good and polite host should accept it. By the same token, a hospitable teacher should politely affirm what students raise questions or discussions in the classroom.

The language of teachers' affirmation of students includes: "yes, that is thoughtful and great question." This is not to say that the students' contributions replace the teachers' criticism. Instead the teachers' affirmation aims at welcoming the voices of students' contribution in the class. If teachers impolitely reject the contributions made by students, that students would feel embarrassed. In order not to happen this, I argue that affirming the students' contributions is a necessary attitude of good teaching. On the other hand, I argue that good teachers should hold a dialectical form of affirmation or praise and criticism where praise addresses students' strengths and criticism their weaknesses. The aim of criticism not to belittle them, but to show them how and what they can improve. Of course, praise is a stimulus for the students, and they want to hear more affirmative.[31] Thus, it is right to conclude that while teachers' revealing task helps students see themselves as the contributors of insights for themselves and hosts, the affirmative language encourages them to keep saying something in the classroom. The hospitable teachers must hold this dialectical form of reveling and affirming tasks.[32]

Dialogical Metaphor of Teaching: Subject-Centered Classroom

Most professors of any field, but especially professors of religion, emphasize the need for dialogical teaching. But, the way the teachers design the classroom remains either a teacher-centered space or a student-centered space. In a teacher-centered classroom, teachers tend toward giving lectures without listening and some even abuse their power. In a student-centered classroom, by contrast, the role of teachers is less and less about forming students, more and more about listening to them without providing them with intellectual skills.[33] The result is not a dialogical teaching. A genuine dialogical classroom must be operated in both teaching and learning.

---

30   Ibid., 87-89.
31   Herman A. Witkin, "The Role of Cognitive Style in Academic Performance and in Teacher- Student Relations," in *Research Bulletin* (June 1973): 1-58, (here p. 32).
32   Nouwen, *Reaching Out to Our Fellow Humans*, 88-89.
33   Palmer, *The Courage to Teach*, 119-123.

What we need in an age of World Christianity is to design a "subject-centered classroom,"[34] to quote Palmer's word. In the subject-centered classroom, both the teachers and students play their respective roles as "active participants and collaborative learners."[35] When I suggest that teachers and students gather in the subject-centered classroom as active participants and collaborative learners, I am not stating that teachers and students share an equal authority; instead, they share an equal opportunity. In the subject-centered classroom, the teachers remain *authoritative* instructors in terms of facilitating the class, giving and assessing assignments, but the main purpose of the subject-centered classroom is to see teachers not as *authoritarian* instructors.[36]

Of course, we must stress the former type of teachers because they hold a dialogical form of teaching and learning without abandoning their authority. Three questions emerge. What makes a dialogical classroom possible? What are the respective roles of teachers and students? What would be the ultimate goal of dialogical teaching?

First, we propose the need for mutual respect. We contend that it is mutual respect that creates a genuine dialogical classroom. Jürgen Moltmann rightly stated;

> Mutual trust is a necessary habit of freedom; its living space. Where other people trust me, I can develop freely and go out of my self. Fish need water to swim, birds need air in which to fly, and we need trust in order to develop humanity.[37]

But how do we attempt mutual respect or trust between North American teachers and global south students of different cultures? We may attempt it by breaking the boundary of different cultures and by building the common bridges of humanity. The assertions are two in number. In the latter sense, teachers need to treat students respectfully as 'humans' regardless of race and nationality.[38] Students must do likewise by treating teachers respectfully as 'humans' regardless of position and status. In other words, one may argue that the subject-centered classroom is to be characterized by the democratic nature of a human-centered atmosphere.

---

34   Ibid., 119.

35   Ibid.

36   Pazmino, *God Our Teacher*, 72-73.

37   Jürgen Moltmann, From a Caaps Lecture, given April 27, 2005, *"In God We Trust, In Us God Trusts: On Freedom and Security in a Free World,"* http://www.theologicalhorizons.org/documents/CAPPStrinscript. pdf, accessed on June 3, 2016.

38   Stephen D. Brookfield and Mary E. Hess, "How Can We Teach Authentically? Reflective Practice in the Dialogical Classroom," in *Teaching Reflectively in Theological Contexts: Promises and Contradictions*, eds. Mary E. Hess and Stephen D. Brookfield (Malabar, FL: Krieger Publishing, 2008): 1:17 (here p. 11).

In the context of belonging to the different cultures, teachers and students need to see their social differences not as contradictions or conflicts, but as gifts of God's creation and as opportunities for complementary and mutual enrichment. This requires boundary breaking and bridge building. Without boundary breaking, we cannot follow Jesus who first breaks the boundary between heaven and earth. Jesus is a dialogical missionary and teacher. In his article *Jesus as Teacher*, Brian Blount argues that "Jesus teaches by engaging and crossing boundaries of His hearers."[39] Peter C. Phan made an even stronger statement which has connection to understanding mission as the act of intercultural studies in an age of World Christianity. He said:

> Intercultural studies or multicultural hermeneutics see social boundaries or boarders as the privileged meeting place where people from both sides of the boundaries or boarders with different cultural backgrounds can come and listen to one another and to create a fuller meaning of theology (text).[40]

If we apply Phan's statement, our task is not only to see the multicultural classroom as a privileged meeting place but also to cross boundaries respectfully. In a similar vein, Lalsangkima Pachuau asserts that "If two or three strangers of different cultures are to meet in the *classroom*, they have to move each other, crossing boundaries and exchanging their different views for mutual enrichment."[41]

In short, it should be noted that breaking boundaries and building bridges are two essential attitudes of mutual respect for the teacher-student relationship. This mutuality of breaking boundaries and building bridges connects to Jürgen Habermas' idea of communicative action. He argues that "communicative action is coordinated not through egocentric or imperial calculations, but through an act of reaching and understanding the other."[42] Habermas' idea of communicative action supports interpersonal, intercultural, interfaith, and ecumenical teaching. Of course, there could also be mutual disagreements on the subject matter of theology, not on humanity. However, mutual respect must always take priority over all kinds of mutual disagreements and debates.

---

39 Blount, "Jesus as Teacher," 189.

40 Peter C. Phan, "Crossing the Boarders: A Spirituality for Mission in Our Times from Asian Perspective," *SEDOS Bulletin*, Vol. 35. (2003): 8-19.

41 Lalsangkima Pachuau, "Vulnerability and Empowerment in Crossing Frontiers: A Christian Theology of Mission," in *Asbury Journal*, Vol. 68, No. 2. (Fall 2013): 78-94 (here p. 78). *Italics* mine.

42 Jürgen Habermas, *The Theory of Communicative, Volume One, The Rationalization of Society* (Boston, MA: Beacon, 1984). 3.

Second, dialogical teaching must be grounded in what noted Christian educator Stephen Brookfield called "Discussion-based participation classroom."[43] By "discussion-based participation," Brookfield referred to a free and open conversation in which teachers and students enter to explore and reflect fearlessly on any kind of theological discipline.[44] The role of teachers is not only to invite students into conversation, but also to lead or guide the conversation.[45] This does not mean that students become the mere objects of learning, but rather they become the invited participants in mutual conversations. In this way, students would express their voices—their identity, their experiences and their understanding of the world and of theology.[46]

Of course, students' expression of their voices in discussion does not necessarily mean "talking a lot or showing everyone else how much they know or have studied."[47] Again we must remember international students whose first language is not English. Mostly they remain on the dialogical periphery.[48] In this context, what the native English-speaking students need to do is let international students speak and listen to their voices patiently. Indeed, dialogical classroom involves sharing students' experiences (context), wrestling with theology (text) and anticipating some comments from teachers and fellow students. It also involves appreciation for all the contributions.[49] By this they teach each other—students teach teachers and fellow students. But I contend that discussion in the classroom should not end with teachers assimilating their students into their own stance.

In my own experience, some teachers have a good attitude of listening to the voices of their students in discussion, but they have a bad attitude of assimilating them into their own stance. This happens especially when teachers and students have their different beliefs of truth. This I would call "truth against truth." How should teachers and students make space for seeking a common truth? To answer this, we need to define what we mean by truth? According to Palmer, "truth is both in us (what we mutually believe is true)—teachers and students—and simultaneously beyond us (the mystery of God)."[50] Truth can be discoverable in the sense that a

---

43 Stephen D. Brookfield, "How Do We Invite Students into Conversation? Teaching Dialogically" in *Teaching Reflectively in Theological Contexts: Promises and Contradictions*, eds. Mary E. Hess and Stephen D. Brookfield (Malabar, FL: Krieger Publishing, 2008): 32-45.

44 Ibid., 44-45.

45 Ibid., 32.

46 Palmer, *The Courage to Teach*, 120.

47 Brookfield, "How Do We Invite Students into Conversation?" 34.

48 Ibid., 47.

49 Ibid., 34-44.

50 Parker J. Palmer, *To Know as We are Known: Education as Spiritual Journey* (San Francisco, Calif, HarperCollins, 1993), 36.

mutual knowing of truth can fit into a synthetic harmony. On the other hand, it is beyond our comprehension.[51] The former demands our compromises, while the latter demands acknowledging our limitations.

Thus, good teachers are not the ones who lead discussions in the classroom toward predetermined conclusions[52] but guide them to a continued discovery of seeking a higher truth. The true meaning of education is not about drawing in but about drawing out. If so, the goal of teachers is not to draw students into their own destiny, but to draw them out with the intellectual skills into a journey of discourse and contemplation on the mystery of God. True dialogical teaching is a space free from assimilation and coercion in which students can discuss, defend, debate, wrestle with, evaluate and come to their own conclusions.[53] In our ongoing journey of dialogical approach to the contemplation of the mystery of God and to the pursuit of truth, David Tracy said well:

> Say only what you mean, say it accurately as you can, listen to and respect what the other says, however different or other; be willing to correct or defend your opinion if challenged by conversation partner; be willing to argue if necessary, to confront if demanded, to endure the necessary conflict, to change your mind if the evidence suggests it.[54]

Third, and perhaps most important, the ultimate goal of dialogical teaching is mutual transformation. This kind of pedagogy has been developed by Brazilian educator Paulo Freire in his seminal book *Pedagogy of the Oppressed*.[55] Freire talked about the need for mutual transformation between teachers (elites) and students (oppressed). For Freire, mutual transformation has to start with the voices of students. Because of this, we have argued earlier that it is imperative for teachers to invite students into conversation. But how does that conversation lead teachers into transformation? The success of teachers' transformation depends on their compassion in listening to the voices and stories of students and their conviction about the voices and stories they heard.

---

51 Ibid.

52 Brookfield, "How Do We Invite Students into Conversation?" 46.

53 David J. Lose, "How Do We Make Space for Students to Seek Truth? Teaching With Conviction," *Teaching Reflectively in Theological Contexts: Promises and Contradictions*, eds. Mary E. Hess and Stephen D. Brookfield (Malabar, FL: Krieger Publishing, 2008): 19-31 (here p. 21)

54 David Tracy, *Plurality and Ambiguity: Hermeneutics, Religion and Hope* (San Francisco, Calif: Harper & Row, 1987), 19.

55 Paulo Freire, *Pedagogy of the Oppressed*, trans. Myra Bergman Ramos (New York: Herder and Herder, 1970).

The nature of true dialogical teaching is built upon a mutual activity of speaking and listening. When teachers speak, students listen, when students speak, teachers listen. When we listen carefully, we always learn something new. The goal of this process is a mutual transformation of both teachers and students.[56] This means that transforming education is not simply to be brought down to students but is directed by the voices of students with the cooperative participation of teachers. In this context, three kinds of transformation could happen on both sides of teachers and students.[57] In order to show how three kinds of transformation could happen, I observe that most students come to seminary for three main reasons: preparation, discernment, and formation/equipment.[58]

First, the task of teachers is to prepare students to be skillful interpreters of the text or theology by connecting with their experience or context. This focuses on how and what are to be interpreted.[59] This is a cognitive transformation (head) involving a new theological understanding. In the process of preparing students, teachers and students are transformed in a new way of thinking about and discussing theology. Second, the task of teachers is to accompany students, praying with them in the process of their discernment. This is an affective transformation (heart), which focuses on God's call, students' spiritual awareness, and their compassionate feeling about ministry. Third, the task of teachers is to form/equip students not only to be skillful interpreters of theology but also to become theological practitioners outside the classroom. This is a behavioral transformation (hand). Three kinds of transformation depend on each other.[60]

Conclusion

If mission is a dialogical discipline, teaching method should also be understood as a two way of communication. One way of communication, that is, teaching without learning, speaking without listening, transforming others without being transformed by others is no longer acceptable in an age of World Christianity. A good teacher of mission must not be the one who merely transfers information to

---

56 Ibid., 23-24, 29, 39.

57 Perry Shaw, *Transforming Theological Education: A Practical Handbook for Integrative Learning* (Cumbria: Lanham Global Library, 2014), 151.

58 I drew the idea made by Dr. Timothy C. Tennent, President and Professors of Mission at Asbury Theological Seminary, Wilmore, KY 40390. My own conviction goes along with him.

59 See Charles R. Foster et al, *Educating Clergy: Teaching Practices and Pastoral Imagination* (San Francisco, Calif: Jossey-Bass, 2006), 167-169.

60 Ibid., 10. See also, Brookfield, "How Can We Teach Authentically?" 4.

students without listening to their voices, but the one who invites students to speak and listen to their voices with the hope of mutual learning and transformation in the process of interaction.

In light of this, I would argue that a good teacher should be characterized by the metaphors of a good shepherd who knows the needs of his or her sheep and knows a method of how to guide them and of a good host who accepts his or her guests with open arm and affirms what the guests contribute. The metaphor of host-guest relationship reminds us that the global south students are not merely impoverished and empty beggars for North American food (education) but the generous guests to whom hospitality and insights must be both extended and received. Teaching mission in an age of World Christianity constantly requires designing a hospitable and subject-centered classroom.

This way of teaching mission reflects the character of Jesus as a dialogical teacher whose teaching is never imposed on the hearers of His messages, but requires for asking the questions and encourages them to keep thinking. This way of teaching mission reflects the nature of Christianity as a world religion thereby western academy or teacher is no longer a referee, but the Bible itself is, and missiology is becoming an intercultural team game with global players in a dialogical and hospitable field.[61]

---

61 I drew the idea by Wright in his forward, Tennent, *Theology in an Age of World Christianity.*

Works Cited

Belenky, Mary F.
  et al. *Women's Way of Knowing: The Development of the Self, Voice and Mind*, 10ᵗʰ anniversary. Basic Books, 1997.

Blount, Brian K.
  "Jesus as Teacher: Boundary Breaking in Mark's Gospel and Today's Church." In *Interpretation: A Journal of Bible and Theology*, Vol. 70. No. 2 (2016): 184-193.

Brookfield, Stephen D.
  "How Do We Invite Students into Conversation? Teaching Dialogically." In *Teaching Reflectively in Theological Contexts: Promises and Contradictions*, eds. Mary E. Hess and Stephen D. Brookfield. 32-45 Malabar, FL: Krieger Publishing, 2008.

  ------. "How Can We Teach Authentically? Reflective Practice in the Dialogical Classroom." In *Teaching Reflectively in Theological Contexts: Promises and Contradictions*, eds. Mary E. Hess and Stephen D. Brookfield. 1-17. Malabar, FL: Krieger, 2008.

Derrida, Jacques.
  De L'hospitalite. Paris: Calman-Levy, 1997.

Foster, Charles R,
  et al, *Educating Clergy: Teaching Practices and Pastoral Imagination*. San Francisco, Calif: Jossey-Bass, 2006.

Freire, Paulo.
  Pedagogy of the Oppressed, trans. Myra Bergman Ramos (New York: Herder and Herder, 1970.

Habermas, Jürgen.
  The Theory of Communicative, Volume One, The Rationalization of Society. Boston, MA: Beacon, 1984.

Jenkins, Philip.
  The Next Christendom: The Coming of Global Christianity, 3ʳᵈ edition. Oxford: Oxford University Press, 2013.

Kinnison, Quentin P.
  "Shepherd Or One of the Sheep: Revisiting the Biblical Metaphorof

the Pastorate." In *Journal of Religious Leadership*, Vol. 9, No. 1. (Spring 2010): 59-91.

Kolb, David.
Experiential Learning: Experience as the Source of Learning and Development. Upper Saddle River, NJ: Prentice Hall, 1983.

Koster, Craig R.
Symbolism in the Fourth Gospel: Meaning, Mystery and Community, 2ⁿᵈ edition. Minneapolis, MN: Fortress, 2003.

Koyama, Kosuke.
"Extend Hospitality to Strangers: A Missiology of Theologia Crucis," In *Currents in Theology and Mission*, Vol. 20. No. 3. (June 1993): 165-176.

-------. *Three Mile an Hour God: Biblical Reflections.* Maryknoll, NY: Orbis, 1979.

David J. Lose,
"How Do We Make Space for Students to Seek Truth? Teaching With Conviction." In *Teaching Reflectively in Theological Contexts: Promises and Contradictions*, eds. Mary E. Hess and Stephen D. Brookfield. 19-31. Malabar, FL: Krieger Publishing, 2008.

Moe, David Thang.
"Nat-Worship and Paul Tillich: Contextualizing a Correlational Theology of Religion and Culture in Myanmar." In *Toronto Journal of Theology*, Vol. 31. No. 1. (Spring 2015): 123-136.

Moltmann, Jürgen,
From a Caaps Lecture, given April 27, 2005. "*In God We Trust, In Us God Trusts: On Freedom and Security in a Free World*," http:/www.theologicalhorizons.org/documents/CAPPStrinscript.pdf, accessed on June 3, 2016.

Nouwen, Henri J.M.
Reaching Out to Our Fellow Humans: The Three Moments of the Spiritual Life. New York: Doubleday, 1966.

Pachuau, Lalsangkima.
"Engaging the Other in a Pluralistic World: Toward a Subaltern Hermeneutics of Christian Mission." In *Studies in World Christianity*, Vol. 8, No. 1. (2002): 63-80.

------. "Vulnerability and Empowerment in Crossing Frontiers: A Christian Theology of Mission." In *Asbury Journal*, Vol. 68, No. 2. (Fall 2013): 78-94.

Palmer, Parker J.
The Courage to Teach: Exploring the Inner Landscape of a Teacher's Life. San Francisco, Calif: Jossey-Bass, 1998.

------. *To Know as We are Known: Education as Spiritual Journey* (San Francisco, Calif, HarperCollins, 1993.

Pazmino, Robert W.
God Our Teacher: Theological Basics in Christian Education. Grand Rapids, MI: Baker Academic, 2001.

Phan, Peter C.
"Crossing the Boarders: A Spirituality for Mission in Our Times from Asian Perspective." In *SEDOS Bulletin*, Vol. 35. (2003): 8-19.

Shaw, Perry.
Transforming Theological Education: A Practical Handbook for Integrative Learning. Cumbria: Lanham Global Library, 2014.

Song, C.S.
Tell US Our Names: Story Theology From An Asian Perspective. Maryknoll, NY: Orbis, 1984.

Tennant, Mark.
Psychology and Adult Learning, 3rd edition. New York: Routledge, 2006.

Tennent, Timothy C.
Theology in the Context of World Christianity: How the Global Church is Influencing the Way We Think About and Discuss Theology. Grand Rapids, MI: Zondervan, 2007.

David Tracy,
Plurality and Ambiguity: Hermeneutics, Religion and Hope. San Francisco, Calif: Harper & Row, 1987.

Walls, Andrew F.
The Cross-Cultural Process in Christian History: Studies in Transmission and Appropriation of Faith. Maryknoll, NY: Orbis, 2002.

Wiebie, Philip H.
God and Other Spirits: Imitation of Transcendence in Christian Experience. Oxford University Press, 2004.

Witkin, Herman A.
"The Role of Cognitive Style in Academic Performance and in Teacher-Student Relations." In *Research Bulletin* (June 1973): 1-58.

Mission Shifts from Pope Benedict XVI to Pope Francis

William P. Gregory

Pope Francis has been in office for a little over three years, and in that time his pontificate has been a big story on many fronts. Part of that story concerns the changes he is promoting in the area of mission. *How is he advancing mission as it has been understood in Catholicism since Vatican II? What teachings in the area of mission is he promoting that are new and distinctive? In what new ways is he leading the church in mission?* This paper seeks to address these questions.

To understand Francis' influence on the topic of mission, it is necessary to begin with a few observations about the influence of his predecessor, Pope Benedict XVI. Following this, I will outline the shifts in mission thinking that I see occurring under Francis.

I - Joseph Ratzinger's / Benedict XVI's Understanding of Mission

The thought of Benedict XVI has had a marked influence upon Catholic mission thought and practice as a result of the combined effect of his twenty-four years as head of the Congregation for the Doctrine of the Faith (1981-2005) and eight years as pope (2005-2013). His numerous writings, speeches, and publications – both on the official and unofficial levels and both as CDF prefect and as pope – express a distinctive theological outlook and set of priorities which have had the effect of emphasizing certain aspects of mission and underemphasizing others. Some many argue that it has had the effect of diminishing mission overall.

What is this theological outlook? Benedict's / Ratzinger's theological outlook is marked by a strong church-world division which reflects a similar grace-nature division. Grace and salvation are predominantly seen by him as in the church but lacking in the "world" –a term which refers most to secular culture but more widely includes other religions and even other Christian denominations. The official "inclusivist" Catholic position, of course, is that grace and salvation are in the world as well as in other religions and other churches, but in a different manner or degree than in the Catholic church. Benedict would not deny this, but his attention is almost always focused on the *dissimilarity* between church and world and rarely if ever on the similarity, almost always on the grace in the church and the sin outside it, rarely if ever on the opposite. His is a particular approach to the Catholic teaching on grace and salvation. It is not technically exclusivist but it is on the exclusivist end of the inclusivist spectrum. His view of the church tends toward the idealistic and his view of the world tends toward the pessimistic.

This way of looking at church and world follows in part from Benedict's way of understanding the relationship between nature and grace. His anthropology is Augustinian, emphasizing that human nature and activity are fallen and deeply marked by sin. Sin for him is *essentially lack of faith* – lack of a lived relationship of dependence upon God – and the assertion of independence from God; hatred, selfishness, injustice, and immorality in general follow from this. God's overcoming of sin as lack of relation to God is God's doing; we don't contribute to our own salvation because our native human tendencies as a result of the fall tend to not have much goodness left in them. Benedict's position is not one of total human depravity, for the Catholic tradition does affirm some goodness left in human nature and activity after the fall and some role for human cooperation with the divine in receiving salvation. But Benedict does not emphasize these much, and he can be critical of the strand of Catholicism that is optimistic about these human potentialities (for example, in Aquinas or Rahner). As a result, he tends to present salvation as a *passive* reception of God's grace, and human activity apart from faith as mostly expressing sinful autonomy from God. Enter the church, acquire faith, and this situation can change.

The reception of grace alters one's nature and one's actions to more and more mirror God's actions, one's life more and more the life of Christ. But apart from grace, outside the church, this shouldn't be so quickly affirmed, and Benedict never chooses to discuss the degree to which it can. So human action informed by faith has the power to reach the heights of love and goodness; human action uniformed by faith does not. It all comes down to the presence of absence of faith – a lived relationship with God, and the place to find this – or to find it fully – is in the church, or to be precise, in the Catholic church.

Benedict's overall theological vision has significant consequences for his understanding of mission. Since the fundamental human problem as he sees it is sinfulness understood as *lack of faith or relationship with God* with all the problems of the world flowing from this basic problem, and since the existence of the church is God's fundamental solution to this problem, mission for him is fundamentally about the continuance of the church in its authentic self, being in the world but not of the world. By extension, mission primarily is about inviting individuals to explicit faith in Christ, existence in the church, and access to the sacraments – in a word, to conversion. Proclamation thus becomes mission's first order of business: "come out of the world and into the church, from the natural human state to the graced human state."

The Catholic understanding of mission, however, includes other elements besides proclamation –dialogue, charity, and working for justice, for example. What place do these have in his thinking?

1) As for dialogue – with other religions, other churches, or the secular world – given Benedict's emphasis on what is lacking in these contexts (grace, or the fullness of grace), he tends to see the value of dialogue mainly in its offering an opportunity for proclamation, religious truth-telling. Dialogue for purposes other than sharing the truth as one sees it has little value for him.

2) As for charitable activity, acts expressing love of neighbor – Benedict affirms the value of these in the strongest terms. They express the deepest nature of the church and are a responsibility of all the faithful. However, his promotion of these activities is overshadowed by his emphasis on proclamation, and he tends to speak of this missionary duty in a way that may not motivate very well. Christians should do these, he says, because such acts are expressive of the true, graced nature of Christian life. We do these to "be ourselves" and to witness to our deepest identity. This may certainly be true theologically, but it is not necessarily a framing of this duty in a way that stings the consciences of the faithful or enflames the moral imagination to action. Francis' approach is much different.

3) Working for structural changes leading to greater justice, peace, and environmental stewardship – Benedict sees these as a subset of charitable activity. As in (2) above, he is affirmative of all these activities; the church (notably the lay faithful, not the hierarchy) must engage in them to express the church's deepest identity. Benedict's framing of these missionary responsibilities, though, tends to be undercut additionally by other elements of his thought.

> • In promoting structural transformations, he insists on the point that our actions don't contribute to or build the kingdom of God (in contrast to the views of various liberation theologians). A strict distinction should be made between the *progress of history*, which will always be fallen however much things may improve from time to time, and the *coming of the kingdom*, which is entirely God's doing. God's kingdom is certainly present incipiently in history now, but this is not as a result of human action, only of divine action. It is present whenever God is loved or whenever God's love reaches us, both of which indicate the presence of faith. For the presence of the kingdom, in other words, look to the church. The most that improved social and material circumstances can provide for people is a better setting for salvation to be received, which is internal and individual.

- Benedict makes these points so strongly because he sees different forms of secular hope in the improvement of the world (e.g. Marxism) as expressing a sinful human hubris and independence from God – a kind of alternate faith to compete with genuine religious faith as dependenceupon God. This concern is understandable, given the influence of Marxism and other philosophies of progress in the twentieth century (though the concern seems a bit dated today). However, Benedict's arguments against these views end up emphasizing innate human sin, evil, and what we cannot change about history to such an extent that the wind is taken out of the sails of his call to missionary activism on these fronts. He so emphasizes what we can't accomplish in the present or shouldn't presume to accomplish in the long run in history, and he so sharply distinguishes social and material improvement from the growth of the kingdom, that it is easy to see Christian faith as necessitating a kind of hopelessness about history in his view, an extreme under-emphasis on what we humans might be able to accomplish, even with God's help. His teachings as a result have been analyzed as giving space to those who would do nothing for the poor or to promote justice.

In sum, Benedict's vision of misson tends to largely center on proclamation and conversion. It includes the other elements just mentioned, particularly charity (of which working for justice is a part). But these other elements seem to function in a mostly supportive role to the main task of communicating the faith in words. This stress on verbal communication was the essence of his "new evangelization" initiative, launched in 2012 and leading to the creation of a new Vatican department. It was an effort to awaken or increase the church's practice of proclamation, particularly in the West, where many have fallen away from the Christian faith and where, in Benedict's assessment, the gospel faces strong resistance from a variety of ideologies (secularism, scientism, relativism, etc.)

Apart from noting the stress he put on words, proclamation, and ideas overall in mission (fitting for a professor become pope), it is worth noting finally that Benedict's overall thinking leads him to take a more defensive posture toward the world. The world is a threat to the church and preserving the church from it is perhaps his greatest concern. The best thing the church can offer the world is its own authenticity.

II – A Few Contrasts Between Benedict and Francis

In comparison to Benedict, Pope Francis has brought a new way of thinking about mission, new ideas and priorities, as well as new leadership. To set the stage for a discussion of these novelties, though without in any way attempting to be comprehensive, let me highlight three important and relevant areas of difference between them which lie at the root of the significant shifts in mission that are occurring under Francis.

First, Francis is much more a man of action than Benedict. Whereas Benedict is best viewed as a theologian-churchman who led most through careful custody of church teaching, Francis is best viewed as a bishop-pastor or mission administrator who leads most by example, service, and attention to actual church functioning and practice. A good deal of Francis' teaching as a result is teaching that attends to, critiques, nurtures, and advances the actual living out of the faith in the church.

Second, I believe Francis sees the center of the Christian faith and practice differently than Benedict. For Benedict, the center of the church is unitary and it is Jesus Christ. The greatest possession of the church is *faith* - the lived experience of relationship to God leading to divinization, union with and conformity to Christ. Jesus established the church as the best means for humans to experience this vertical or mystical dimension of life, which overcomes sin. The church's mission then is to preserve and pass on this treasure of new life in Christ.

Francis would certainly affirm this mystical and Christic center of the faith, but for him it is more binary than unitary. As a man of deep prayer and spirituality he sees transforming vertical relationship with God as non-negotiable and essential. But this transforming relationship for him necessarily extends into the horizontal dimension of relationship with others in the manner Christ related to others – it extends into love. There can be no thinking about the vertical apart from the horizontal. In fact, the measure of one's growth and authenticity in the vertical dimension is the measure of one's growth and authenticity in the horizontal. Christian action in love of others in imitation of Christ, in other words, is as significant and as central to the faith as drawing close to and being changed by God. They are two sides of the same coin. The one is God's gift to us, the other is our gift to God and others in return. The one takes us to the resurrection and to the source of new life in Christ, the other to the ministry of Jesus and to the cross.

This difference between Benedict and Francis can be put in a few other ways. One way is in terms of dominant Christology – Benedict's is definitely Johannine. The center of the faith is sharing in the life of Jesus, discovering this gift and passing it on; Jesus is the kingdom in person. To know Christ is salvation and life in the kinfgdom. Without denying this, Francis would add more Synoptic elements: Christian life includes following in the way of Christ, imitating him in his actions of love and compassion for all, especially the poor and the marginalized. Benedict's Christ is mystically encountered in prayer. Francis' is too, but Francis adds the Christ we also encounter in the poor and the suffering, which he calls "the suffering flesh of Christ." A final way to put this is in terms of visible and invisible. Benedict's Christ is invisible, the one encountered in prayer and liturgy. Francis' is this, but in addition is also visible – the suffering of the earth. Our Christian calling is to be with Christ in both forms, according to him.

A third and final difference between these two popes. Francis attends to the realities of sin and grace in ways very different than Benedict. Instead of lopsidedly focusing on sin in the world and grace in the church in the stark dualism of Benedict who sought to highlight the supernatural distinctiveness of the church, Francis (a) sees and affirms the good outside the church where it is to be found, and (b) is unhesitating in exposing the depths of sin he sees as much in the church as in the world. For Francis, judgment of sin and grace comes down to discerning particular cases, whereas for Benedict the analysis of church and world operates on a level of abstraction from history and particular cases.

In terms of grace and nature, Francis' anthropology is definitely more positive than Benedict's. He is not Augustinian but stands more in the theological tradition of Aquinas and Rahner – humans, even in their fallen state, retain a notable capacity for the good. That doesn't necessarily lead Francis to a more rosy assessment of the depth of sin in the world, but it does enhance his assessment of the possibilities for free human action. There is a lot of good that humans can do apart from faith, he believes, and therefore are responsible for doing. Francis thus speaks with a much louder voice to the world on moral issues than Benedict who harbored more pessimism about human change apart from faith. He more happily carries on Vatican II's recognition of grace and the activity of the Spirit at work in the world than Benedict who read this inclusivist teaching perhaps in the most exclusive way he could.

These basic theological differences lead Francis to frame and advance mission in the Catholic church with a whole new kind of force and focus. In the final section of this paper, I will outline the major features of Francis' rejuvenation of mission.

III – The Francis Shift

What new ideas and practices in the area of mission is Francis promoting? Now, over three years into Francis' pontificate, there is quite an extensive and significant list of items to enumerate. But let me try to present them roughly in their order of importance, as I see them. I will make eight points.

First, Francis is reemphasizing Christian identity in the Catholic church fundamentally in terms of missionary identity. Vatican II taught that "the church is missionary by its very nature" (AG 2) and subsequent popes including Benedict have all affirmed this. However, in practice and in terms of the church's day to day operating theology, this teaching has not been deeply encouraged and promoted. For two generations of Catholics have not been strongly raised to understand that they have a mission and church leadership in this time has often tended to stress the importance of participation in the sacramental life over participation in mission.

But Francis is challenging this. He has introduced a first in Catholic magisterial teaching - *a vivid portrait of the ideal missionary* to guide and challenge the church's self-understanding. He has simultaneously said (1) that this is what the church as a whole should be and (2) what every baptized person is called to become. In other words, like every pope, he has a vision for the church as a whole, and his is a vision which is fundamentally missionary and which he pointedly insists must be lived out on the individual level. Francis is making the missionary the standard and ideal for all the baptized. We are all, in his words, "missionary disciples." There is no being a disciple of Jesus without also being a missionary.

I will explore Francis' vision of mission in more detail below, but let me just add a few more points detailing how, for him, this is a vision which applies to all the faithful and in a fundamentally equal way.

A great deal of Catholic magisterial teaching prior to Francis (one might say, all of it?) has made much of the distinctions between clergy and laity – bishops and priests have been seen to operate on one level and laity on the other, with religious men and women and deacons somewhere in between. Read Catholic magisterial documents and one often finds separate sections addressing these different groups in different ways. To an extent, certainly, there is a place for such distinctions since there are differences in ministry in the church. But notice how dwelling too much on these distinctions takes attention away from the fundamental identity and equality of all of the baptized. Francis seeks to bring us back to this basic equality. In his 2013 apostolic exhortation, *Evangelii Gaudium*, he does something new. He dispenses with addressing different groups and simply speaks of "pastoral workers" – a term broad and inclusive enough to encompass bishops, priests, religious, and lay people working in all their varied capacities. In many different speeches and addresses he also is clarifying what it means to be a priest, a bishop, or a cardinal essentially in terms of being a pastoral worker. The church is a church of pastoral workers, and priests, bishops, and cardinals are to be the models of service and pastoral activity par excellence, not something other than servants and pastoral workers, and certainly not little lords or princes. In this respect, Francis has spoken out intensely against clericalism – any sense of superiority clergy may feel over laity which would entitle them to assign special privileges to themselves, especially those which would bring them away from meaningful pastoral activity and outreach. No, Francis insists, every individual baptized person is called to be a missionary disciple in the church, especially the ordained, and no individual ordained person may see himself as dispensed from this obligation as a consequence of some supposedly higher function within the church. There is no higher function within the church than pastoral ministry and the pope himself has modelled this by keeping up as pope his pastoral outreach to different groups.

So– first - Francis is powerfully promoting the missionary identity of all the baptized and of the church as a whole. Now – second – what does this identity look like? What is his *vivid portrait of the ideal missionary?*

His description is striking. He calls Christians to tend the wounded of the world, to go to all the places of pain and isolation, exclusion and desperation humans find themselves in and bring hope, comfort, friendship, and the light of the gospel. His primary image of the church is of a field hospital after a battle and the gospel passages he cites most are Matthew 25 and the parable of the Good Samaritan. Individual Christians are called to communicate God's compassionate care and mercy in a world which so often leaves the poor, the weak, and the wounded alone to fend for themselves and in many cases die.

This description of the missionary identity of the church is striking for several reasons.

> a) *It is focused.* By comparison, as one reviews what has counted as missionary activity in Catholic teaching on mission since Vatican II, one sees an extensive and diffuse list – proclamation, catechesis, sacramentalization, inculturation, dialogue in various forms (ecumenical, interreligious, and with secular culture), charitable activity, and promotion of peace, justice, and the common good, etc. All these have been understood to form part of the church's mission; moreover they are to be seen together and not separated from each other.

Now Francis is not at all doing away with this cohesive and interconnected list – he supports and advances every one of these individual activities as part of the church's mission - but he does something quite unique, which is to raise up and highlight for the church as a whole the one kind of activity that every baptized person can take part in – person to person acts of mercy. Anyone can do this, even a child. In contrast, consider the difficulty of mission as promoted by Benedict in the form of the new evangelization, which highlights informed and skilled proclamation and directs people inwardly toward personal encounter with the invisible God. This is not an easy task for you're average Christian. Many will find it too esoteric a task, because in a pluralist age speaking adequately and with conviction on faith in the context of the mysterious aspects of life is not easy. Not so Francis' focus on the suffering and needy. This focus will certainly challenge one, but it doesn't present immediately intellectual difficulties.

b) *It is focused on the poor, the vulnerable, and the needy*, in all the forms these states take – from the economically poor (such as the hungry, migrants, and the unemployed) and the physically poor (such as the elderly and the unborn), to the socially and spiritually poor (slaves and trafficked human beings, criminals and those in prison, the lonely and forgotten). This emphasis on helping those in need is known in Catholic social teaching as "the option for the poor," and together with "solidarity" (identification with, personal relationship with, and assistance to vulnerable groups and individuals) - Francis is promoting it as a basic mark or criterion of the life of every baptized Christian, every missionary disciple. Here we see Francis presenting mission as an encounter with "the suffering flesh of Christ" in the world.

c) *It restores authenticity to the church's proclamation.* A person's words always signify in the context of their actions, and the same is true of institutions – churches. At first blush Francis' action or witness-focused paradigm of church mission may appear to underserve or detract from energy spent on proclamation, but in fact the opposite is true. According to Francis, the church's efforts at proclamation and passing on the faith are currently lagging because of a lack of authenticity in the realm of action. The church on the whole, and too many Catholics individually – including priests, bishops, and other church leaders – aren't walking the talk, and so they send a powerful contrary message about the meaning of being Christian. Francis would like to turn that around to give significance to the church's proclamation, and his ideal missionary identity is the means.

Having described Francis' rooting of Christian identity in mission (first), and having examined his core conception of what that identity looks like (second), let's now move on to consider several additional aspects of his thought on mission. I will consider in turn the topics of proclamation, the gospel, sinfulness within the church, sinfulness outside the church, dialogue, and finally conversion.

Third, and speaking of proclamation, Francis is promoting a return to the kerygma in all aspects of the church's self-communication. This necessarily includes both words and actions. The field-hospital plan described above covers the action part of this self-communication: Francis wants the church to so consistently reach out to the wounded of the world that people will know without a doubt that Christianity most stands for the compassionate love and mercy of God, which reaches out to and assists all humans in their travail.

He wants the same focused message to ring out loud and clear in the church's verbal communication of its message. In this respect he has made clear that prior exercises of proclamation, in his view, have in many cases been wanting. Church leaders and Christians in general have emphasized things other than the kerygma and thus obscured the gospel, likely unintentionally. He especially singles out the church's moral and sexual teachings which have often been stressed to the point where the church becomes more known for what it is against than what it is for. Here in this country, for example, one thinks of the US Catholic bishops' strident and vocal opposition to abortion, contraception, and gay marriage which were trumpeted to such a degree that, in the words of one of my teachers, "the good news of Jesus Christ got turned into the bad news about sex."

This transformation of the way the church proclaims its message isn't about changing doctrine or adopting more liberal positions on various issues. Church teaching remains the same. Rather, it is about emphasizing primary things (the kerygma) most and communicating secondary and tertiary church teachings in proportion to their relative importance within the whole body of the church's message, and with sensitivity to how the church's overall message is being perceived by outsiders. This involves a political or public relations kind of awareness – a sensitivity to and care for how one is being perceived and an associated self-discipline over one's intended public communications, so that what the church most stands for wis hat is most frequently communicated, and not something else.

Fourth – But what then is the good news, the kerygma, or the gospel, according to Pope Francis, and does it allow any room for prophetic critique?

Alongside his depiction of the paradigm missionary activity of the church (a field hospital tending the wounded of the world), Francis also provides a clear statement of what he believes the fundamental message of the church is (as well as should be in its public expressions). The key ideas are mercy and justice for the poor. "The name of God is mercy" as the title of a book-length interview with him expresses. God offers to each of us the grace of forgiveness and reconciliation. No matter how gravely we have sinned, God passionately desires to forgive us and to fill us with his love. He comes out to meet us in love. Like the father of the prodigal son, he waits for us.

Sin also exists socially, though, in vast networks that oppress and harm human beings. In his mercy and outreach to the world, God therefore also passionately desires the transformation of sinful human structures and the establishment of true justice and peace on earth. The proclamation of the gospel as "good news for the poor" thus implies a strong critique of all those forms of bondage which hold humans hostage – sinful structures of privilege and exploitation and indifference. We receive God's mercy fully in our own lives to the extent that we are drawn into the works of mercy which express God's passionate outreach to the world in love. And to the extent that we are indifferent or uninvolved in works of mercy, or worse, complicit in structures of injustice, we have not yet fully received the mercy of God. This is a point Francis makes by speaking of Christian life as involving two kinds of encounter or two forms of transcendence beyond the self: (1) the transcendence into encountering God in prayer and (2) the transcendence of outreach and encounter with others.

This brings us– five – to what ails us, or how Pope Francis conceives of sinfulness within the church – that which disfigures and undermines our deepest identity. Characteristically, he describes sin in the church as fundamentally anti-missionary in nature and structure. The core sin he speaks of is an ecclesial self-centeredness which locks individual Christians and the church as a whole into a selfreferential way of being. What is left out, in either case, are other people and the poor. The church's core problem, in other words, is that it doesn't "go out" to encounter and serve others, and part of the cause of this is its failure to encounter God in prayer, who always calls us out of ourselves. The church, in his estimation, is like a closed room, whose air has become stale and lifeless. Or, to provide another image, the church is no longer existing before God as "the mystery of the moon." It is not reflecting the light of the sun, God's divine mercy. This is a very concrete assessment of the church, quite unlike Benedict's idealistic way of reflecting on it. Once again, Benedict focused on the invisible, supernatural dimension of the church as the place of grace. Without denying this, Francis turns to the visible, concrete human dimension and calls us out for failing to live the mission.

Francis' internal critique of the church is extensive, unrelenting, and quite unlike anything the Catholic church has heard in modern times. Anyone who reads paragraphs 76-109 of *Evangelii Gaudium* on the "Temptations Faced by Pastoral Workers" or his 2014 and 2015 "Christmas Greetings" to the Roman Curia will be amazed at the breadth and intensity of his criticisms. Every church worker, in his view, should aspire to embody the missionary ideal. Instead, however, one sees far too much self-concern, careerism, disengagement from the church's evangelizing mission, and joyless pragmatism – an anxious and narcissistic tomb psychology and a sterile pessimism. Even worse, one sees in-fighting, rancor, and profound perversions of Christian spirituality which boil down to spiritual elitism and condemnation of others. The gospel cannot be communicated when this characterizes so many of us. The church itself must be converted before there is to be any new chapter of evangelization in its history.

Several observations are in order here regarding Francis' internal critique of the church.

(a) Once again, it is a critique that challenges everyone in the church to live up to an identical missionary ideal assigned to all the baptized. Cardinals, bishops, and priests are not measured by a different standard. Rather, they are measured more intensely and severely given their greater responsibilities. Connecting back to the first point made – that mission is everyone's responsibility – Francis also seems to be implicity critiquing a kind of "parlour general" mentality on the part of clergy. A bishop or priest isn't doing his missionary duty just when he is calling the shots. He needs to be a foot soldier on the ground who also interacts with people and gets his hands dirty. Francis clearly does this as pope, sending a message to other bishops.

(b) Given the importance and necessity of a continuing internal critique for the sake of the church's mission, one wonders whether Francis has inaugurated a new form of missionary activity analogous to inculturation, interreligious dialogue, or service to the common good of society. This would be a specifically internal intra-ecclesial form of mission centered on drawing the church and individual Christians back into the mission of God.

Six – and sticking with the topic of sinfulness – this brings us to the question of how Francis addresses sinfulness outside of the church, in individuals, cultures, and in social structures.

Francis here is nuanced. On the one hand, he is unrelenting in his prophetic denunciation of larger cultural trends which foster violence, injustice, and disregard for human life. He thus speaks often of the evils of consumerism, of a global economy that disregards human beings (creating vast unemployment and exclusion of many from the necessities of life), of war, and of the trade in arms, drugs, and human persons, among many other issues. In speaking of larger sinful social structures, he pulls no punches.

In regards to sin in the lives of individual human beings, though, he tends to take a very different approach. Except in the worst cases of human corruption (drug lords, the mafia, traffickers, certain kinds of church leaders – and here he addresses classes of people, not individuals) he strictly avoids condemnation. Rather, as noted above, he emphasizes the mercy of God and asks that the church "accompany" people – meet them where they are at in their spiritual journeys and love them like a mother. This point applies to proclamation as well – the key is to communicate what is most essential of the gospel – God's infinite love – to an extent and in a measure that the particular person hearing it can positively understand and assimilate it given their specific history and current capacity for change. This requires of the witnessing Christian care, discernment, and an understanding that God deals patiently with all of us as sinners. The opposite of this is an approach that hurls stones and condemns people for sins – whatever they may be. This Francis sees as a betrayal of mission and a distortion of the gospel, a Pharisaic elevation of rules over the mercy of God and the dignity of the individual. This approach, along with point three above on the need to focus on the kerygma, seem to mark real advances in Catholic thinking – teachings on effective vs ineffective proclamation.

Seven – now what about interreligious dialogue or dialogue with those without any religious identity?

Francis' approach, as noted above, is marked by a positive anthropology and by an affirmation of the presence of the Spirit enlivening all peoples and religions. In contrast to the approach of his predecessor Benedict XVI who tended to see religious and non-religious others more as a threat and who defensively stressed the specialness and superiority of Catholicism over alternative ways, Francis sees others as no threat. Rather they have goodness and gifts of God which we get to discover in coming to know them. This is true both on the macro level of religions and cultures and the micro level of specific individuals – everyone has some gift to share with us, some unique insight into life or quality of heart. The Christian in dialogue should focus on this. She doesn't need to be anxious about the non- Christian or non-religious identity of the other, but rather, secure in her own identity and certainly not hiding it, she should engage in an exchange of gifts, keeping in mind the goods of friendship, greater mutual understanding, and cooperative effort on some common cause that dialogue can achieve.

Returning to the theme of ecclesial self-criticism and correction, Francis believes the overly inwardlooking, self-referential character of Catholic church culture has resulted in a church body relatively unaccustomed to dialogue, to going out of itself, and to engaging creatively and meaningfully with difference. This needs to be replaced by a new, outward-looking culture of encounter and dialogue within the church. One might call this a true missionary culture.

With regard to dialogue with other Christians, Francis' approach is even more affirmative of the other. He doesn't call other Christians to all become Catholic, but affirms their Christian identity and prizes the gifts they have to share with Catholics, and vice versa. While recognizing the real obstacles to Christian unity that exist, he seeks a unity that acknowledges the diverse expressions of the Christian faith – what he calls a "reconciled diversity."

Eight - But what about conversion, Benedict's deepest concern? Isn't the church called to go out to the world, to proclaim the gospel, and to make disciples of all nations? Yes, Francis would say. Absolutely. But his affirmation of the goodness of the other is joined to a recognition that conversion works mainly by attraction and that one's primary job as a Christian witness is to authentically represent Christ. The rest is in the hands of the other and God. And in many cases the grounding of the other person in their particular religious or non-religious identity is deep, putting conversion quite out of consideration. So the main work of Christian witness is instead to focus on Christlike action in the world (especially for the benefit in the needy and forgotten) and the good of encounter itself. When opportunities for proclamation arise, one should take them, but there is a great deal of good in other realms that Christians are also called to do.

Conclusion – In sum, Francis has issued a powerful call to the church to live its mission. All the baptized, from priests and religious to bishops and lay people, have a missionary responsibility. And to focus the challenge upon all, he presents a focused missionary ideal – all should go out to the margins, to the existential and economic and social peripheries and tend to the suffering flesh of Christ. All also should take a thoughtful, sensitive approach to encountering others who aren't Christian or Catholic, valuing first the goodness that is in them, communicating with wisdom and respect the kerygma when appropriate, and seeking with all the common good of humankind.

Select Bibliography

John L. Allen,
   The Francis Miracle: Inside the Transformation of the Pope and the Church
   (New York, NY: Time Books, 2015)

James Corkery, S.J.,
   Joseph Ratzinger's Theological Ideas (Mahwah, NJ: Paulist Press, 2009).

Austen Ivereigh,
   The Great Reformer: Francis and the Making of a Radical Pope (Picador, 2015).

The Elephant in the Room:

Towards a Paradigm Shift in Missiological Education

SARITA D. GALLAGHER, PH.D.

About the Author

Sarita D. Gallagher, Ph.D. is Associate Professor of Religion at George Fox University in Newberg, OR. She is the author of: *Abrahamic Blessing: A Missiological Narrative of Revival in Papua New Guinea* (Pickwick Publications, forthcoming 2014).

Abstract:

In this paper, I identify the critical need within Western academia to move from an ethnocentric understanding of theology to a global theological framework. Western missiological and theological education is often restricted to solely Western hermeneutics, methodologies, and worldview. While the rich diversity of the global Church is sprinkled throughout traditional Western education, the real vibrancy of global missiology, theology, and ecclesiology has yet to fully impact Western academia. In reflecting on this lack of diversity and inclusivity, I identify two paradigm shifts that need to take place before Western academia can engage in a true global dialogue. I argue that by re-determining who has a voice in academia and by listening to global theology in transformative ways, the West can begin to engage meaningfully and humbly as an equal partner in global academic discourse.

As I sat in the small Bible School classroom in Adelaide, Australia, I couldn't help but notice the Papua New Guinean pastor sitting behind me. The topic of the day was church planting and along with a handful of other Australian pastors and leaders, I was spending the afternoon learning about the challenges and potential strategies for planting churches. Our lecturer for the day was a highly experienced church planter by Western standards, having started several churches during his decades in ministry. However, as I listened to him speak, my thoughts turned again to the Melanesian pastor behind me. Would he be asked to share? Would we hear his story? For the Christian leader seated behind me was not merely a member of the course but a visiting minister on a practicum exchange from the largest church in our denomination. Moreover, the irony was not lost on me that he was an experienced church planter who had helped plant not one or two churches but over forty churches during his lifetime. As the minutes of the class dwindled down, I started to realize the obvious; our visitor would not be asked to speak. It was in fact a one-sided practicum; one in which pastors were sent to the West, to learn from the West, but not the other way around.

While there may be exceptions to this scenario, an unfortunate and uncomfortable truth resides within this narrative. I join the increasing number of scholars and institutions, who are on a journey of revisiting and reimagining Western missiological and theological education. In this paper, I outline several ways in which Western theological institutions can increasingly listen to and learn from the collective experience and wisdom of the global Church. In the first section, I draw our attention to the core of the issue; the critical need within Western academia to move from an ethnocentric understanding of religious education to an inclusive and holistic global theological framework. In the following sections

I identify two steps that need to take place before this goal can be reached: 1) Re-determining who has a voice in religious education and 2) Listening to global theology in transformative ways.

Moving from a Western Theology to a Global Theology

Recently, in a casual conversation with my friend's teenage daughter, the young girl confidently explained to me that she was the best softball player on her team. She went on to explain objectively that she wasn't joking; she was literally the best player. Although all the other players tried very hard, she just had natural talent and thus was the most valuable competitor. Although we may smile at this unbridled confidence often seen in our youth, this belief in many ways mirrors the sense of superiority so often reflected in our Western theology. We simply, even if unwittingly, believe that we are the best. Non-western scholars may try to exegete the Scriptures, apply biblical hermeneutics, and contribute to missiological and theological conversation, but really, we are the best. Our ability to interpret Scripture is superior, as are the methods we use to do so. Our theological conclusions are more accurate, more in-line with Christian tradition, more theologically orthodox, more hermeneutically reliable, freer of cultural bias, and just downright correct. Although this ethnocentric belief is more often implied than stated, until recent decades it has been the presiding assumption in our Western-centric academies. The primary problem with this mindset isn't only its myopia; it is its discontinuity from patterns of biblical faithfulness. Wilbert R. Shenk highlights the problem when he states: "the global domination of Western theology remains largely unaddressed. Theological education in the non-Western world is still captive to the Western tradition and curriculum."[1] Nevertheless, while Western theology and curriculum has dominated recent decades of theological conversation, the geographical and theological shifts within the global church demand a radical change.

Although the West still boasts an abundance of educational resources, theological scholars, and prestigious institutions, much of the cutting edge theology-on-the-ground is taking place among the fruitful churches of the global South and East. The tremendous numerical growth of the Church in Latin America, Asia, and Africa has birthed a vibrant theological discussion that is contextual, engaged with current issues of injustice, poverty, and materialism, and is biblically grounded. More than simply offering a marginal hearing of these voices, a new theological paradigm needs to be created in which Western theologies are understood to be a voice, rather than *the* voice of theological thought.

In order to fully make this shift, there are several preliminary changes that need to take place on both an individual and institutional level. First, the limitations and inadequacy of relying upon one contextual theological perspective need to be acknowledged. From its inception, Christianity has addressed the specific concerns of its adherents within their socio-cultural, political, and historical context. Whether we consider the prophet Elijah sharing the love of God with the Sidonian widow at Zarephath or the 1st century Early Church leaders addressing the polytheistic concerns of new believers, God's truth is shared within a cultural context, to a specific people, within a particular time period. While God's truth is universal, theology is by its very definition, humanity's perception and understanding of God and religious truth. Thus, while adhering faithfully to the gospel of Christ, there naturally exists within the global Church "differences in religious experience, in ways of thinking and arguing about theology, in views as to the tasks of the Church, in individual and communal life-styles."[2] While the extent of this theological diversity has not been fully evident largely due to centuries of geographical isolation, the contemporary

---

1   Shenk, "Recasting Theology of Mission," 98.

2   Bosch, "An Emerging Paradigm for Mission", 496.

Church faces an increasingly complex reality within its theological discourse.[3] No longer can one theological voice assume that its perspective is universal; instead the validity of other theological perspectives must be brought to bear on our vision of the future of Western theological education.

In discussing this major transition, David J. Bosch acknowledges the need for Western scholars to make this shift and the potential challenges that theologians will face in making it. He explains:

> It is, therefore, presumptuous for persons of one culture and tradition to dictate the "normal" signs of conversion for another culture and context. To accept this, not only intellectually but also existentially and practically, may be a traumatic experience for Christians from the west. It makes our own views and convictions vulnerable. It de-absolutizes them. And even if we have assured ourselves and others a thousand times that it does not matter, that all along we have been working and hoping for a genuine contextualization of the gospel in the younger churches, we cannot rid ourselves of the nagging fear that, perhaps, they may have missed the real essence of the gospel.[4]

While this "nagging fear" reveals the ethnocentric nature of the West's theological assumptions, it also emphasizes the necessary realignment of the West as it considers the Church and its mission. The Church does not direct God but God the Church. Likewise, theological truth is not bound to one specific people group, region, or time period. Instead, theological truth is bound to God. It is therefore infeasible for one nation, people group, or individual to hold the exclusive rights as interpreter of God's truth. This reality does not undermine the universal nature of God's truth but instead considers the biases and cultural context of those who interpret it. As Kevin J. Vanhoozer notes: "theology in an era of world Christianity is still hermeneutical, but hermeneutics now means not 'rules for interpretation' but 'reading from one's lived experience' ... Today, it is hermeneutically incorrect to claim that one's interpretations are immune to cultural conditions and hence applicable to all times and places."[5] Thus, as we consider the realm of theology, biblical exegesis and hermeneutics cannot be, and should not be, the property of one global region or a limited group of scholars.

Second, it is crucial to understand that the study of God is a collective global activity. As we consider historical accounts such as the establishment of the Moravian *Unitas Fratrum* in 18th century Herrnhut and the development of Pastor Xi Shengmo's ministry to opium addicts in 19th century China, it is evident that developing theology has been a characteristic of Christian communities throughout Church history. However, in contrast to this rich and diverse theological heritage in

---

3   Bosch, "An Emerging Paradigm for Mission," 496.
4   Ibid., 496.
5   Vanhoozer, "One Rule to Rule them All," 95.

our age, Western theology is often pushed to the forefront of theological discussion. In writing of this current overemphasis on Western theology, Shenk argues that contrary to popular belief, theology developed in the West is often the least helpful to Majority World churches. He points out that "it is more promising to cede to the Asian, African, and Latin American churches the freedom to seek out natural links between their experiences and those historical periods when the church confronted similar issues."[6] Shenk explains, "great cultural and historical distance separates the early church and the modern Western church, whereas contemporary Asian, African, and Latin American Christians have considerable affinity with those of the first and second centuries."[7] The author notes that the religious and cultural pluralism familiar to Majority World Christians allows them to relate to the socio-cultural context of the early church.[8] As such, lessons drawn from early church realities may be more applicable to Majority World churches than the realities of the West. However, as the author concludes, "this limitation has not inhibited Western theology from assuming that it is uniquely qualified to determine the theological canons by which contemporary African, Asian, and Latin American churches ought to live."[9] As the author so aptly states, Western theology does not, and cannot, answer all the urgent questions of the global Church. Instead, Western theology brings insight as it contributes to the entire body of theological thought. It is in the collective study of God and Scripture throughout history that the global Church can learn, grow, and flourish.

Finally, in moving towards a global theological framework, Western scholars must embrace the role of being co-learners rather than theological teachers. Solomon Aryeetey, a Ghanaian medical doctor and co-founder of Pioneers-Africa, addresses this issue head on in his timely article "Sebi tafratse (with all due respects): A Word to the West from the Rest." He writes:

> Enough is enough! This is the 800 lb. gorilla in the room every time groups of Christians in the Majority World sit around the table with their Western counterparts to talk about partnership. It is time to call a spade a spade, and not a big spoon! A dear friend of mine stated it this way: 'As a representative of the non-Western segment of the Body of Christ, I refuse to be a second-class citizen in my own Father's house!'[10]

Aryeetey's poignant words ring true, and present a challenge to the Western Church. In order to become co-laborers and co-learners in Christ, Western and Majority World churches need to develop mutual partnerships, partnerships in which both of their academic and missional pursuits are given equal standing and voice. This move does not mean, however, that "third world theology should now

---

6   Shenk, "Recasting Theology of Mission," 100.

7   Ibid., 100.

8   Ibid., 100.

9   Shenk, "Recasting Theology of Mission," 100.

10   Aryeetey, "*Sebi tafratse*," 171.

become the norm for the entire world … Neither does it mean that third world Christianity does not also face dangers on all sides and that it is not as susceptible to distortion as first world Christianity was and still is."[11] But it does imply that our own Western theologies have limitations and "that third world Christians do not need anyone's authorization before they theologize."[12]

As co-learners, the Western church can glean wisdom from fellow believers around the world. David D. Ruiz, in conjunction with Majority World leaders at the 2004 Lausanne Forum for World Evangelization, addresses both the current changes in Majority World churches and the lessons that can be learned from these growing missional movements. He writes:

> The growth of the Majority World Church and its vitality have transformed it into a new missionary force. For example, The Nigeria Evangelical Mission Association (NEMA), founded in 1982, is formed by 90 missionary agencies and denominations and has more than 3800 missionaries in 38 countries. Indian Mission Association is connecting almost 200 national agencies and COMIBAM in Latin America is connecting 26 different countries in a mission movement. These agencies and churches today have some contributions to offer to the contemporary mission of the church.[13]

Ruiz continues, noting that various characteristics of Majority World mission such as the direct relationship between the missionary and their sending church and the reemphasis on long-term mission, are valuable practices that contribute to global mission theory and praxis.[14] In his discussion, Ruiz also acknowledges the areas of growth facing the Majority World mission movement. He notes the shared challenges of raising financial support, the over-popularity of high harvest mission fields, and "the tendency to send missionaries where the same language is spoken."[15] It is in this acknowledgement of both the limitations and contributions of the Majority World mission movement that Western Christians can take their rightful positions as co-laborers in Christ. It is also in this mutual position of humility and respect that balanced and insightful global theological discussions can develop.

This movement towards a global theology requires decisive action as well as a conceptual paradigm shift. Although many steps can be noted as potentially contributing to this shift, in the following sections I highlight two crucial steps needed to reach this goal. First is the re-determination of who has a voice in academia. Second is the need to listen to Majority World theologians in transformative ways.

---

11   Bosch, "An Emerging Paradigm for Mission," 501.
12   Ibid., 501.
13   Ruiz, "The Two Thirds World Church," 9.
14   Ibid., 9.
15   Ruiz, "The Two Thirds World Church," 9.

Re-Determining Who Has a Voice

The first move towards this change is re-determining who can and should speak. I will never forget the uncomfortable feeling of inadequacy as I stood in front of the Institute of Evangelism Students at Bethel Centre in Port Moresby, Papua New Guinea, teaching the course *Revival for Today*. As a recent seminary graduate, I was assigned the task of instructing the first year evangelism students on the signs and wonders, healings, exorcisms, and nature miracles of the gospel narratives. My class was filled with pastors and church leaders from around the nation who were actively involved in church planting, healing ministries, prison ministries, and local evangelism. As the days and weeks passed, it quickly became apparent to me that while I was very familiar with the intellectual concepts presented in the gospels, I had limited knowledge as to how God used the miraculous in his Church today. While I could readily supply the missional motifs, socio-cultural background, and structure of the text, it was my students who had experience living out the biblical realities in their contemporary context. Similarly, as we consider developing a more global theological outlook in the West, we must consider the full diversity of wisdom and knowledge that is present in our world. In the West, we have long valued theory over praxis, science over experience, and literature over oral history. But, as the center of Christianity continues its geographical shift to the Global South and East, the assumed superiority of this approach, and the cultural values and assumptions behind it, must be reassessed. The rules of our theological discussions must be revised to allow for the diversity of thought and methodological approach reflected in the growing global Church.

During the past few centuries, theological clout has been pre-determined exclusively by Western educational standards and ideals. Academic degrees earned, institutions attended, texts published, and academic societies joined all determine who can speak, to whom, and where. As long as one plays by these rules, she or he can have a voice in academia. This academic structure has been created for the West by the West and then exported as a definitive model to the Majority World. Per Frostin comments on how this reality has played out within his context:

> In discussing Third World Theologies with Scandinavian colleagues, I have frequently encountered arguments of the following character: It is interesting that Third World Christians create new types of theology, but I can dialogue with them only on the condition that they state their critique of Western theology in a manner understood by me as scientific. In other words, the prerequisite of a dialogue is that the other party accepts "our" rules, since only these rules are genuinely scientific. This prerequisite for dialogue is ... the hegemony postulate.[16]

---

16 Frostin, "The Hermeneutics of the Poor," 131.

Expanding on Frostin's thoughts, Tite Tiénou explains, "the West's self-perception that it is the center of scholarship is a corollary of the hegemony postulate. Here the assumption is that the West represents the center of scholarship and the rest (usually Africa, Asia, and Latin America) fits in the margins. The assumption is seen in the reflex of dismissing third world scholarship without real or adequate basis."[17] At its core, this dismissal of Majority World scholarship and the demand for conformity in theological method is based upon the assumption that Western scholarship is superior to that of the Majority World. As Shenk states "the Western intellectual framework assume[s] the primacy of Western culture."[18] Is this true? Is Western scholarship and culture really superior? A growing number of scholars are adamantly proclaiming: "No!"

While historically Western nations are not alone in their claims of mental superiority, such beliefs have always proven to be shortsighted, ethnocentric, and ignorantly pronounced. Addressing this unspoken assumption of Western intellectual superiority, Aryeetey points out the inherent inaccuracy of such a claim. He explains:

At the heart of Western culture is a tendency to presume that there is little that can originate from a culture outside of the West that could be described as better than what the West offers. "*Sebi tafratse*" [with all due respect], this is baloney! It is insulting to the creativity, ingenuity, and sovereignty of the God who so delicately made the other cultures for his glory. Unwittingly, Christians in the West have believed this lie that makes them feel a sense of entitlement to a biblically untenable position of first-class citizens in the Kingdom of God. The result is that they then expect all other cultures to automatically assume the subservient and inferior role of second-class citizens. This is heresy.[19]

As the author so accurately relates, non-Western Christians are not second-class citizens in the Church, and I would add neither are they second-class citizens in academia. Therefore, if Western theoretical constructs are not inherently superior, then it can be inferred that neither is Western scholarship or methodology. If this is true, the question quickly becomes: "why ... Christian theologians from other parts of the world must play by Western Christianity's rules in order to do theology."[20] Similarly, if Western theological models, degrees, and methodologies are not inherently superior, "how [then] do we do theology 'after the West'"?[21]

---

17 Tiénou, "Christian Theology in an Era of World Christianity," 47.
18 Shenk, "Recasting Theology of Mission," 100.
19 Aryeetey, "*Sebi tafratse*," 171.
20 Vanhoozer, "One Rule to Rule them All," 88.
21 Ibid., 91.

In noting this transition away from Western biblical methods, Vanhoozer explains "the very notion of method may itself be too Western a category to embrace for some." He notes that "it may be that theology in an era of world Christianity inhabits a situation 'after method,' that is, a situation in which no one method dominates."[22] The author continues:

> Non-Western theologies question the form, content, and categories that have become default setting of academic theology. In this respect, non-Western thinkers have become surprising bedfellows with certain Western postmoderns. Both groups ... agree on the need for a genealogical analysis of Western intellectual systems to unmask their apparent universality and on the need to listen to others. And both groups agree that the West's discourse on God and salvation is ultimately only a "local" theology.[23]

This act of separating theology from methodology is an important step towards facilitating a global theological discourse. Thus, in moving forward, the boundaries of who speaks in theological circles must also be expanded to include a wider expression of theology.

This transition is by no means new to Christianity. Throughout Church history theologians have routinely adopted new methods to study and convey theology. As Christianity has spread across the world, the avenues through which believers have expressed their faith have been as diverse as their linguistic and socio-cultural backgrounds. The authors of Scripture reflect this diversity in their expression of theological thought through a wide spectrum of genres: poetry, song, the law, narratives, proverbs, theological discourse, letters, and prophetic writings. Acknowledging the various ways in which communities understand and articulate truth, Bosch highlights the growing understanding among Western scholars of these diverse theological constructs:

> Now, at long last, we are beginning to rediscover what is sometimes referred to as the Hebrew way of experiencing reality as contrasted with the Greek way. This has led to an appreciation of 'narrative theology' and 'oral theology' as legitimate complements to conceptual theology. Walter Hollenweger argues that the Bible uses narrative theology predominantly; here the medium of communication is 'not definition, but description, not thesis, but dance, not doctrine, but hymn, not the learned book, but history and parable, not the formulation of concepts, but the celebration of banquets' (Hollenweger 1979:80-81; [Bosch] translation). He is aware of the limits of narrative (or 'analogical') theology; it is imprecise and ambiguous, so it needs to be supplemented (not replaced!) by 'catalogical' or conceptual theology. It is not enough to enunciate the correct doctrine, nor

22 Ibid., 91.
23 Ibid., 89.

to be logically consistent. There should be room for intuition and imagination. Descartes'‘I think, therefore I am,’ has to be supplemented with ‘I experience’ and ‘I participate, therefore I am.’[24]

While noting the validity of "narrative," "oral," and "conceptual" theologies, Bosch rightly emphasizes the complementary nature of each expression of theological thought. As Bosch indicates, the inclusion of a variety of theological models does not eliminate the necessity of any one method but instead each model contributes to the wider spectrum of theological understanding.

In recent decades scholars have increasingly embraced the complementary nature of theological methodologies. Texts such as Stanley Hauerwas and L. Gregory Jones's, *Why Narrative: Readings in Narrative Theology* (1997), and W. Jay Moon's, *African Proverbs Reveal Christianity in Culture* (2009), highlight the contribution of narrative theology within theological research. Similarly, oral theology - theology expressed through song, drama, proverbs, poetry, sermons, and story - is also gaining its place within global theological education. In *The New Faces of Christianity: Believing the Bible in the Global South*, Philip Jenkins recounts numerous examples of oral theology in churches around the world. In the author's comments on contemporary African churches, Jenkins writes:

> Modern African churches have made great use of music, both imported and autonomous; and at least since the beginning of the twentieth century, believers across the continent have deployed local musical traditions to the service of praise and worship. So central, in fact, is music to African cultures that institutions of all kinds are commonly riven between the official head and the music leader, whether the musician is a church worship leader or a school choirmaster: music matters.[25]

As the churches in the South and East continue to grow in their global influence, the richness of their oral and narrative traditions will become more accessible to Western scholars. While not replacing the West's own theological heritage, these fresh modes of theological expression have the potential to add a layer of depth and wisdom to the global Church's understanding of God and his kingdom.

I witnessed first-hand the impact of one of these rediscovered methodologies, narrative theology, while attending a church service in Port Moresby. Papua New Guinea is a nation united by its love of stories. When locals spend time hanging out with their friends, the common expression used is "We are going to tell stories together." Knowing Papua New Guineans love of narrative, I was surprised while living in the capital how rarely narrative was incorporated in Sunday sermons.

24 Bosch, "An Emerging Paradigm for Mission," 499.

25 Jenkins, *The New Faces of Christianity*, 32.

Preachers, perhaps mirroring their missionary counterparts, often overlooked the narratives of Scripture and instead focused on systematically exploring biblical motifs. However, this Sunday morning was different. We were all sitting together in the open-air auditorium of Bethel Centre, and the preacher before us was weaving a spellbinding tale. The young evangelist was telling the story of a large, Papuan black snake that had crawled into the upper rafters of his family home. Between describing his attempts to keep his mother from walking into the room and the snake's adventures in the ceiling, the preacher had the entire audience riveted between fearful apprehension and uncontrollable laughter. The preacher then moved with conviction, highlighting the parallel between the snake and the presence of sin in our lives. The entire auditorium of 2,000 people fell silent. The obvious comparison hit us all like a brick. No logical explanation of the negative consequences of human sin could have impacted us in the same way that the speaker's powerful narrative had. While Western academia often dismisses the adequacy of narrative as a vehicle of theological ideas, the power of story cannot be denied. In 1st century Israel, Jesus chose to teach hundreds of his followers spiritual truths through story. Generations of Christian scholars have followed suit expressing significant theological treaties in famous works such as St. Augustine of Hippo's *Confessions*, Dante Alighieri's *Divine Comedy*, Teresa of Ávila's *The Interior Castle*, John Milton's *Paradise Lost*, Paul Bunyan's *Pilgrim's Progress*, and C.S. Lewis' *The Chronicles of Narnia*. What we witnessed during that Sunday service in Port Moresby exemplified the validity and continued potency of this ancient tradition of narrative theology.

Listening to Global Theology in Transformative Ways

The second step towards facilitating a global theology is listening to and learning from non-Western theologians. During a recent academic conference, I witnessed some of the challenges that this paradigm shift poses for both parties. It was the final afternoon session of the conference, and the last academic papers were being read to the tired but congenial audience. After reading my own paper, one of my non-Western colleagues presented his current research in which he examined contextualization models within his own indigenous community. As the scholar opened up the conversation to the audience, hands flew up around the room, and the strong resistance of the academic crowd became quickly apparent. While such a passionate response is not at all unwelcome or unfamiliar in the iron-sharpening-iron discussions of academia, it was the scene that followed that caught my attention. As the questions came to a close, the next presenter stood up to present his parallel research; this time the scholar was from the West. Per the theme of the afternoon, the speaker also presented his research on the same people group. His specific topic was a historic analysis of the indigenous church and their continued governance by outside Western bodies. After the paper was read, the same audience responded with overwhelming support for the scholar. One of the previously dissenting audience members even adamantly expressed the injustice of the situation stating that "members of [this non-Western community] really needed to be allowed to govern themselves and speak for themselves." I sat there in stunned silence. The obvious disparity between the two responses was simply too clear to ignore. Only a few minutes before the same audience member had forcefully dismissed the perspective of a member of that exact community. After the session ended, I approached my non-Western colleague who had originally presented and asked him if he often received this hostile of a reception. He smiled knowingly and explained that this response had become a common occurrence within his academic career.

There is something wrong with this scenario. Something is askew when Western scholars can only welcome non-Western perspectives when they are filtered, packaged, and interpreted by our Western peers. True dialogue, while the more challenging path, needs to provide an equal platform for each voice. By engaging in open theological dialogue with the full body of Christ, each party is apt to hear points of view with which they agree and disagree, and positions that align with and oppose their own. Nevertheless, this vibrant intersection is healthy and vital for the growth of the global Church. Moving ahead in global dialogue can be challenging as "habits formed over years, and even centuries, cannot change overnight."[26] However, one significant step forward in this journey is listening with openness and respect to our brothers and sisters around the world.

When considering theology from the global South and East, there are several common themes that emerge. One of these themes, the importance of embracing the organic relationship between theology and missiology, is of unique significance. In analyzing the historic development of Western theology, Shenk explains the current separation between theology and missiology that exists in the West. He writes:

> From as early as the fourth century Western theology has pursued an inward-focused, intellectual, and pastoral agenda rather than an outward-looking evangelistic and missional agenda ... As Western theology moved into the university and was professionalized, it became increasingly detached from ecclesial reality and cultural context. In the twentieth century it was left to missionary statesmen and a few theologians sympathetic to mission to develop the theology of mission; the academy—in both its dominant seminary and university forms—largely ignored it.[27]

26 Tiénou, "Christian Theology in an Era of World Christianity," 50.
27 Bosch, "An Emerging Paradigm for Mission," 490.

Emphasizing this same historical predicament, Bosch explains, "When, approximately a century ago, missiology was admitted as a subject into the field of theology, this was done not because it was intrinsically necessary to have a separate theological subject called "Missiology," but because western theology had forgotten its very raison d'être."[28] Quoting Martin Kähler, Bosch continues that "the early Christian mission was 'the mother of theology' and even today theology, truly defined, should regard itself as a 'companion of the Christian mission, not a luxury of the world-dominating Church.'"[29] While the separate study of theology and missiology has its benefits, the separation of the Church from its mission does not. Bosch rightly states that Western theology, in losing its connection to the mission of God, has forgotten its very reason for existence. As Shenk rightly notes: "It is time to listen to voices from the non-Western world that can help construct a theology capable of empowering the global church for participation in the *missio Dei*."[30]

While the West's "missionless theology and churchmanship"[31] was originally exported overseas, many churches in the Majority World have since reestablished the holistic connection between the Church and the mission of God. In C. René Padilla's article "The Fullness of Mission," the Latin American scholar calls attention the need for a universally action-based Christian faith. He explains:

> The Christian mission is concerned with the development of the whole person and of all people. It includes, therefore, the shaping of a new lifestyle … The need is for models of mission fully adapted to a situation characterized by a yawning chasm between rich and poor. The models of mission built on the affluence of the West condone this situation of injustice and condemn the indigenous churches to permanent dependence. In the long run, therefore, they are inimical to mission. The challenge both to Christians in the West and to Christians in the underdeveloped world is to create models of mission centered in a prophetic lifestyle, models that will point to Jesus Christ as the Lord over the totality of life, to the universality of the church, and to the interdependence of human beings in the world.[32]

This practical outworking of one's Christian faith against the real systemic injustices of the world recalls the marriage of 'word' and 'deed' in the pre-Christendom church. While not entirely absent from the Western Church, the organic connection between right belief and right action can be found at the forefront of Majority World mission theology. Noting this trend, Vanhoozer writes: "Increasingly, theologians in Africa, Latin America, and Asia are more interested in orthopraxis than orthodoxy. Theology must be relevant, and it must make a difference; it must

---

28 Bosch, "An Emerging Paradigm for Mission," 490.

29 Bosch, "An Emerging Paradigm for Mission," 490; Kähler, *Erfahrungen der Leibhaftigkeit,* 189.

30 Shenk, *Write the Vision,* 98.

31 Bosch, "An Emerging Paradigm for Mission," 490.

32 Padilla, "The Fullness of Mission," 10-11.

address people's concerns, and it must transform the structures of everyday life."[33] As Bosch confirms, this revolt "against [the] intellectualization of theology ... [has] made an 'epistemological leap' from a hermeneutic of abstract reflection on the truth to a hermeneutic of praxis. One *does* theology, one does not simply *write* it."[34] This embodied faith reunites the body of Christ with its original mission to love God and love its neighbors (Matt 22:37-39).

The importance of adopting a missional theology was highlighted anew when I attended the Third Lausanne Congress on World Evangelization in 2010 in Cape Town, South Africa. While at the conference, I was one of 4,000 Christian leaders from over 198 countries attending the global conference. After one of the afternoon sessions, I struck up a conversation with two Latin American church leaders attending the conference. Standing in the busy hallway we exchanged pleasantries in Spanish, and I asked them about their impression of the congress so far. In answer to my question, the two women hesitated slightly and then proceeded to tell me what they had just observed. Directly after one of the sessions focused on "Wealth, Power, and Poverty," they had walked outside of the convention building with the bustling conference crowd to the waiting buses. Scattered amidst the coaches were several women and men begging for money. The women explained with surprise and shock, "we had just left the session focused on compassion for the poor, and as we stood there, individual after individual passed the poor without offering assistance. It was as if no one even saw the poor."

As we continued our conversation, their observation struck me: "It was as if no one even saw the poor." In a few minutes, these women had pinpointed a major flaw in Western theology: the pervasive dualism that has long separated word and deed; the dualism that enables us to discuss compassion for the poor, without being compassionate; that enables us to theorize about evangelism, without evangelizing. And, in theological education, the dualism that allows us to focus on intellectual theory without ever participating in the mission of God. However, unless we engage in theological conversations like this one in Cape Town, our theological blind spots will continue to be our blind spots. It is only in listening and learning from our brothers and sisters in Christ that we can experience the full insights of the global body of Christ.

Conclusion

When I think back to the Bible School classroom in Adelaide, Australia, I am saddened and embarrassed by the paternalistic attitude extended towards the visiting Papua New Guinean pastor. This sense of superiority and privilege that so seamlessly permeates our Western mindset is damaging to the entire body of

33 Vanhoozer, "One Rule to Rule them All," 96.
34 Bosch, "An Emerging Paradigm for Mission," 499.

Christ and also detrimental to the Western Church. Like a table with two legs, the absence of a global theological discussion can only result in a lop-sided theology. While hiring non-Western faculty members and including diverse perspectives in academic texts is a step in the right direction, it doesn't address the systemic problem: the intellectual hierarchy that pervades Western academia. It doesn't challenge the "assumption…that the West represents the center of scholarship and the rest (usually Africa, Asia, and Latin America) fits in the margins."[35] In researching for this paper, it was sobering to note the early publication dates of the articles and texts that first raised this issue. Over thirty years have passed since prominent Western and non-Western scholars initially called for a comprehensive theological paradigm shift. Even more eye opening is the present lack of Western seminaries promoting non-Western theologies at an institutional level. In searching for best practices in Western seminaries, I eventually had to concede that currently there are none.

As a professor of religion at a Christian undergraduate institution in the United States, I look forward to the day when my theology students are as familiar with the thoughts of Orlando Costas and Kosuke Koyama as they are with those of Karl Barth and John Calvin. While the rich diversity of the global Church can be seen sprinkled throughout traditional theological education, the real vibrancy of global missiology, theology, and ecclesiology has yet to fully impact Western academia. Therefore, as we consider the future, indeed the very nature and mission of theological education in North America, there is one urgent need that rises above all others: the need to let the global Church speak! - to speak into our understanding of God, Scripture, and the Church –to speak into not just what we teach our students, but how, why, and to what end we teach them as well - to speak into our theologies, methodologies, and traditions.

---

35 Tiénou, "Christian Theology in an Era of World Christianity," 47.

Bibliography

Aryeetey, Solomon.
"Sebi tafratse (with all due respect): A Word to the West from the Rest." *Evangelical Missions Quarterly* (April 2013) 166-174.

Bosch, David. J.
"Theological Education in Missionary Perspective." *Missiology* 10:1 (Jan. 1982) 13-34.

_____ "An Emerging Paradigm for Mission." *Missiology* 11:4 (1983) 485-510; idem, "Missionary Theology in Africa." *Indian Missiological Review* 6:2 (1984) 105-39, republished *Journal of Theology for Southern Africa* 49 (December 1984) 14-37.

Frostin, Per.
"The Hermeneutics of the Poor: The Epistemological 'Break' in Third World Theologies." Studia Theologica 39:2 (1985) 127-50.

Hauerwas, Stanley and L. Gregory Jones eds.
Why Narrative: Readings in Narrative Theology. Eugene, OR: Wipf and Stock, 1997.

Hollenweger, Walter J.
Erfahrungen der Leibhaftigkeit Munich: Chr-Kaiser Verlag, 1979.

Jenkins, Philip.
The New Faces of Christianity: Believing the Bible in the Global South. New York: Oxford UP, 2006.

Kähler, M.
Schriften Zur Christologie Und Mission. Munich: Chr-Kaiser Verlag, 1971 [1908].

Moon, W. Jay.
African Proverbs Reveal Christianity in Culture: A Narrative Portrayal of Builsa Proverbs Contextualizing Christianity in Ghana. American Society of Missiology Monograph Series. Eugene, OR: Pickwick, 2009.

Padilla, C. René.
    "The Fullness of Mission." *Occasional Bulletin of Missionary Research* 3:1
    (Jan. 1979) 6-11.

Ruiz, David D.
    "The Two Thirds World Church." Lausanne Occasional Paper No. 44
    (paper presented at Lausanne Committee for World Evangelization, 29
    Sept. to 5 Oct. 2004. Pattaya, Thailand) Online:
    http://www.lausanne.org/documents/2004forum/LOP44_IG15.pdf.

Shenk, Wilbert R.
    "Recasting Theology of Mission: Impulses from the Non-Western World."
    International Bulletin of Missionary Research (July 2001) 98-105.

    _____ *Write the Vision: The Church Renewed.* Valley Forge, Pa.: Trinity
    Press International, 1995.

Tiénou, Tite.
    "Christian Theology in an Era of World Christianity." In *Globalizing
    Theology: Belief and Practice in an Era of World Christianity.* Ott, Craig and
    Harold A. Netland eds. Grand Rapids: Baker Academic, 2006.

Vanhoozer, Kevin J.
    "One Rule to Rule Them All?: Theological Method in an Era of World
    Christianity." In *Globalizing Theology: Belief and Practice in an Era of World
    Christianity.* Ott, Craig and Harold A. Netland eds. Grand Rapids: Baker
    Academic, 2006.

Historic Models of Teaching Christian Mission:

Case Studies Informing an Age of World Christianity

ROBERT L. GALLAGHER

Introduction

Christian higher education today occurs within a global context. Effective mission studies will recognize today's age of world Christianity within its educational goals. Instructors should teach missions accordingly, using appropriate andragogical strategies. If the first expansion of the Christian faith spread across Europe and then from the continent towards the Global South, are we teaching mission in western colleges, universities, and seminaries aware of this explosion of Christianity? Are the global experiences that have shaped the contours of Christianity in Africa, Asia, the Caribbean, Latin America, and Oceania appreciated in our teaching institutions in North America? Can we learn lessons from these cross-cultural pathfinders in order to adapt resources for teaching mission in our age of world Christianity? I believe that there are historic mission movements that immersed themselves in a global vision that do provide models for teaching contemporary intercultural studies. We should allow these past paradigms to inform our approach to mission studies today, and select case studies that best promote practices of world missions.

In this paper, I will consider six case studies of educational institutions within five movements of Christian expansion from post-apostolic times to the beginning of modern missions. Because of their far-reaching influence on world Christianity, I will examine the Church of the East, Celtic Christianity, the Franciscan Friars Minor, the Reformation, and the modern mission platform of Pietism. Drawing from these findings, my essay will explain observable patterns across the movements, including the holistic training of students together with the emphasis of theology and languages. Historic perspectives of God's past work through educational institutions can guide us toward a Spirit-inspired twenty first century of teaching Christian mission in an age of world Christianity.

Church of the East Mission Education

The Church of the East has been described as "the most missionary church that the world has ever seen," providing the earliest missionary thrust to the east into Asia (Stewart, 1928: 141). This movement spread beyond the borders of the Roman Empire from the third to the fourteenth centuries across Persia and Mesopotamia to Arabia, India, central Asia, Siberia, China, and Japan. One of the key reasons for this growth of Christianity was the use of training schools. After the Council of Ephesus in 431, a number of the Eastern bishops rejected the decision to anathematize Nestorius, and subsequently formed a separate church movement.

Its center was a school of theology developed in Edessa, Upper Mesopotamia at the end of the second century and expanded under Ibas (bishop of Edessa, c. 435-57), a friend of Nestorius. The school's curriculum majored in theology, philosophy, languages, and music.

In 489, the Christian theological and scientific center in Edessa was closed by the Byzantine emperor Zeno because of its Nestorian teachings. Students and teachers who believed in the claims of Nestorius transferred to the School of Nisibis (present-day Turkey), under the supervision of Barsauma, a pupil of Ibas. This led to a wave of Nestorian immigration into the Persian Empire. At Nisibis Church of the East scholars together with Hellenistic philosophers banished from Athens by Justinian in 529, carried out important research in medicine, astronomy, mathematics, and theology (Cochrane, 2014: 80-82).

Another significant educational center was at Gundeshapur (present-day Iran). Under the rule of Khosrau I (531-579), the Sasanid emperor, the city offered training in medicine, philosophy, mathematics, science, and theology. Before 376, the Church of the East had established a monastery in Gundeshapur, yet under Khosrau I, the city became famed for its theological school. During the sixth century, Gundeshapur gave refuge to Greek philosophers and Syriac-speaking Nestorian Christians fleeing religious persecution by the Byzantine Empire. Emperor Khosrau I commissioned the refugees to translate Greek and Syriac texts on medicine, astronomy, and philosophy into Pahlavi, an exclusively written form of various Middle Iranian languages.

Gundeshapur was the most important medical center of the ancient world during the sixth and seventh centuries. Even though almost all the physicians of the medical academy were Persians, they wrote their treatises in Syriac since medicine had an established tradition in this dialect of Middle Aramaic that became a major literary language throughout the Middle East from the fourth to the eighth centuries. Additionally, qualified physicians systemized and transferred medical practices to their students who worked under supervisors in hospitals, and were required to pass exams in order to practice as accredited Gondeshapur medical doctors (Lewis, 2015: 1-10).

Khosrau I, furthermore, invited Indian and Chinese scholars to Gondeshapur who translated Indian texts on astronomy, astrology, mathematics, and medicine and Chinese texts on herbal medicine and religion. With educational centers in Nisibis and Gundeshapur, the Church of the East began to branch out beyond the Persian Sasanian Empire. For five hundred years, these educational institutes continued as major centers of theological and scientific education (Moffett, 1982: 248; Winkler, 2003: 26).

The Persian curriculum focused on instructing people in biblical understanding. Guided by its most famous teacher, Narsai of Nisibis in the fifth century, the teaching institutes combined the doctrine of Christ's salvation with a universal calling modeled after Peter, Paul, and Jesus. Narsai was one of the most important Syriac poet-theologians whose poetic approach revealed the deep mysteries of the Christian faith. At the school in Nisibis, Syrian theology emphasized sharing the gospel to all peoples, which made it as much a training ground for missions as for the priesthood. A person needed to be a missionary to follow in the footsteps of Christ (Philip, 1996: 513-514, 518). Followers submitted to austere rules of spiritual discipline, and performed manual labor to support their educational outlay. A "son of the covenant" was a student who took an oath regarding celibacy, monastic life, and community sharing, whereby a person's responsibility was as serious as receiving God's grace (Jenkins, 2008: 77).

A number of the early writings in Edessa show the missional thinking of the education centers. Tradition proposed that the apostle Thomas sent Thaddaeus to share the gospel to the people of Syria. Consequently, the story of Thomas' journey to India, *The Acts of Thomas*, was widely read, which indicates, "Edessa's heroes were missionaries" (Moffett, 1975: 419). Even though the work was full of exaggerated miracles, the gospel message was central. The book begins, "And when all the apostles had been for a time in Jerusalem . . . they divided the countries among them, in order that each one of them might preach . . . in the place to which the Lord sent him. And India fell by lot and division to Judas Thomas the apostle" (Klijn, 1962: 65).

Another writing that shows the mission theology of the Eastern Church was *The Odes of Solomon*. Written in Syriac at Edessa during the first century, this Christian hymn was influential in Syrian Christology. Portrayed as the Savior of the world, Christ gathered the nations. In *Ode 10* Christ proclaims, "I took courage and became strong and captured the world, and it became mine for the glory of the Most High and of God my Father. And the Gentiles who had been dispersed were gathered together" (Charlesworth, 1977: 48). Christ saves all people and the knowledge of the Lord flows like a river. "For there went forth a stream and it became a river great and broad . . . for it spread over the surface of all the earth and it filled everything. Then all the thirsty upon the earth drank. . . . Blessed, therefore, are the ministers of that drink" (*Ode 6*, Charlesworth, 1977: 30).

The training schools of eastern Christianity not only provided biblical education for the laity, but also for the leaders of their monastic communities. After prescribed study, monks could become teachers at the monasteries, or live as anchorites. Historians now consider that monasticism first started in Syria and Persia, independent of any Egyptian stimulus. Although Church of the East monasteries were similar to those of Egypt and southern Europe, there were differences with respect to education and mission (Philip, 1996: 505).

Beginning in the third century, the eastern monastic network grew throughout Persia and Central Asia, producing hundreds of celibate missionaries who proclaimed the good news of Christ, together with a love of Scripture, education, and mission. These monasteries were not only centers of prayer, worship, copying Scripture, and missionary activity, but also functioned as schools, inns, and medical facilities. John Stewart describes the monks as "men of great faith, mighty in Scriptures, large portions of which they knew by heart, fervent in prayer, gentle and humble in manner, and full of love to God on the one hand, and love to their neighbor and all mankind on the other" (1928: 47).

Celtic Mission Education

Parallel to the early monastic tradition of the Church of the East was the ascetic Christian movement of Ireland. Over the course of 800 years, thousands of Celtic men and women traveled across Scotland, England, and throughout Europe bringing the good news of Jesus to peoples ravaged by paganism and violence. They also transformed societies by establishing monastic centers of mission and education. Patrick of the early fourth century was the first major figure of missions in Ireland: a man who founded numerous monasteries, ordained priests, brought literacy, eradicated slavery, and cared for the poor. Patrick and his followers formed the Irish monasteries as centers of community, education, and missionary outreach.

In these monastic communities, the Celts did not separate the sacred and the secular since they were holistic in their ordered life of prayer, work, worship, and study. As men and women came and dedicated themselves to service, they would build a "church, refectory, kitchen, guesthouse, library, and workshops" (McNeill, 1974: 75). Within these committed communities that attracted scholars from Britain and the rest of Europe, the students were educated in reading and writing Latin (McNeill, 1974: 120). Some of the Irish monasteries, such as Clonard (founded in 520), were well known for their scholarship, and attracted pupils from as far away as Asia (Zimmer, 1969: 45-46). Many of the societies had extensive manuscript collections of classical literature, writings of the early church fathers, and the New Testament. The transcription of these works was of prime importance to the Irish monasteries from the sixth century (Ryan, 1972: 380).

Celtic monasticism was responsible for not only influencing Irish people to follow Christ, but also the inhabitants of England, Scotland, and parts of Europe such as Germany, Holland, and Italy. Ireland—this small nation that had only recently accepted Christianity—became the new mission center, flooding Europe with God's word. Monks left their Irish monastic schools and planted monasteries outside their homeland to propagate their faith and learning. Seeking favor with local rulers, they cooperated with secular authorities wherever possible, even while keeping their freedom of opinion. They not only preached the gospel, but also spread an understanding of the creative arts, languages, history, and the sciences; relaying the foundations of western culture after they were destroyed by the invasions of the northern tribes.

After Patrick, Columba became one of the first notable Irish missionaries to preach outside his country. He had established forty monasteries in Ireland, such as those at Derry, Durrow, and Kells before he led a team of twelve monks to the island of Iona off the west coast of Scotland in 563. Iona became a major missionary educational center, resulting in the establishment of twenty three monasteries in Scotland and thirty eight in England by the time of Columba's death in 597 (Zimmer, 1969: 19-20).

Another remarkable Irish monk that wandered beyond his homeland was Columban. With his twelve Irish monks, Columban traveled to Brittany around 590, and preached to the populace with such success that Sigebert, the local king, gave them land to build a monastery. The monastery at Luxeuil became a center of Christian learning and western culture where scholars and artisans worked side-by-side. For Columban, the teaching of the Christian worldview included the secular sciences, as well as theological subjects. Unfortunately, King Sigebert was offended by the Irish monk's preaching against immorality, and forced him to leave Luxeuil, as well as the other monasteries he had founded at Burgundy and Fontaines in Gaul. In spite of Columban's banishment, monks from Luxeuil established another fifty three monasteries, and influenced the establishment of two hundred more. Jonas, Columban's biographer, claims that 620 French missionaries left Luxeuil in one generation alone, establishing monasteries throughout France, Switzerland, and Italy.

After Columban's dismissal from Luxeuil, he traveled further into the European continent, where he established a monastery that dominated the European intellectual scene for nearly a thousand years. Bobbio, in northern Italy, became a center of education with an international reputation due to the work of the Irish monks. At Bobbio, scholars devoted themselves to study, writing, and teaching in both the spiritual and natural domains. They studied doctrine and creeds, and memorized Scripture, while learning the fundamentals of Latin grammar. In addition, these monks also considered rhetoric, classical writings (such as Virgil, Homer, and Ambrose), mathematics, music, and astronomy. The monastery became an academy of theologians, historians, artists, poets, and musicians—living in ascetic devotion to God.

The abbey of Saint Gall (St. Gallen in present-day Switzerland), the sister monastery to Bobbio, was described by J. M. Clark as being full of both scholarly and cultural activities. Established by Gall, a disciple of Columban, this monastery became the intellectual center of Germany by 610, and remained so for three hundred years. The monks wrote, copied, and illuminated books in the scriptorium as well as composed musical works, and taught the theory of music. They also observed the sun and the stars to calculate the dates of church festivals, and diligently studied all the sciences known in that day. Nor did the ascetics neglect the more practical arts and handicrafts: painting, architecture, sculpture in wood, stone, metal, and ivory, together with weaving, spinning, and agriculture were all objects of industrious attention (1926: 91).

Columba and Columban, as well as those who followed them, were only the first of thousands of Irish missionaries who came to educate Europe. By the beginning of the seventh century, Irish monks were the preeminent scholars and educators on the continent. From Britain and Germany to northern Italy, they trained national leaders, developed the educational systems, and spread the Christian message to faraway places such as Iceland, Greenland, and Russia. Slowly and steadily, the monks and their students took dominion over the scholarship of Europe, as well as the leadership structure of the Catholic church. The majority of church leaders during the Early Middle Ages (c. 5th-10th centuries) were Irish monks, including a number of bishops in Austria, France, and Gaul. By the end of the seventh century, ninety four monasteries in Europe had sprung into existence directly attributed to the Irish invasion.

Franciscan Mission Education

Echoing the monasticism of Celtic Christianity and the Church of the East, the educational efforts of the early mendicant Franciscans set the stage for an explosion of Catholic mission throughout the thirteenth century. Ramon Llull followed in the footsteps of Francis of Assisi, dedicating his life to bring Muslim heretics to Christ by way of his apologetic writings, missionary training colleges, and willingness to embrace martyrdom. He endeavored to establish monasteries where monks could learn the languages of non-believing peoples, and receive appropriate instruction to preach the gospel.

For Llull, missionary education was essential in reaching the unbeliever, especially training in languages, theology, geography, and ethnography. His desire was to create monasteries in order to teach monks and laity Arabic, Hebrew, and other languages of non-Christians to share "the holy truth of the Catholic faith, which is that of Christ." In *Felix, the Book of Wonders*, Llull wrote that he hoped that God would send apostles who knew science and languages to convert unbelievers, and set an example to the church (Llull, 1985b: 781).

After Llull's conversion in 1263, he spent the next nine years in Majorca studying contemporary sciences, Latin, and Arabic (from a Muslim slave), as well as Christian, Islamic, and Jewish theologies and philosophies. Despite these extensive preparations, he struggled with feelings of inadequacy as he pursued knowledge of the Arabic language (Llull, 1985a: 15-17). The Catalan influence in southwestern Europe, together with Llull's aristocratic connections, however, enhanced his emergence as a respected scholar and prolific writer in interdisciplinary fields, and enabled him to gain access to ecclesiastical leaders and monarchs.

The prevailing European attitude to Mohammedanism (Islam) during the Middle Ages was one of "gross ignorance and great hatred," with violence and torture considered justifiable in the spread and defense of Christianity (Zwemer, 1902: 50). In contrast, Llull believed that the first attempts to convert the Muslim nonbeliever should be of love and compassion, and called himself the *procurator infidelium* ["advocate of nonbelievers"] (Lorenz, 1985: 20). In his *Book of Contemplations*, he avowed, "Wherefore, it appears to me, O Lord, that the conquest of that sacred land [Palestine] will not be achieved other than as Thou [Christ] and Thy apostles undertook to accomplish it, by love, and prayer, and the shedding of tears as well as blood" (Mackensen, 1920: 29; Peers, 1969: 30-31). In other words, attempts at Muslim conversion should be through apologetics and dialogue by using principles common to Islam, Judaism, and Christianity.

In 1276, Llull founded his first missionary training school, Trinity College at Miramar, Majorca through the assistance of James II of Majorca, and the support of John XXI, the Portuguese Pope. There he established a curriculum for thirteen Franciscans in the liberal arts, theology, oriental languages, and Islamic doctrines, as well as his own teachings. The Catalan missionary tried to communicate the Gospel in a way that was most appropriate to his audience.

For instance, Llull wrote his novel, *Libre de Blanquerna*, in Catalan for Catalonians, incorporating narrative with theology and philosophy. *The Book of Contemplation*, though, he first composed in Arabic for the Muslim world, and later translated it into Catalan. He not only used the vernacular in written communication (Arabic, Catalan, and Latin; his writings were also translated into French and Italian), but also sought to use a commonality of thought in philosophic style and content. By way of illustration, Llull styled his work, *The Book of the Lover and the Beloved*, after the manner of Muslim Sufi writings; and well versed in the Qur'an and Muslim doctrine, he wrote about Saracen (Islamic) beliefs in his *Book of the Gentile* (Bonner, 1985: vol. 1: 20).

During the Middle Ages, religious scholars influenced each other and often embraced shared views. Because of the philosophic strength of Islam and Judaism in the age of scholasticism, Llull used Augustinian reason and logic to understand faith in dialogue with the Saracen and Jewish philosophers. He held that if a scholar could be overwhelmingly convinced of the truth of the gospel through philosophy and rational debate, then that person would convert to Christ. Ironically, Llull's approach was at odds with his own complex conversion process, which unfolded not through philosophical debate, but through a series of supernatural interventions and traumatic encounters with people. He held firmly to the belief, nevertheless, that divine reason had placed in God's creation an order that people could discover by the disciplines of language, mathematics, and poetry, in addition to music, geometry, and astronomy. Since the educated wealthy aristocrats were the shapers of society, Llull was convinced that in converting these elites there would follow a mass conversion of Jews and Muslims.

Ramon Llull sought endorsement of his training facilities in various cities without success since the popes (e.g. Nicholas IV) were more interested in fighting the Saracens than saving them. It is unclear, though, what happened to the students trained in his college at Miramar, which was the only training school established in his lifetime. Political changes forced Llull to abandon the program when James II's elder brother, Peter III of Aragon, came to the throne in 1292 (Lorenz, 1985: 20). The insufficient support of the church for Llull's training colleges was one of his major disappointments, and the prime catalyst for his missionary trips to North Africa. His educational appeals continued, until finally, at Pope Clement V's Council of Vienne in 1311, his proposal aroused support for academic chairs in the study of Arabic, Chaldean, and Hebrew in cities where the papal courts resided; and at the universities of Bologna, Oxford, Paris, and Salamanca. The Council's decision, regrettably, died with the martyrdom of Llull in 1316: all for the glory of God.

Reformation Mission Education

Similar to Llull's motivation for the glory of God, Jean Calvin and Martin Luther during the early sixteenth century played crucial roles in the spiritual reawakening of Europe driven by a passion for the church, and a desire to see the kingdom of Christ established. A key component in achieving their Reformation goals was the belief that missional education was essential for the salvation of Europe.

Calvin's Geneva Academy

As a result, Calvin established his Academy in Geneva, Switzerland to educate pastor missionaries who upon graduation were sent to teach the Reformation message throughout Europe and abroad. The training school was an important contributor to the Reformed movement because Calvin believed that as long "as this objective [the establishment of the Academy] was not realized, no permanence was assured for the work of reform" (McNeill, 1954: 192). In 1557, Calvin entreated the city council for land and a building; and two years later, he conducted the inaugural service. With the establishment of the Academy in Geneva, "Calvin had achieved his task: he had secured the future of Geneva making it at once a church, a school, and a fortress. It was the first stronghold of liberty in modern times" (McNeill, 1954: 196).

The aim of the Geneva Academy was to make the church educationally self-perpetuating; and as such, Calvin established a school for children run by Antoine Saunier. The Geneva city ordinances of 1541 speak of the need to raise seed for the time to come, in order not to leave the church a desert to their children, and an obligation to prepare youth for the ministry and civil government. The opening of the Academy created stability to the Reformed message that it previously did not possess. Without such an institution, the Swiss Reformation might have died with its reformers.

The school began with an enrollment of 162 students, mainly Frenchmen, and in six years, the numbers had increased by ten-fold. In the first four years, out of 160 male students, thirteen were Swiss (three from Geneva), ten Dutch, ten German, 13 Italian, and 114 French (Lewis, 1994: 49-50). For the students, "the purpose of the Academy was mainly preparation for the ministry, with law and medicine as secondary interests" (McNeill, 1954: 194). This institution trained them to understand and propagate Calvin's teachings. The Academy divided the pupils according to their location within the four sectors of the city, and arranged the sectors into seven grades. In the style of a renaissance school, the students learned French, Latin, and Greek New Testament languages, accompanied by Virgil, Ovid, and Cicero, with rhetoric and dialectic from classical texts. In addition, the students sang Psalms in French daily for one hour at eleven in the morning (McNeill, 1954: 194).

As early as 1555, Calvin trained French immigrants at his Academy in ethics, homiletics, and theology, sending them back home as pastor missionaries ("the gatekeepers of the Kingdom"). He believed that for proper gospel proclamation, trained ministers needed to establish churches. Carl D. Stevens writes, "Calvin's interest was not the sending of men into France to preach the gospel to anyone who might listen; rather, Calvin's intention was to restore the church in France as a gospel-preaching institution" (1994: 201). Further, Paul E. Pierson reflects, "Calvin was more intentional [than Luther] in encouraging mission. In some areas, Calvinism became the religion of the state; in other areas, local churches were established amidst persecution. Pastors were trained in Geneva and sent as missionaries; many were martyred" (2000: 814).

An example of Pierson's assertion of pastors trained in Geneva and sent as missionaries occurred in Brazil. The Catholic Nicolas Villegagnon (a French naval officer)—from 1555 until they returned to France three years later—persecuted French Calvinists (Huguenots) trained in Geneva who had attempted the first Protestant missionary outreach beyond Europe (Hughes, 1966: 317). Calvinists such as Guillaume Charretier, Jean de Léry, and Pierre Richer had intended to colonize the Island of Serigipe in the Bay of Guanabara (present-day Rio de Janeiro, Brazil). In the words of de Léry, "As much as out of an earnest desire that God had given to serve His glory, as out of curiosity to see this New World . . . for the extension of the realm of Christ into so distant a country, even into so strange a land, and among a nation that was indeed completely ignorant of the true God . . . so we were fourteen in number who left the city of Geneva to make this voyage" (*History of a Voyage to the Land of Brazil*, quoted in Whatley, 1990: 5-6).

Luther's University of Wittenberg

In comparison to Jean Calvin's Academy in Geneva, I will now examine Martin Luther's educational center at the University of Wittenberg, Saxony, which will challenge Paul Pierson's assessment of Luther's missional intent. Kenneth Scott Latourette argues that in the newly formed Protestantism, Luther, in forsaking Catholic monasticism, lost a valuable vehicle of missionary expansion. Consequently, there was an absence of mission practice, and no replacement structure for early Protestant missions (1975: 3). Yet, I find evidence of the mission praxis of Luther in the cavalcade of students sent from the University of Wittenberg that became a committed community of lay missionaries, and the subsequent unfolding of Lutheranism in northern Europe.

The Christian Church has not always been successful at looking ahead in a dangerous world. Ernest G. Schwiebert in his work, *Luther and His Times*, describes the impact that Luther had on Europe radiating out from the University of Wittenberg. In 1514 Paul Lange, a Benedictine monk, traveled through central Germany looking for promising young university theologians to include in his *Schriftstellerlexikon* ("Who's Who among Germany's Teachers"). Lange did not even interview Martin Luther, a thirty-one year old Augustinian monk. Unnoticed by the academy, Luther from 1514-17 affected the faculty at the University of Wittenberg with his views on Scripture, the church, and justification by faith. The October 31, 1517 nailing of the *Ninety Five Theses* on the cathedral door was not an isolated act of a rebellious priest, but was the culmination of ideas forged from the faith community at Wittenberg (1950: 293). Martin Luther deeply embedded himself in the relationships of a small provincial town in Saxony-Anhalt, and we should not view him as a solitary genius. Heiko A. Oberman highlights this Saxon context in his *Luther: Man Between God and the Devil*: "Luther is to be regarded not so much as a lonely prophet—let alone as the Hercules of the humanists—but as a leading member of the Wittenberg team which, in keeping with the motto of the university, initiated its program 'in the name of St. Paul and St. Augustine'" (1990: 151).

The teaching at Wittenberg was rebellious: overturning the tables of the medieval church and transforming Christendom. Luther's theology was the key catalyst of the change, especially his idea of justification by faith alone (MacCulloch, 2016: 1-14). Theologians preached his doctrines from an ever-increasing number of pulpits in the country. Monks and priests were leaving their religious vocation to proclaim the new reformation. Young humanists such as Philipp Melanchthon (the first systematic theologian of the Lutheran Reformation) were joining the "wild boar loose in the vineyard" at Wittenberg from all over Europe. Students at the University of Wittenberg had observed the rebel burning Leo X's papal decrees. It was unrealistic that they would be content with only watching the uprising from the sidelines. Even though Luther disdained riots and violence, his writings and preaching accidentally unleashed a religious freedom within people that careered them towards tumult. "If there is a single thread running through the whole story of the Reformation, it is the explosive and renovative and often disintegrating effect of the Bible, put into the hands of the commonality and interpreted no longer by the well-conditioned learned, but by the faith and delusion, the common sense and uncommon nonsense, of all sorts of men" (Elton, 1964: 52). Between 1521 and 1523, rioting mobs of Wittenberg students stormed through Saxony threatening priests, destroying church altars, removing church pictures and side-altars, giving congregants both kinds of communion (bread and wine), simplifying the liturgy, and distributing the responsibility of church revenue into the hands of the laity (Chadwick, 1964: 58-59); and then Luther had to try to reign in the genie of his revolutionary ideas that had leapt out of the bottle.

Throughout these turbulent years, Luther remained committed to train young men for Christian ministry and to send them from the university in order to spread his Reformation message. Conversion of the unsaved was paramount for Luther, and he knew that education could play an important role in this goal. At Wittenberg, Luther emphasized understanding true doctrine, and at the same time took a personal interest in the students; realizing that on leaving the university, they would face hostile opposition. His mentoring of the students even included finding their first ministry appointments (Coats, 1969: 603).

Between 1520 and 1560, approximately 5,000 of the 16,000 at Wittenberg's university were from nations other than Germany, making the institution an important center for missions' training (Bunkowske, 1985: 170). Through his teaching at the university, Luther promoted a renewed interest in the gospel, and many of his students returned to their home countries across Europe bringing the Reformation, which resulted in social transformation. This was especially true of Scandinavia, which, similar to Germany, wanted to discard papal dominance. David J. Valleskey confirms, "Luther's teaching at the University of Wittenberg also served the purpose of missions' work. Students came from all over Europe to study under Luther and Melanchthon. When they returned to their homes, they brought along with them the restored gospel of salvation" (1995: 100).

The transforming effect of the Wittenberg students in northern Europe was considerable, and played a major role in the unfurling of Lutheranism. The Wittenberg influence in Denmark, for example, came through students and faculty such as John Bugenhagen, Andreas Carlstadt, Peder Palladius, Martin Reinhart, Hermann Tast, Hans Tausen, Eberhard Weidensee, John Wendt, and Wolfgang von Utenhof. In Finland, the reformer Mikael Agricola had studied at Wittenberg under Luther and Philipp Melanchthon. Moreover, in Sweden, Laurentius Andreae, Georg Norman, the brothers Olaus and Laurentius Petri, and Nicholas Stecker had attended Wittenberg, and on returning home, proclaimed and secured the Reformation message and methods. These reforming student-missionaries reinforce the notion that Luther's mission theology at Wittenberg was practically effective (Gallagher, 2005: 131-32; cf. Peters, 1970: 40-46).

Pietist Mission Education

The Pietist movement of seventeenth-century Germany continued the tradition of missional educational institutions such as those founded by the Church of the East, Celtic Christianity, the Franciscans, and early Calvinism and Lutheranism. Pietism emphasized the practice of Christianity from a subjective and emotional perspective in contrast to the rational and intellectual manner of German Lutheranism. Pietists desired to transform society by improving the living conditions of the poor, reforming the prison system, abolishing slavery, reducing class distinctions, reforming education, increasing mission activity, and fostering programs for social justice. Philipp Jakob Spener, a leading reformer in this movement, influenced the formation of the University of Halle in Saxony-Anhalt, Germany in 1694, which became a formative location of Pietist missionary and church leadership development in the next century.

August Hermann Francke was similarly involved in the beginnings of the Pietist movement in educating and sending cross-cultural workers from the University of Halle to Greenland, Iceland, India, Lapland, and beyond. Francke became a professor of Greek and Oriental languages at Halle, and the pastor of St. George church at Glaucha, a poverty-stricken suburb of Halle. Because of Francke, Halle became a center of social ministry, cross-cultural mission, and Jewish outreach. His published correspondence inspired the church in Europe and North America to be involved in mission through prayer, giving, and fieldwork (Sattler, 1982: 78). At Halle, he established a Bible Society to study and apply the word of God as he had done in Leipzig and Erfurt. Francke upheld the Bible as the only rule of faith and doctrine, and taught the application of the Scriptures. He was not without his critics since many of the professors believed that their task was to make students more learned and not more pious.

The institutions at Halle included a free elementary school, trade school, classical school that prepared people for university, royal school for the nobility, teacher's seminary, the Oriental College of Divinity (where Eastern languages were studied for Bible translation), an orphanage, drugstore, museum and bookstore, house for widows with chaplains, and a Bible Society. The university distributed Bibles and other Christian literature, and under Francke's influence, many students converted to Christ, and were inspired to serve God in some of the most inhospitable places on earth. With Francke's goal of bringing Scripture to every part of the globe, he established the Canstein Bible Institute in 1712; and in one hundred years, the Institute had printed and distributed two million Bibles and one million New Testaments. He maintained a tolerant attitude towards Catholicism, Reformed denominations, and Eastern Orthodoxy, which allowed the spread of his ideas throughout continental Europe.

Until August Francke's death in 1727, he continued to appoint student missionaries who went out from the University of Halle; held correspondence with them, published accounts of their missionary endeavors, and demonstrated particular interest in mission to the Jewish people. Halle University was the heart of Pietist mission, sending young men from its academic halls to German settlements in eastern and southeastern Europe and colonial outposts in Africa, Asia, and the Caribbean. In 1695, for example, the university sent teachers and students to the courts of Peter the Great in Russia where Francke cultivated friendships with several ministers in the Tsar's government. Shaped by Franke and Halle, a parade of Pietists followed in cross-cultural ministry. I will now briefly refer to six student missionaries: Bartholomew Ziegenbalg and Henry Plütschau, the Norwegian Hans Egede, Count Nikolaus Ludwig von Zinzendorf, Anton Wilhelm Böhme, and Christian Friedrich Schwartz.

In 1705, it was the University of Halle in partnership with Frederick IV of Denmark that sent the first Pietist missionaries, Bartholomew Ziegenbalg and Henry Plütschau, to evangelize the people in Tranquebar, along the southeast coast of India. The king and his Pietist wife, Queen Louise of Mecklenburg-Güstrow, concerned for the spiritual care of their colonial subjects, commissioned Franz Julius Luetkens, a German Pietist and the Danish court chaplain, to find suitable ministers to go to southern India. Luetkens contacted August Francke at Halle in Germany who recommended Ziegenbalg and Plütschau as worthy candidates.

One year later, the two Halle University students became the first Protestant missionaries to India for the express purpose of evangelizing the indigenous people. Putting into practice the principles and teachings learned at Halle, they sought to share the Scripture with cultural sensitivity. Their message was a blend of Lutheran theology and pietistic relevance believing that the word of God was "efficacious and powerful" for personal conversion and holiness; and their cross-cultural adventures inspired a procession of Protestant missionaries. One of the participants in the procession was the Norwegian Lutheran Hans Egede.

While studying theology at the University of Copenhagen, Egede acquired an interest in missions and connected with Pietist believers in the court of the Danish king, Frederick IV. Egede witnessed the ordination of the Halle university students Ziegenbalg and Plütschau and their departure to the Danish colonies in southern India. This event ignited his mission desires. As a result, Egede, "Greenland's Apostle," became a colonist and trader for the Danish monarchy in early eighteenth-century Greenland motivated by his desire to pastor the descendants of forgotten Norwegian settlers and interact with the indigenous people.

Another Lutheran Pietist influenced by Ziegenbalg and the Danish-Halle mission was Count Nikolaus Ludwig von Zinzendorf. Pietist missionary letters from Tranquebar were read in meetings at Zinzendorf's grandmother's castle at Gross-Hennersdorf in Upper Lusatia in 1708. "There and then the missionary impulse arose in my soul," reflected Zinzendorf (Hutton, 1895: 179). From ten to sixteen years of age, Francke influenced the Count as he attended the Royal Paedagogium at Halle University. It was in Francke's home that the Halle student met Ziegenbalg and Plütschau, which "increased my [his] zeal for the cause of the Lord in a powerful manner" (Gallagher, 2008a: 238-39). It was during this time that Zinzendorf, with four of his friends, formed a small group known as the Order of the Grain of Mustard Seed at Halle University, which focused on prayer and the cause of Christ. With one of his university friends, Count Frederick von Watteville, Zinzendorf vowed to "do all in our power for the conversion of the heathen, especially for those for whom no one cared, and by means of men whom God, we believed, would provide" (Hutton, 1922: 7). The Halle Pietists shaped the young Count's theological views. They emphasized the heartfelt religious devotion of the individual, belief in the Bible as the Christian's guide to life, and a complete commitment to Christ that would manifest itself in ethical purity and charitable activity. In doing so, they stressed the importance of experiencing God.

Count von Zinzendorf in 1722 founded the Moravian missionary movement at Herrnhut, near Dresden in Saxony. He offered a part of his estate as a refuge for a group of persecuted believers from Bohemia and Moravia. From these Brethren came the first organized Protestant mission. By 1760, the year Zinzendorf died, the Moravians had sent 226 missionaries to ten different countries. Mission stations had been established in Danish St. Thomas, in the West Indies (1732); Greenland (1733); Georgia, North America (1734); Lapland (1735); Surinam, or Dutch Guiana, on the north coast of South America (1735); Cape Town, South Africa (1737); Elmina, Dutch headquarters in the Gold Coast (1737); Demarara (present-day Guyana), South America (1738); and the British colonial islands of Jamaica (1754), and Antigua (1756). In 1760, there were forty nine men and seventeen women serving in thirteen stations around the world ministering to over six thousand people (Hutton, 1922: 55, 58; Latourette, 1975: 893, 897, 951, 956; Neill, 1986: 201-202; Tucker, 2004: 99-105). Even so, the greatest of the Moravian's contributions, was to awaken Protestantism to its responsibilities for cross-cultural ministry. Over the years, for example, the Moravian influence extended to the lives of eighteenth-century leaders such as John and Charles Wesley, and William Carey (Gallagher, 2008b: 185-86).

Other Halle University influences include the following. Anton Wilhelm Böhme, a Halle graduate, in 1710 became the Lutheran chaplain at St. James' Palace, London in the courts of Queen Anne of England and her husband, the Danish Prince George. Böhme translated many Pietist devotional tracts into English, including Ziegenbalg's annual letters reporting on the Danish Tranquebar mission called *Propagation of the Gospel in the East*; and distributed the publication to Pietist communities in Germany, Denmark, and England (Zorn, 1933: 101, 103). This compilation of letters reached the courts of Denmark and England, the Archbishop of Canterbury, and John and Charles Wesley, to name a few, and served as a catalyst to encourage financial giving and sending to the mission field. In addition, Böhme suggested to the Anglican Society for Promoting Christian Knowledge that they should send a printer and printing press to India for the service of the Danish mission to translate the Scriptures into the languages of southern India. Ziegenbalg, a German Lutheran in the service of a Danish monarch, eventually translated the New Testament into Tamil, and had it printed on an English press; funded by an Anglican mission society. Francke also used the Tranquebar Mission to promote missions and raise support. For instance, he published letters from his Halle missionaries in Germany and England that generated interest and financial assistance, especially among the nobility and royalty (Stoeffler, 1973: 34-35).

In 1713, Francke began sending Bibles, hymnals, and scriptural tracts, in addition to money, to Swedish prisoners of the Great Northern War (1700-21) in Siberia. In succession, Pietism established itself among the prisoners, and upon returning to their homeland, they formed schools modeled after Halle, including the Copenhagen Royal College of Missions of 1715, which became a significant Protestant missionary training center (Brown, 1978: 155). Further, there was a lack of trained pastors in the Lutheran churches of the American colonies in the eighteenth century, and Halle supplied the need. Justus Falckner, for example, studied theology under Francke in 1693, and ten years later began pastoring German and Swedish Lutheran immigrants in Philadelphia, New Jersey, and New York for twenty years (Stoeffler, 1976: 14-15).

The final Pietist Lutheran missionary I would like to review is Christian Friedrich Schwartz who inspired by the writings of August Francke and the pioneering work of Ziegenbalg and Plütschau began his studies at the University of Halle in 1746. It was at Halle—as he grew in his understanding of Pietism under the guidance of Benjamin Schultz who had been a missionary in southern India—that Schwartz dedicated himself to serving Christ in that part of the world (Frykenberg, 1999: 130). Even before Schwartz left for India, he had learned Greek, Latin, and Hebrew through his secondary education; and at Halle University under Schultz, he had studied English and Tamil. He arrived in southern India in 1750, and began his missionary career as a chaplain in the English garrison. Less than four months after his arrival he had preached his first sermon in Tamil on Matthew 11:25-30. For over forty eight years, he witnessed to non-Christians, discipled new believers as he studied languages and committed himself to the physical needs of the people, trained indigenous pastors, and served in various diplomatic roles. With Schwartz's unique ability to forge friendships with Muslims, Hindus, and English settlers and soldiers alike, the Halle alumni sought to transform society one person at a time, as did Francke his predecessor (Genischen, 1998: 606).

Implications

Following my exploration, I believe that we should study historic models of teaching mission to glean insights in order to incorporate Majority World Christianity in our teaching; and then ask the question: how do the cultural contexts and theological traditions of the historic movements examined affect our teaching and learning in North America?

Mission schools such as those of the Pietists at the University of Halle, the early Reformers, and the Church of the East, together with the monasteries of Celtic Christianity and the Franciscans were influential in the expansion of Christianity throughout Europe, and around the world. In this paper, I reviewed the training strategies of these early mission movements to provide insight into effective methods of contemporary mission teaching and learning. A number of patterns emerged across the five historic case studies.

First, the renewal movements that affected global missions had educational centers. That is, they provided resources to train their cross-cultural workers, and did not withhold the energy and effort involved to do so. All of the movements believed that furthering education was vital to their effectiveness and sustainability. In today's milieu of financial stress for both mission candidates, agencies, and denominations, often preparation is the first issue deleted. The current inertia towards missional education is not because of a lack of opportunity. There are over seventy graduate programs in missiology in the United States alone, and others available in another thirty countries, compared to one graduate program in 1965 facilitated by Donald A. McGavran and Alan R. Tippett at Fuller Theological

Seminary in Pasadena, California. Moreover, with advances in technology, field workers can conveniently study missions through online and hybrid delivery systems anywhere around the globe.

Yet, crippling undergraduate loan debt, a pragmatic millennial ethos, overcapitalization of short-term missions, and a continuing financial recession has hampered suitable preparation of cross-cultural workers. A few years ago, mission agencies considered it appropriate to train their candidates for nine months or more before allocating their intercultural assignments. Because of changes in western culture, people are more resistant to allotting time and money towards preparation; and coupled with advances in technology whereby instructors conduct assignments via the internet, many mission organizations have gradually reduced their training periods from six to four months and then from three to two weeks; most of which concerns organizational branding, security training, and human resource information such as health insurance, financial reports, and payroll. There is no time for foundational teaching such as biblical theology of mission, the history of mission, contextualization, intercultural communication, or world religions.

Second, in many of the training schools, faculty trained students holistically—teachers expected students to excel not only academically, but also in character, discipline, and spirituality. As representatives and reconcilers of Christ, character and spiritual formation matter. The Church of the East school at Nisbis, for example, had students follow strict rules of spiritual discipline and oaths of celibacy. In Celtic monastic communities, the life of the monks revolved around their missional education, as they spent each day in prayer, work, worship, and study. Other teaching schools such as the University of Halle encouraged care of the poor and needy as well as academics. The schools connected this pattern of holistic training to the belief that a missionary's work required faith and servanthood; submitted to the Lord's will. Before committed communities sent their cross-cultural workers, they had opportunity to grow in character, ethics, discipline, and perseverance, together with experiencing a renovation of the soul as they sought the Lord Jesus in prayer and worship while practicing an ascetic lifestyle.

Third, the academic focus of the training schools explored was on theology and languages. Celtic monasteries educated students in reading and writing Latin; Calvin's Reformed Academy at Geneva taught students French, Latin, and Greek New Testament languages, as did Luther's University of Wittenberg; Llull's Franciscan curriculum included theology and Oriental languages; and Pietist Francke also taught theology, Greek, and Oriental languages. These courses prepared students to minister cross-culturally with their language skills, and educated them in Christian theology to communicate to non-Christians the relevancy of the gospel of Jesus. Throughout the history of missions, the cross-cultural workers—whether Protestant, Catholic, or Orthodox—who were successful in contextualizing the gospel across cultural and ethnic barriers always spent extensive time in biblical studies, and learning the language and customs of the people before embarking on their mission.

Lastly, the purpose of the educational institutions was to raise up leaders and missionaries, who would not only evangelize, but disciple new Christians. The preparation in missions was cyclical, with cross-cultural ministries raising up indigenous leaders, so that as many people as possible would change their allegiance to Christ. Church of the East and Celtic Christianity infected the national leaders of Asia and Europe with the gospel of Jesus. The leaders in turn, affected their people towards adherence to Christianity. During the Reformation, Calvin intended the formation of the Geneva Academy to make the church self-perpetuating. Thus, Calvin sent his workers with the Reformed message to start churches across Europe, especially in the Netherlands and France. Likewise, Luther intentionally branded his Wittenberg students with his Reformation ideas who upon returning home to places such as Denmark, Sweden, and Finland, influenced the national king and church to break from Catholicism and embrace Lutheranism. Mentoring of younger leaders, both men and women, and providing opportunities for them to exercise their God-given gifts, is imperative for the survival and flourishing of the Christian faith.

Conclusion

In this essay, I reviewed historic cases of mission training to guide today's church towards God's future for missions' education. For followers of Christ to spread the gospel effectively, they should contextualize the message of Christ in a way that allows the hearers to receive the Good News with understanding. This is especially important in today's age of world Christianity. Instructors of mission today, therefore, need to recognize the global context of Christian education by incorporating educational goals and using effective andragogical strategies similar to the historic precedents investigated. I discovered that the historic preparation of missionaries took time and effort, and included holistic development of character and spiritual formation, alongside rigorous academics, especially in theology and languages. As we move forward into the twenty first century of teaching Christian mission, we should learn from these past educational institutions, and adapt their effective methods of cross-cultural training to our mission context.

References Cited

Bonner, Anthony
(1985). *Selected Works of Ramon Llull (1232-1316)*, vols. 1 and 2. Princeton, NJ: Princeton University Press.

Brown, Dale W.
1978. *Understanding Pietism*. Grand Rapids, MI: Eerdmans.

Bunkowske, Eugene W.
1985. "Was Luther a Missionary?" *Concordia Theological Quarterly* 49 (April-June): 161-79.

Chadwick, Owen.
1964. *The Reformation*. The Pelican History of the Church, Vol. 3. Baltimore, MD: Penguin Books.

Charlesworth, J. H., ed. & trans.
1977. *The Odes of Solomon*. Chico, CA: Scholars Press.

Clark, J. M.
1926. *The Abbey of St. Gall as a Centre of Literature and Art*. Cambridge: Cambridge University Press.

Coates, Thomas.
1969. "Were the Reformers Mission-Minded?" *Concordia Theological Monthly* 40 (October): 600-11.

Cochrane, Steve.
2014. "East Syrian Monasteries in the Ninth Century in Asia: a Force for Mission and Renewal." *International Bulletin of Missionary Research* 38:2 (April): 80-83.

Elton, Geoffrey R.
1964. *Reformation Europe: 1517-1559*. Cleveland, TN: Meridian Histories of Europe series.

Frykenberg, Robert E.
1999. "The Legacy of Christian Friedrich Schwartz: Missionary and Raj-Guru/Regent of Thanjavur," in *International Bulletin of Missionary Research*, 23:3 (July): 130-135.

Gallagher, Robert L.
    2005. "Present to Potential Prospect." In *Changing Worlds: Our Part in God's Plan*, eds. Nathan Bettcher, Robert L. Gallagher, and Bill Vasilakis, 129-142. Adelaide, South Australia: CRC Churches International.

Gallagher, Robert L.
    2008a. "Zinzendorf and the Early Moravians: Pioneers in Leadership Selection and Training." *Missiology: An International Review* 36:2 (April): 237-44.

Gallagher, Robert L.
    2008b. "The Integration of Mission Theology and Practice: Zinzendorf and the Early Moravians." *Mission Studies: Journal of the International Association for Mission Studies* 25:2 (October): 185-210.

Genischen, H. W.
    1998. "Schwartz, Christian Friedrich," in *Biographical Dictionary of Christian Missions*, Gerald H. Anderson, ed., 606. New York: Simon & Schuster Macmillan.

Hughes, Philip Edgcumbe.
    1966. *The Register of the Company of Pastors of Geneva in the Time of Calvin*. Grand Rapids, MI: Eerdmans.

Hutton, J. E.
    1895. *A Short History of the Moravian Church*. London: Moravian Publication Office.

Hutton, J. E.
    1922. *A History of Moravian Missions*. London: Moravian Publication Office.

Jenkins, Philip.
    2008. *The Lost History of Christianity: The Thousand-Year Golden Age of the Church in the Middle East, Africa, and Asia—and How It Died*. New York: HarperCollins.

Klijn, A.F.J.
    1962. *The Acts of Thomas*. Supplements to *Novum Testamentum*, Vol. 5. Leiden, the Netherlands: E. J. Brill.

Latourette, Kenneth Scott.
    1975. *A History of Christianity, Volume II: Reformation to the Present*. San Francisco: Harper & Row.

Lewis, Gillian.
    1994. "The Geneva Academy." In *Calvinism in Europe, 1540-1620*, eds. Andrew Pettegree, Alastair Duke, and Gillian Lewis, 35-63. Cambridge: Cambridge University Press.

Lewis, Paul W.
    2015. "Hermeneutics and the Church of the East in First Millennium Missiological Context of Central/East Asia: Lessons for the Contemporary Globalized Church." Paper presented at the North Central Evangelical Missiological Society. Deerfield, IL: 1-19.

Llull, Ramon.
    1985a. "Contemporary Life," in *Selected Works of Ramon Llull*, vol. 1, Anthony Bonner, trans. Princeton, NJ: Princeton University Press.

Llull, Ramon.
    1985b. "Felix, the Book of Wonders," in *Selected Works of Ramon Llull*, vol. 2, Anthony Bonner, trans. Princeton, NJ: Princeton University Press.

Lorenz, Erika, ed. & trans.
    1985. *Ramon Llull: Die Kunst, Sich in Gott zu Verlieben*. Freiburg im Breisgau, Germany: Herderbuecherei.

MacCulloch, Diarmaid.
    2016. *All Things Made New: The Reformation and Its Legacy*. New York: Oxford University Press.

Mackensen, H.
    1920. *Raymund Lull: A Missionary Pioneer in the Moslem Field*. Minneapolis, MN: Lutheran Orient Mission.

McNeill, John T.
    1954. *The History and Character of Calvinism*. New York: Oxford University Press.

McNeill, John T.
    1974. *The Celtic Churches: A History A.D. 200 to 1200*. Chicago: The University of Chicago Press.

Moffett, Samuel Hugh.
    1975. "The Earliest Asian Christianity." *Missiology: An International Review* 3:4 (October): 415-30.

Moffett, Samuel Hugh.
　　1982. "Mission in an East Asian Context: The Historical Context."
　　The Princeton Seminary Bulletin 3:3 (July): 242-51.

Neill, Stephen.
　　1986. *A History of Christian Missions*, 2nd ed. London: Penguin Books.

Oberman, Heiko A.
　　(1982) 1990. *Luther: Man Between God and the Devil.* Trans. Eileen
　　　　Walliser-Schwarzbart. New Haven, CT: Yale University Press.

Peers, E. Allison.
　　1969. *Ramon Lull: A Biography.* New York: Burt Franklin Publishing.

Peters, Paul.
　　1970. "Fruits of Luther's Mission-Mindedness." *Wisconsin Lutheran*
　　　　Quarterly 67 (January): 40-46.

Philip, T. V.
　　1996. "The Missionary Impulse in the Early Asian Christian Traditions."
　　　　International Review of Mission 85:4 (November): 505-21.

Pierson, Paul E.
　　2000. *Evangelical Dictionary of World Missions*, gen. ed. A. Scott Moreau,
　　　　s.v. "The Reformation and Mission," 813-814. Grand Rapids, MI:
　　　　Baker Books.

Ryan, John.
　　1972. *Irish Monasticism: Origins and Early Development.* Ithaca, NY:
　　　　Cornell University Press.

Sattler, Gary R.
　　1982. *God's Glory, Neighbor's Good.* Chicago: Covenant Press.

Schwiebert, Ernest G.
　　1950. *Luther and His Times.* St. Louis, MO: Concordia Publishing House.

Stevens, Carl D.
　　1994. "Calvin's Corporate Idea of Mission." Ph.D. diss. Ann Arbor, MI:
　　　　UMI Dissertation Services.

Stewart, John.
　　1928. *Nestorian Missionary Enterprise: The Story of a Church on Fire.*
　　　　Edinburgh: T. & T. Clark.

Stoeffler, F. Ernest.
　　1973. *German Pietism During the Eighteenth Century.* Leiden, Netherlands:
　　　　E. J. Brill.

Stoeffler, F. Ernest.
    1976. *Continental Pietism and Early American Christianity*. Grand Rapids, MI: Eerdmans.

Tucker, Ruth A.
    2004. *From Jerusalem to Irian Jaya: A Biographical History of Christian Missions*. Grand Rapids: Zondervan.

Valleskey, David J.
    1995. "Luther's Impact on Mission Work." *Wisconsin Lutheran Quarterly* 92 (April): 96-123.

Whatley, Janet.
    1990. *History of a Voyage to the Land of Brazil, Otherwise Called America*. Berkeley, CA: University of California Press.

Winkler, Dietmar W.
    2003. "The Age of the Sassanians: Until 651." In *The Church of the East: A Concise History*, eds. W. Baum and Dietmar W. Winkler, 7-41. London and New York: Routledge Curzon.

Zimmer, H.
    1969. *The Irish Element in Medieval Culture*. Jane Loring Edmands, trans. First published in 1891 by The Knickerbocker Press. New York: G. P. Putnam's Sons.

Zorn, H. M.
    1933. "Bartholomaeus Ziegenbalg," in *Men and Missions*, L. Fuerbringer, ed., vol. 10. St. Louis, MO: Concordia Publishing House.

Zwemer, Samuel M.
    1902. *Raymund Lull: First Missionary to the Moslems*. New York: Funk and Wagnalls.

How the West Was Won:

World Christianity as Historic Reality

Professor of Intercultural Studies, Kingswood University, Sussex, NB, Canada
Adjunct Professor, Asbury Theological Seminary, Wilmore, KY, USA

Abstract

Since the end of the previous century, there has been an increasing realization that the Church in the Majority world now forms the "majority" of the Christian population worldwide. To read much of the literature regarding this phenomenon, one would think that the idea of the church being a worldwide community was something which has arisen recently. As one glances back at the history of Christian faith, however, one is struck by the reality that the mission of the Church has *always* been "from everywhere to everywhere," and that the Gospel was brought to the West itself (insofar as the "West" could be understood to have even existed at that time) by people from "colonies" in other parts of the world. Far from mission from outside the West being a "new" thing, the situation can now be understood as a return to the historic norm, in which followers of Jesus from any part of the world can expect to be engaged in God's work among people anywhere else. In this paper, I will seek to trace this reality, and note both its resurgence as well as its trajectory into the future.

Since the end of the twentieth century, there has been an increasing emphasis in Christian and in missions circles on the rise of the "Global South" in the Christian community worldwide, and the reality that Christians from outside of areas traditionally considered to be part of the "West" now form the majority of Christians worldwide. This has been perhaps most famously underlined in volumes such as Philip Jenkins' *The Next Christendom: The Coming of Global Christianity* (third edition 2013; originally published in 2002), and more recently as the Anglican and Methodist communions have found their large African contingents working to uphold historic orthodoxy in Western settings where biblical authority has sometimes been regarded as secondary to more modern social trends.

When the perspective of such developments is that the churches in Asia, Africa and South America are the "younger" results of earlier mission work carried out by those in the West, it would seem that there is a trajectory of the Gospel and of Christian community moving from the West to the "East" (or South), and that even as the Gospel declines in the former, it has grown dramatically in the latter. When, however, one takes the longer view of Christian history, one begins to see that the reality is that Christian faith has *always* been rightly understood as a worldwide phenomenon, and that influence within the Church has been correctly understood multidirectional as well as multicultural. Jenkins himself has noticed this to an extent, with his subsequent (2009) volume, *The Lost History of Christianity: The Thousand-Year Golden Age of the Church in the Middle East, Africa, and Asia--and How It Died.*

In analyzing this topic, one difficulty which arises is in regard to the *definition* of the "West": In modern times, we tend to define the West as, loosely, the regions and countries of Western Europe, and those which were settled primarily by those of Western European stock in North America (the United States and Canada) and Oceana (Australia and New Zealand). This definition is somewhat difficult to sustain when we are discussing the world of the first millennium in which the northern reaches of Europe remained the unreached hinterlands, and the key centers of Christianity were in centers of power such as Rome and Constantinople, as well as places which were less central politically such as Edessa and the Egyptian desert.

The story of the Gospel begins, of course, away from the corridors of power, and in the relative backwaters of the Levant. Beginning primarily among Jewish people in their native land, and then spreading among both the Jewish Mediterranean diaspora, the message and life of the risen Christ began to spread among non-Jews in the region as well, with the initial agents being Jewish followers of Jesus. Early Church history is replete with examples of the influence of theologians from Egypt, North Africa and Syria on the development of Christian thought and theology, and interacting freely with those from the upper Mediterranean.

In this brief essay, however, we are going to examine three examples of influence of those from outside of the "center" of Christian life in the upper Mediterranean which had something of a missional turn. First, we will examine the influence of the Desert Fathers (and Mothers) of Egypt on the development of the monastic movement, and especially of the influential and widespread biography of the early monk Anthony authored by Athanasius (e.g., Athanasius 1979).

We will then turn to another key figure in the development of Egyptian monasticism, but more to the writings which we pseudonymously circulated under his name in the fourth century: Macarius of Egypt. Likely originating in Syria, and written in Greek, these *Homilies* had an influence throughout the Christian world as devotional literature, and apparently on the theology of both contemporary and later theologians. As we will see, in Europe, the *Homilies*, especially the second collection of fifty of them, also had an influence on the founders of Pietism and Methodism.

Finally, these examples are mainly *centripetal* in that they drew people from across the Christian world to engage in monastic asceticism, and to carry the teachings and practices of the monks of Scete and the Nitrian Desert back to Europe. Most fascinatingly, however, we will see that some of these monks may have gone as missionaries to the as-yet-unreached British Isles and Ireland, and engaged in cross-cultural mission themselves in this very different context.

The Influence of Egyptian Monasticism on the West

The monastic movement within Christianity has often quite famously been traced to Egypt, though it's possible that this was preceded by Syrian monasticism (MacCulloch 2009: 203), or at least appeared at roughly the same time in both Syria and Egypt (Guillaumont 1991: 5:1663). Some have speculated that Egyptian monasticism may have some connections with the communities of Jewish monastic *Theraputae* mentioned by Philo of Alexandria in his *On the Contemplative Life* (comparing them as more solitary contemplatives to the more communal, but also monastic Essenes)(Scouteris N.d). Others insist that this was more of an indigenous Egyptian development, possibly initiated by Paul of Thebes initially seeking relief from the Decian persecutions of 249-250, but eventually settling into the desert to pursue the solitary life (Guillaumont 1991: 5:1661). Paul was followed by Antony (c. 251-356), who came to be considered the "father of the monks" (Ibid.), and the most famous of the early monastics in Egypt. Antony and those following him (and many of those described in the collected writings of the

Desert Fathers [E.g., see Waddell 1962]) were referred to as those who practiced *anachoresis* (solitude; thus often transliterated "anchorites"). Generally speaking, however, those following Antony's example actually practiced what one writer has referred to as "semi-anchoritism," where the monks would live alone in their cells and united only on Saturday for a communal meal and to partake of the Eucharist (Guillaumont 1991:5:1661).

Not too long afterward, former soldier Pachomius (c. 292-348), an Egyptian who had served with the Roman military in Gaul, entered the monastic life as an anchorite. He later led in the development of *cenobitic* monasticism (Ibid.), focused less on individual solitude than on communal life. Pachomius applied some of the organizational skill that he had learned in the military, and providentially utilized abandoned villages along the Nile to establish monastic communities which practiced a very austere asceticism (MacCulloch 2009:203-204). Worth noting is that Pachomius' sister, Marie, founded a parallel order for women, too (Ibid.: 204). Both forms of monasticism were significantly indigenous, with the majority of the monks being native Egyptians whose first language (and in many cases, *only* language) was Coptic (Neill 1986: 33).

The key influence which Egyptian monasticism was to have on the West, and on the development of Christianity in the West, was initially by means of the distribution of a biography of Antony, written in Greek by his friend, bishop Athanasius of Alexandria (296-373). Containing an account of Antony's "spiritual athleticism" in terms of his asceticism, miracles, spiritual combat with the powers of darkness, and great wisdom, Athanasius wrote it particularly with an eye to influencing the Western Church with this account (Meinardus 1992:1), and the volume was copied and widely distributed in Greek, cited as an influence by the likes of Gregory Nazianzen (329-390) (Ibid.). Translated into Latin by Evagrius (345-399), it spread even further, influencing the likes of Jerome (347-420) and Augustine (354-430) (Ibid.); it has been suggested that it may have been the "most read book in the Christian world after the Bible" (MacCulloch 2009: 205). While questions have been and can be raised about both the accuracy and the motivation of the account (Ibid.: 206), this is ultimately not as important as the influence which the biography of Antony had in spreading the ethos of monasticism across the Christian world, and particularly to the West.

A generation later, another figure arrived on the scene who further illustrates the largely *centripetal* manner of the influence of Egyptian monasticism on the West. Born in what is now Romania, John Cassian (360-435) came initially to Palestine and was initiated into monastic life in Bethlehem. He became intrigued with the reports which he heard out of Egypt, however, and decided to travel there and learn from the desert monastics. For seven years he remained there, absorbing the wisdom of the monks, and interviewing them at length in what would eventually be compiled toward the end of his life as the his *Conferences*. These consisted of his recollection of interviews with various monks in Lower Egypt, which he wrote at the request of his colleagues in the monastery in Marseilles where he settled (Guy 1991: 2: 461). John is understood to form a kind of bridge between the Eastern and Western Church of the time. This is not only because he sought wisdom from the monks of Egypt, but because in providing this for a Western audience, he sought to communicate this wisdom into their cultural idiom, effectively *contextualizing* the message. Guy writes,

> Under the guise of a simple compiler who might allow himself only some slight adaptations to the Western climate and context, Cassian in reality laid the foundation of the first coherent pedagogy of Christian experience, and he did so by reworking and transposing into a new culture the experiences received from the monks of Egypt. (Guy 1991:2:463).

Thus the message of the life of the monks and of spiritual formation in the context of the monastic life, and the wisdom which John Cassian had sought from those who they perceived to be Christian elders in the more marginalized fringes of the Roman Mediterranean was thus effectively brought to Europe – both to what were considered more central areas such as Constantinople, and to places which might have been perceived as being elsewhere "on the fringes" such as in Marseilles (Meinardus 1992:3).

Another of the most famous and influential of the early Egyptian ascetics was Macarius (c. 294-394), who was said to be a disciple of Antony (Meinardus 1992: 3). He is said to have been instrumental in establishing monasticism in Scete, into which thousands followed him (Ibid.: 33). While his fame as a pioneer of monasticism is significant, of greater influence were three collections of writings, the *Spiritual Homilies*, as well as a "Great Letter" attributed to him. As scholars have by now almost universally affirmed, however, this collection of writings was not the work of Macarius, but rather of an anonymous Syrian (Maloney 1992: 6-8), *possibly* identified as Symeon of Mesopotamia (Dörries 1941: 7-8). His writings may have been circulated anonymously due to a suspicion of connections with Messalian groups in Syria (who prioritized religious experience over the sacraments, and who may have been extreme in their asceticism) (Maloney 1992: 8).

In spite of the apparent anonymity of the author, however, these writings have been some of the most influential in Christian history, including in the West. Macarius scholar Marcus Plested asserts that "The Macarian writings are one of the principal fountainheads of the Christian ascetic and mystical tradition" (Plested 2004: 1); Plested goes on to describe the influence the Macarian writings had on key figures in the development of especially Eastern Christian traditions: Maximus the Confessor (c. 580-662), Symeon the New Theologian (949-1022) and Gregory Palamas (1296-1357) (Ibid.). George Maloney adds to this list the great Cappadocian theologian Gregory of Nyssa (335-394), citing recent scholarship which notes that parallels between Gregory's *De Instituto Christiano* and the Macarian "Great Letter" likely point to the former having borrowed from the latter, rather than the other way around (Maloney 1992: 250).

More fascinating as well is that while the Macarian writings, especially with their emphasis on themes of union with God, sanctification, and Holy Spirit empowering (Friedman 2012), continued to circulate and maintain and influence in both the East and in the West, this influence extended into the Reformation, too, with early "proto-Pietist" Johann Arndt (1555-1621) having memorized the *Fifty Spiritual Homilies* (Plested 2004: 1-2, n. 2), with their contents influencing his landmark *True Christianity* (1605-1610). *The Spiritual Homilies* also had an influence, both directly and indirectly via Arndt, on the development of the early Methodist theology of sanctification (Friedman 2012: 98-100). Thus the anonymous writings of a fourth-century Syrian monk had a remarkable impact on the development of both Eastern and Western theology, all the way into the later Reformation.

The question then arises, however: In addition to this extensive *centripetal* influence by means of others coming to Egypt and returning, was the Egyptian Church involved in any significant *centrifugal* mission – that is to say, were Egyptians involved in outreach to as-yet-unreached regions? While it's difficult to be completely certain, there is evidence pointing to their having been involved in outreach into Europe. Some of the most fascinating speculation on this subject is in connection with the influence of Egyptian monasticism in England, Scotland and Ireland.

Egyptian influence on Christianity in the British Isles is easily grasped through artistic, literary and liturgical parallels (Meinardus 1992:4). There are examples of early Christian iconic art in Britain and Ireland which replicate Egyptian models. William Dalrymple, for example, shows an image representing Paul of Thebes and Antony of the desert breaking bread together, depicted in a rather stylized manner. Dalrymple places two examples of this image side by side: One is from the monastery of Saint Antony in Egypt, and the other is on a Pictish symbol stone in Scotland (Dalrymple 2004: photo plate), which also includes an image of Christ which is said to resemble a similar icon from St. Catherine's monastery in Sinai (Dalrymple 2008). The late eighth century *Stowe Missal* in Ireland, the oldest missal in the country, includes references to the Egyptian anchorites (Meinardus 1992: 4). This Egyptian influence in British and Irish monasticism goes back to at least the fifth century (Ritner 1976: 65). The *Antiphonary of Bangor*, the oldest Irish liturgical manuscript of any kind (late seventh century) includes the following lines:

> This house full of delight
> Is built on the rock
> And indeed the true vine
> Transplanted out of Egypt. (Dalrymple 2008).

Certainly the degree of ascetic intensity followed by the Egyptian monastics seems to have been replicated in Irish monasticism (Ritner 1976: 67), and in communities subsequently influenced, as Irish monks went forth in evangelistic mission across northern Europe. Further evidence has been indicated for the presence (and martyrdom) of Egyptian Christian missionaries in Switzerland at an early date (Ibid.: 81-82). Moreover, there is reference in the "litany of St. Oengus" in the *Book of Leinster*, asking for the aid of the "seven Egyptian monks in Disert Ullaigh" (Ibid.: 83; sic), noting the development of a kind of "equivalent" of a desert monastery (Ibid.).

While the indirect *influence* of the Egyptian monks is fairly certain, the idea of Egyptian *missionaries* seeking to bring the Gospel and discipleship as they understood it to the wild reaches of northwest Europe imply something about the nature of World Christianity – it moves in multiple directions, and will continue to do so. That European Christians in the "younger" churches sought wisdom from their Egyptian brothers might sound odd to Western Christians of the colonial era, but within their time, it would have been business as usual. May their example inspire us as well to learn well from one another, across the global body of Christ, and to teach our students the same.

References Cited

Athanasius.
    1980.   *The Life of Anthony and the Letter to Marcellinus.* Translated by Robert C. Gregg. Mahwah, NJ: Paulist Press, 1979.

Dalrymple, William.
    2004.   From the Holy Mountain: Journeys in the Shadow of Byzantium. New Delhi: Penguin Books.

    _____. 2008. The Egyptian Connection. *In New York Review of Books*, October 23. http://www.nybooks.com/articles/2008/10/23/the-egyptian-connection/.

Dörries, Hermann.
    1941.   *Symeon von Mesopotamien: Die Überlieferung des messalianischen Makarios-Schriften.* Leipzig: J.C. Hinrichs Verlag.

Friedman, Matt.
    2012.   A Macarian-Wesleyan Theology of Mission. *The Asbury Journal* 67, No. 1 (93-111).

Guillaumont, Antoine.
    1991.   Monasticism, Egyptian. *In Claremont Coptic Encyclopedia.* Edited by Aziz S. Atiya, 5:1661-1664. New York: Macmillan. http://ccdl.libraries.claremont.edu/cdm/ref/collection/cce/id/1381.

Guy, Jean-Claude.
    1991.   Cassian, Saint John. *In Claremont Coptic Encyclopedia.* Edited by Aziz S. Atiya, 2:461-464. New York: Macmillan. http://ccdl.libraries.claremont.edu/cdm/singleitem/collection/cce/id/428.

Jenkins, Philip.
    2009.   *The Lost History of Christianity: The Thousand-Year Golden Age of the Church in the Middle East, Africa, and Asia--and How It Died.* New York: HarperOne.

    _____. 2011. *The Next Christendom: The Coming of Global Christianity.* Third edition. The Future of Christianity Trilogy. New York: Oxford University Press, 2011. (Orig. Pub. 2002).

MacCulloch, Diarmaid.
    2009. *Christianity: The First Three Thousand Years.* New York: Penguin Books.

Maloney, George A.
    1992. Introduction and Notes to *The Fifty Spiritual Homilies and the Great Letter*, by Pseudo-Macarius. Mahwah, NJ: Paulist Press.

Meinardus, Otto F. A.
    1992. *Monks and Monasteries of the Egyptian Deserts.* Revised Edition. Cairo: American University in Cairo Press, 1992. (Orig. Pub. 1961).

Neill, Stephen.
    1986. *A History of Christian Missions.* The Penguin History of the Church, Vol. 6. Second Edition. London: Penguin Books.

Plested, Marcus.
    2004. *The Macarian Legacy: The Place of Macarius-Symeon in the Eastern Christian Tradition.* Oxford: Oxford University Press.

Ritner, Robert K.
    1976. Egyptians in Ireland: A Question of Coptic Peregrinations. *Rice Institute Pamphlet - Rice University Studies*, 62, no. 2. Rice University: http://hdl.handle.net/1911/63225.

Scouteris, Constantine. N.d.
    The Therapeutae of Philo and the Monks as Therapeutae according to Pseudo-Dionysius. *Biblioteca Theologica "Porphyrogenitus."* (Orig. Pub. University of Athens). http://www.apostoliki-diakonia.gr/en_main/catehism/theologia_zoi/themata.asp?contents=selides _katixisis/contents Theological.asp&main=SK_13&file=13.9.htm.

Waddell, Helen, trans.
    1962. *The Desert Fathers.* The Fontana Library: Theology and Philosophy. London: Fontana Press.

The World's Christians:

Strategies for Teaching International Graduate Students in Kenya's Christian Universities

JANICE HORSAGER RASMUSSEN

About the Author

Janice is a Phd candidate in Education at Africa International University. A missionary since 1995 in Tanzania and Kenya, she teaches church leaders and researches international education issues. Previously, she was a University of Minnesota Extension Assistant Professor.

The experiences of international graduate students in Africa are nearly nonexistence in the literature. In a case study of one Christian university in Kenya, I interviewed international graduate students and conducted participant observations. I aimed to understand their learning experiences. I found that low English proficiency plagued many students, as did lack of academic writing and critical thinking skills. Students appreciated teachers who utilized the diverse learning community, gave clear guidance, and mentored them. In a follow-up study at four Christian universities in Nairobi, international graduate students and their teachers provided further strategies for promoting learning for this population.

Introduction

As globalization increases, faculty, students and ideas are crossing borders at faster rates than ever before. Yet, little research has been conducted on the effects of globalization on educational institutions and students in Africa. International student research has often focused on Africans studying in the USA or in Europe (McLachlan & Justice 2010; Terkla, Roscoe, & Etish-Andrews 2007; Zhao & Wildemeersch 2008). Yet many Bible schools, seminaries and Christian universities in Africa have had always been international. At the Christian university in Nairobi studied here, internationals (non-Kenyan passport holders) constitute 23% of the student body (Rasmussen 2014:4).

Research Purpose

Much money, time, and opportunity cost is spent to educate international students. Families, sponsors and churches sacrifice to send their members across borders for graduate education. Yet, little is known about the graduate international students' learning experiences. I sought to explore this. Later, I expanded the inquiry into three more Christian universities and included faculty members. I investigated the factors that hindered and facilitated their learning as well as effective teaching strategies.

Methodology

To better understand the learning experiences of international students at one Christian university, I designed a qualitative, interpretive case study. I conducted a preliminary study of five international students, after which I revised the interview guide. Then in 2013 I interviewed thirteen graduate students living on the campus, who had studied there at least one term. The sample upheld my desire for nearly maximum variation in program, family status and country of origin. They spoke 13 languages, came from eight countries and had lived in seven others. Likewise, students had been influenced by various colonial educational systems. They came from a variety of previous schools, including denominational Bible schools, liberal arts colleges, secular universities, schools of ministry, and other theological schools (Rasmussen, 2014).

I also participated and took notes in the community for four years as a graduate student and as International Student Coordinator. After transcribing verbatim and coding all of the interviews and field notes using WEFTQDA software, I identified themes.

In a follow-up study, I built on this research by expanding my population to four evangelical Christian universities in Nairobi. I focused my inquiry on learning and teaching, still with international graduate students. To date in 2016, I have 33 faculty members and 27 students at four Christian universities in Nairobi. They represented an additional nine countries. I have taken notes on the interviews, but I am still in the process of transcribing and analyzing them.

Therefore, all findings and quotations are from the original study, but some preliminary findings from the follow-up study are included in the pedagogical implications. While specific to Christian universities in Nairobi, others from similar settings may explore whether some of the findings may be cautiously transferred.

Findings

I will discuss my findings from my original case study using an adaptation of a model (below) developed in the UK which describes international student experiences in higher education. The term "culture" is a bit vague here, but it highlights that there are agreed upon norms a group may expect without stating them. The three main categories include: academic expectations and study skills, communication issues and language skills, and cultural expectations: roles, values, and intercultural skills.

Academic Expectations and Study Skills

Academic institutions develop their own micro-cultures, with beliefs, values, expectations, practices and behaviors. These are often implicit, which is confusing for students who have not been a part of that culture. They may even clash with students' previously experienced academic cultures (Cortazzi & Jin, 1997:77; Carroll, 2005:26–27). Students in this case study experienced some of these expectation clashes in the structure of learning, the level of learning and the heavy work load.

Structure of learning.

Since the structure of learning was different from past experiences, most international students had to adapt their approaches to learning. Many came from systems that provided more guidance, so they had expected more direct teaching from their professors. This gap left them feeling somewhat abandoned. According one student, "You are teaching yourself, you have to teach yourself. That's the kind of learning process here. They just guide you" (M. Democratic Republic of Congo 2013). Those from French-speaking systems especially seemed to expect more guidance.

The faculty members in this study often challenged students to think critically in class. One student admitted, "Wrestling with professors in class about issues - at times I question myself and never thought that way .... It has just really changed me in thinking a different way" (Y. Malawi 2013). Some students had come from classes where rote learning was the norm. Students had been expected to recite back information to teachers. They were punished if they questioned their teachers (e.g. South Sudan). Classroom environments in the study varied and some Westerners had to learn not to challenge some of their teachers.

Various administrative issues in the education troubled students. Some had to adjust from semesters to terms. Overlapping demands stressed some. For example, many master's students felt overwhelmed researching and writing their theses while doing coursework. Doctoral students were surprised to have proposals and competency exams due simultaneously. Grading systems varied from their past experience, so it took time to figure out the meaning of grades. The credit transfer system confused some. Also, the meaning of "on time" varied. Some found that deadlines were more flexible than expected.

The small size of classes generally contributed to students' learning. Small class sizes enabled quality interactions between lecturers and students, and among students. This allowed for varied growth opportunities, such as oral presentations in seminars. Likewise, individualized attention from professors promoted learning.

> The teacher seem to be more friendly than in Congo. They are much more authoritative there. But here . . . you contribute, you become more friends, which is, for me, very positive . . . . You build a course together. You also bring your findings, your discovery on the table. And also I like small classes. . . . It's give good room for good interaction [*sic*]. (M. Democratic Republic of Congo 2013)

At this university, professors as well as students came from many different educational systems. The variation of standards and expectations between professors confused students. Standards for referencing and writing papers varied from professor to professor. One student observed, "You can have different lecturers; everyone . . . has his own system of writing papers, even of referencing. . . . We are using Turabian as a main, but some are like parenthetical, some footnotes" (M. Nigeria 2013).

Organization and coordination of programs was inconsistent. Sometimes courses were not offered in the expected time, causing students to over-stay. Some students felt that professors seemed relatively free to teach as they liked, without much coordination or accountability from the broader system. Some professors sent syllabi out irregularly, without much time to prepare read and write papers for seminar classes. They wanted clearer instruction. One student complained, "You keep saying, 'write a good paper.' That is somehow confusing . . . but if you give me guidelines, follow these guidelines correctly, then I can do better" (T. Tanzania 2013).

Level of learning.

Of course, students felt the difference when they entered into graduate, compared with undergraduate studies. Most lecturers pushed them to think more independently and more critically. While this was demanding, they appreciated this approach. At the other end of the spectrum, students had a few teachers who just gave out basic information, did not challenge them, and did not seem prepared to teach at the necessary level. Students varied in their level of preparedness for studies. For some, many classes built on their bachelor's studies. For others, the topics were entirely new. This necessitated that teachers review basic concepts before moving on.

> One of the least favorite has also been the best. There was one particular assignment where we really were pushed . . . using only primary sources . . . we were just groping in the dark to try and figure it out and produce a decent paper, so that was a really tough exercise, but it was also one of the best learning experience, without very much guidance . . . so it was just kind of being thrown into the deep end . . . Most of it was on our own. (P. Canada 2013)

Heavy work load.

Nearly all of the students found the work load and pace daunting. The amounts and levels of reading and writing, along with the proofreading and editing required, shocked many students, although they had expected a challenge.

> The whole of the first year, I would say that I didn't learn much, because it was just like cramming knowledge in class and even writing papers without digesting. . . . We were given a lot of stuff in a very short period, so before you will digest that, the term is over. You're given another pile of courses and by the end of the day, I didn't know if I was learning. (D. Malawi 2013)

Students coped with the work load by getting advice, praying, learning to manage their time, and developing their study skills. Some determined to persevere. Though it cost their grades, some overloaded their schedules to finish early, especially if their spouses were ready to return home. Others stayed because they dreaded the shame and disappointment they would cause to their families and sponsors if they quit. Some took fewer courses or cut out other activities, such as socializing or time with family. Many found that gradually, they grew accustomed to the system (including the professors' accents and expectations) and they learned to study more effectively.

New study skills were required. Some students come to school with fewer basic study skills than their colleagues, so they were more overwhelmed. For instance, some had to learn how to use computers, the library, and internet resources.

> I struggled like the first three terms. I was like totally confused between the IT, and the library, and the classes and actually in my undergraduate we don't use computers. This was one of the hard things. Sometime I can write and in the middle of my assignment, I lost it. You can just feel the frustration. (L. Democratic Republic of Congo 2013)

Many had to learn to write better and to read faster and more selectively. One student had never done a book review. Others learned about plagiarism the hard way. E-learning was new to many. One noted, "We have been raised in a culture where story-telling is very important ... you have to ask him [the teacher] questions or her questions. But in e-learning ... actually it's good, but it is quite challenging" (I. Tanzania 2013). They appreciated learning to do e-learning, but they also missed face-to-face interaction with their lecturers.

Communication Issues and Language Skills

Cultures of communication relate to the ways in which people express and interpret ideas in their cultures (Cortazzi & Jin 1997:76). Language proficiency can be a major stress point for international students, but the actual communication problems can be much deeper, relating to the content being communicated, not just the way in which it is being communicated (Egege & Kutieleh 2004:75–76; Hofstede 1986:314–316; Lacina 2002:22). Like many other international students elsewhere, graduate students had to learn new communication skills. Academic writing and critical thinking challenged many.

English difficulties.

English plagued many students, especially those who had not schooled much in English previously. This language difficulty was compounded by the high level of academic work, the different schooling systems, and the heavy work load mentioned above. Students who struggled with English felt disadvantaged compared to other students fluent in English.

> That's another challenge, in fact, to write in a good way, since we are from different countries . . . we don't have English. Our people, they do not speak English But here, since we are from different countries, our teachers, they look to our work, according to their standards or according to the other students, not understanding our problem, or our weakness in English. (E. Ethiopia 2013)

For many students, improving their English and accessing English materials was one of their goals in attending university in Kenya. Some students from Rwanda or the Democratic Republic of Congo had study options in French, but they felt the university in Nairobi was superior. Some sought international friends and attended English church services to improve their fluency.

Cultural Expectations: Roles, Values, and Intercultural Skills

The culture of the learning environment relates to expectations in the classroom, roles of students and teachers, basic values and beliefs regarding learning and teaching. Issues of pedagogy and assessment are also important parts of cultures of learning (Cortazzi & Jin 1997:76, 85).

Credible, diverse faculty.

Though challenging at first, many students came to value the international diversity and exposure from their professors. One student reported, "I've been really blessed by the professors and the range of professors. Like last term, I had a South Korean, Kenyan, West African, and an American ... that wouldn't happen in too many other places" (Y. USA 2013). Their different experiences and approaches to teaching enhanced the learning process. A number of professors had been international students. Doctoral students appreciated working with well-known visiting professors/authors. Others liked the credibility of professors who were missionaries teaching missions classes.

Several metaphors surfaced to describe faculty. One was seen as a father who modeled patience and encouraged his students. Others were referred to as elders or gurus.

> He was like a father, a teacher, very encouraging. . . . I like that approach. It challenged myself, if I will be a teacher, or a pastor, tried to care for those who are down, those who they don't think they can do something. So that was a good experience to learn from my lecturer [sic]. (P. Tanzania 2013)

Approachable faculty.

Students compared their professors with their past experiences. Most expected more power distances between professors (and their spouses) and students (Hofstede, 1986:307). Most found the faculty friendly, approachable and available.

> This is one university that I learn that it is possible for me to interact with your professors one on one, to take tea together. In my background, is almost impossible ... The system here kind of creates an atmosphere where you can chat ... you can express yourself more freely to the professor. He will even ask you questions ... It is open and the professors themselves are also hoping to engage you. (M. Nigeria 2013)

Students often found teachers who were willing to mentor them, though not all faculty members were so available. They appreciated being included in conferences and professional networks as well as getting experience teaching and researching with faculty.

> So the faculty, most of them, have been very, very generous and gone out of their way to give advice and counsel outside of the classroom which has been very, very helpful, ... more mentoring. They have given the students the feeling that we're more like colleagues than a strict teacher-student division ... I wasn't expecting it would be that collegial. (P. Canada 2013)

Contextualized African teaching.

Having various Africans teaching on African issues within an African context brought authenticity to the learning process. Dealing with real African issues assisted students in thinking through their worldviews and their own responses to these issues. Some noted the mixture of influences on the university (British, American, Kenyan) but they appreciated that faculty dealt with local realities and helped students apply learning in their context. Interestingly, it was mainly Western students and faculty who wished for more African authors on the syllabi.

> But coming here to this school ... I found it taking me back to my roots ... the courses that I've taken here, the lecturers. They really push us back to our African roots to value our culture, to appreciate a lot of cultural aspects of our communities. (D. Malawi 2013)

Learning in an international community.

In addition to faculty, students appreciated the community of learning and their fellow students. Small class sizes lent themselves to frequent discussions in class. They learned from each other's experiences and perspectives, in class and outside of class. As one student expressed this, "I've really appreciated knowing classmates. ... It's been really good, the benefits of learning here and understanding spiritual points of view from classmates. That's been really rich" (Y. USA 2013).

Living on campus gave students numerous opportunities to interact. They made friends and developed international networks. Learning and living in an international, inter-denominational community also required some adjustments. For example, it did not take too long to learn new ways of greeting friends but it took a long time to feel really greeted in the new way.

> You get to know how other people approach life from their different countries and how they see what you don't see, through interaction with one another, learning from what they are doing out there to their countries, how they approach life, how they see things, their system in education. (P. Tanzania 2013)

Summary and Discussion of Findings

International Student Research

In summary, these international students experienced many issues common to international students elsewhere, but they also faced some unique situations.

Like others, they were initially quite disoriented by the different system of learning they met. The case study university's unique mix of international influences (American, British, and Kenyan) confounded the issue. As in other places, the new role expectations of teachers and students mystified many at first. A study at Trinity International University noted similar challenges and benefits for their theological graduate students (Charter, Guth, Lopes, & Theonugraha 2010).

Other internationals struggled to learn to think critically and write academically. Teaching these explicitly, as helpful tools to survive university, often helped students grasp them (Egege & Kutieleh 2004:77–81; Davies 2006:16–37). While students were expected to take a class in writing, it was not enough for many. More support (writing center, tutoring, proofreading) was needed than was available at the university. Like others, language difficulties plagued many throughout their studies. They may have had less English support than at some other bigger, more resourced international universities (Cammish 1997:143–146). Perhaps to boost enrollment, some students were admitted with seemingly low English skills, which contributed to low learning levels and poor grades, especially at first. Still, nearly all gradually improved their English.

Generally, Kenyans were seen to be quite friendly and helpful when approached. Internationals sometimes had to pursue contacts with them, but the gap seemed smaller with hosts than in many of the other studies. These international students also reported less racism, although some Westerners felt some xenophobia (Terkla et al. 2007:1; Zhao & Wildemeersch 2008:57). Off campus, African internationals also felt some discrimination, especially if they could not speak Kiswahili. Like other sojourners around the world, they felt lonely, missed home, and experienced culture shock. As in other places, many struggled immensely with finances, as support sometimes dropped off and they could not rely on family members or church members to help from afar.

Like other internationals, students encountered cultural differences in class and living on campus, such as variations in time/event orientations, individual/communal orientations, power distance variations, and varying levels of tolerance towards ambiguity (Hofstede 1986:307–310). Though uncomfortable, they tried to adapt to some of these differences. For example, individualistic students learned to appreciate study groups. Teachers were more approachable and accessible than students from high power distance cultures expected, but before long, they appreciated this. Deadlines were renegotiated with teachers. Students requested more specific guidelines when needed.

Like many internationals, they broadened their perspectives and networks by studying at this university. Close, continual interactions with fellow students and faculty influenced these changes. Students appreciated the African focus of their studies, which was not the case for many international students studying abroad (Hyams-Ssekasi 2012:197; Noronha 1992:57–58; Barker 1997:109–112).

Multicultural Pedagogies

Many experts recommend becoming a critically reflective teacher to improve one's teaching of international students. Hofstede recommends teachers must first understand their own cultures and then recognize that others learn in different ways. His anthropological approach to teaching embraces the world's cultural variety (1986:316). To do this, teachers must examine their own assumptions. Cortazzi and Jin advocate aiming for *cultural synergy* when teaching, where teachers and students try to understand the other's principles of interpretation. Teachers and students can learn from each other while still maintaining and affirming each other's cultural identity (1987:88–89). They must recognize the cultural underpinnings of their own teaching and assessments, including their subliminal expectations. They then must reflect on how these may affect others from different groups. This can help teachers decide what is essential and what can be adapted to suit the needs of their students. Being explicit also helps students to understand expectations and to express their learning (Carroll 2005:27–28; Ryan 2005:96; Weinstein & Obear 1992:41–61; Ramsay 2005:22; Ford & Dillard 1996: 232–236; Banks 2001:64; McLaren & Sleeter 1995:35–45; Gorski 2010:2–4).

Pedagogical Implications

Teachers play a critical role in facilitating international graduate student learning. Their attitude, modeling, and competence are critical for learning. Below are some suggestions for teachers of graduate students at Christian universities in Nairobi, based on the follow-up study of internationals and faculty.

Academic Expectations and Study Skills

- Learn about different educational systems (e.g. British, Arabic, French, Ethiopian).

- Explore students' past experiences and expectations for student and teacher roles.

- Teach needed competencies (e.g. academic writing and critical thinking) explicitly.

- Grade mostly for content. Correct writing and grammar, in increasing detail.

- Keep explicitly educating on plagiarism.

- In thesis writing, go slowly, even paragraph by paragraph, if needed.

- Be patient.

- Help students develop confidence academically. Reward positive steps.

- Give examples of excellent work.

- Give clear guidelines and expectations for learning and assessments.

- Prioritize the most important readings and assignments.

- Help students access resources (e.g. more books on reserve, on-line resources)

Communication Issues and Language Skills

- Speak clearly, slowly and audibly. Be aware of your accent. Don't mix in Kiswahili.

- Write the main points when lecturing. Give notes and/or use powerpoint.

- Refer students to language support services (e.g. English, writing centers).

- Give students simple books to read for practice.

- Encourage them to have a dictionary or electronic translation device handy.

- Teach students presentation skills.

- Learn some greetings in students' languages.

- Be humble, accessible, and approachable. Encourage them to ask questions.

Cultural Expectations: Roles, Values, and Intercultural Skills

- Recognize culture shock and transition overload. Give extra grace at first.

- Be aware of different expectations of power distance, ambiguity, time orientation, individualism versus communalism, and ascribed versus achieved authority (e.g. be careful of correcting elders in groups).

- Learn about students' contexts and roles. Help them apply their learning to these.

- Critically reflect on your own values, beliefs, experiences and teaching practices.

- Utilize the international community as a learning environment.

- Use disorienting situations for learning.

- Be a role model and mentor.

- Be self-aware and Holy-Spirit aware. Let the Holy Spirit teach.

- Show you care, holistically (ask about family, give credit to call home, visit them, help them financially, lend books, listen, or pray with them).

- Treat students as adults. Engage students.

- Avoid local jokes. Give appropriate examples.

- Encourage students to learn from each other (i.e., discussions, small groups). Use oral and social methods.

- Use a variety of methods. Mix lectures with practical activities.

- Help students apply content to their contexts (e.g. Africa, country).

- Give case studies or have them share their experiences.

- Drink tea, eat together, host students at home and discuss life issues.

Notes

Some of the content of this paper was presented at the International Conference on Education in Nairobi, Kenya in July 2015.

Acknowledgements

My deep appreciation goes to all of the international students and faculty members whose stories informed this research.

All interview quotations use a pseudonym to protect the privacy of the student. Interviews conducted by Janice R. H. Rasmussen:

2013   Learning experiences at AIU interview [digital recording, transcribed].
        Canada, Paulo (April 29).
        Democratic Republic of Congo, Luka (May 13).
        Democratic Republic of Congo, Marco (May 20).
        Ethiopia, Emmanuel (April 26).
        Malawi, Daudi (May 27).
        Malawi, Yohanna (May 10).
        Nigeria, Matteo (May 15).
        Tanzania, Isaka (May 20).
        Tanzania, Pierre (May 8).
        Tanzania, Timeteo (May 3).
        USA, Yakobo (May 20).

References Cited

Banks, James A.
2001   *Cultural Diversity and Education: Foundations, Curriculum, and Teaching.* Needham Heights, MA: Allyn and Bacon.

Barker, John
1997   "The Purpose of Study, Attitudes to Study and Staff-Student Relationships." In *Overseas Students in Higher Education: Issues in teaching and Learning.* D. McNamara & R. Harris, eds. Pp. 108–123. London: Routledge.

Cammish, Nadine K.
1997   "Through a Glass Darkly: Problems of Studying at Advanced Level Through the Medium of English." In *Overseas Students in Higher Education: Issues in Teaching and Learning.* D. McNamara & R. Harris, eds. Pp. 143–155. London: Routledge.

Carroll, Jude
2005   "Strategies for Becoming More Explicit." In *Teaching International Students: Improving Learning for All.* Pp. 26–34. London: Routledge.

Charter, Miriam, Guth, Cheryl, Lopes, Cesar, & Theonugraha, Felix
2010   "Communicating for Learning Across Cultures." Summary of Findings from Phase One of Research, (October). Trinity Evangelical Divinity School, Chicago.

Cortazzi, Martin, & Jin, Lixian
1997   "Communication for Learning Across Cultures." In *Overseas students in higher education: Issues in teaching and learning.* D. McNamara & R. Harris, eds. Pp. 76–90. London: Routledge.

Davies, W. Martin
2006   "Cognitive Contours: Recent Work on Cross-cultural Psychology and its Relevance for Education." (December 12) [Springer Science + Business Media B.V. 2006].

Egege, Sandra, & Kutieleh, Salah
2004   "Critical Thinking: Teaching Foreign Notions to Foreign Students." *International Education Journal 4:* 75–85.

Ford, Terry L., & Dillard, Cynthia B.
1996   "Becoming Multicultural: A Recursive Process of Self-and Social Construction." *Theory into Practice, 35*(4): 232–238.

Gorski, Paul. C.
2010   "The Scholarship Informing the Practice: Multicultural Teacher Education Philosophy and Practice in the United States." *International Journal of Multi-Cultural Education, 12*(2).

Hofstede, Geert
1986   "Cultural Differences in Teaching and Learning." *International Journal of Intercultural Relations 10:* 301–320.

Hyams-Ssekasi, Denis
2012   "The Transition of International Sub-Saharan African Students into the UK University System with Reference to a University in the North of England." Doctoral dissertation, University of Huddersfield, UK, Huddersfield, UK. Retrieved from http://eprints.hud.ac.uk/16428/.

Lacina, Jan Giudry
2002   "Preparing International Students for a Successful Social Experience in Higher Education." *New Directions for Higher Education, Internationalizing Higher education: Building Vital Programs on Campuses* 117: 21–27.

McLachlan, Debra A., & Justice, Jessica
2010   "A Grounded Theory of International Student Well-being." *The Journal of Theory Construction and Testing, 13*(1): 27–32.

McLaren, Peter, & Sleeter, Christine E.
1995   "Introduction: Exploring Connections to Build a Critical Multiculturalism." In *Multicultural Education, Critical Pedagogy and the Politics of Difference.* Pp. 5–32. Albany, NY: State University of New York.

Noronha, June
1992   "International and Multicultural Education: Unrelated Adversaries or Successful Partners?" *New Directions for Teaching and Learning, Promoting Diversity in College Classrooms: Innovative Responses for the Curriculum, Faculty, and Institutions* 52: 53–59.

Ramsay, Nancy J.
2005   "Teaching Effectively in Racially and Culturally Diverse Classrooms." *Teaching Theology and Religion, 8*(1):18–23.

Rasmussen, Janice R. Horsager
    2014 "Learning Experiences of International Students at Africa International University." Unpublished MPhil thesis draft, Africa International University.

Ryan, Janette
    2005 "Improving Teaching and Learning Practices for International Students." In *Teaching international students: Improving learning for all*. J. Carroll & J. Ryan, eds. Pp. 92–100. London: Routledge.

Terkla, Dawn Geronimo, Roscoe, Heather S., & Etish-Andrews, Jane
    2007 "Voices from Around the World: International Undergraduate Student Experiences." *Association for Institutional Research (AIR) Professional File*, 104:1–12.

Weinstein, Gerald, & Obear, Kathy
    1992 "Bias Issues in the Classroom: Encounters with the Teaching Self." *New Directions for Teaching and Learning* (Promoting Diversity in College Classrooms: Innovative Responses for the Curriculum, Faculty, and Institutions) *52*:39–50.

Zhao, Miao & Wildemeersch, Danny
    2008 "Hosting Foreign Students in European Universities." *European Education, 40* (1):51–62.

Gendered Mission:

Educational Work or Itinerating Preaching? The
Mission Practice of the Presbyterian Church
USA in Barranquilla, Colombia, 1880-1920

ANGEL SANTIAGO-VENDRELL

Two gendered based evangelistic approaches developed in the Barranquilla mission of the Presbyterian Church USA in the beginning of their missionary work to Colombia in the nineteenth century.   One was directed towards the proclamation of the gospel through preaching and the establishment of churches. The missionaries who used this method were more conservative in their theology and worldview. They were interested in the salvation of the soul, but never took care of the daily affairs of life.   The other group also thought that they were evangelizing the Colombian people through education. This group of missionaries was theologically more liberal and their agenda of educating the middle and upper classes to influence the elites of the nation was well received by those social sectors. Even though both approaches differ in their methodology, the final goal was the same, to bring them to the blessings of Western civilization through Jesus Christ.

As the majority of missionaries in the Barranquilla station in the last part of the nineteenth and early twentieth centuries were single women, their missiology predominated in the station. Dana L. Robert argues that "as women's groups founded their own journals to disseminate missionary intelligence to their constituencies, a common missiology emerged, known as Women's Work for Women."[1] The goal of the emerging missiology was to bring salvation to native women and uplift their lives in society. The best method for uplifting and evangelizing native women was through education. Robert notes, "Women's Work for Women aimed to put into place instruments of education, medical work, and evangelization that would raise women to the status they presumably held in Christian countries."[2] For the female missionaries there was no separation between church and school work because the educational system was their best evangelistic tool. For example, in her personal report of 1908, Dora Lee stated, "Another feature of the school work in Barranquilla which made the school particularly evangelistic in its tone was the fact that the missionaries themselves have had charge of the boarding departments. We have thought that by living with the children, eating food with them at the school tables, and sleeping with them in the dormitories, we could exert a deeper influence over them."[3] The first part of the article will give a Historical Overview of missionary work and the formation of the Presbyterian Church in Colombia. The second part is a narrative of the missionary work in Barranquilla, Colombia. In this section, the female missionaries faced great setbacks and attacks against their mission theory by male missionaries. The third part addresses the ministry of Bible women who converted through the missionary efforts of the single female missionaries. The final part presents the missionary efforts to trained national leaders. One of the

---

1   Dana L. Robert, *American Women in Mission: A Social History of Their Though and Practice* (Macon, Georgia: Mercer University Press, 1997), 130.

2   Robert, *American Women in Mission*, 133.

3   Dora T. Lee, Personal Report to the Board of Foreign Missions, January 13, 1908. The Colombia Mission, 1833-1911. Boston University School of Theology Library. Microform Archive.

disparities that the section reveals is that women were not invited to participate in formal theological education while they were fierce educators, evangelists, and pillar of their communities.

Brief History of the Presbyterian Church in Barranquilla, Colombia

The Presbyterian Church was the first Protestant ecclesiastical body from the United States to send a missionary to Bogota, Colombia, in 1856. The Colombian Mission commissioned in 1888, the Rev. Thomas and Mrs. Candor to form a mission station in the city of Barranquilla. After three months in the city, Mrs. Candor organized the first school for girls in the North American Consulate. The school began by the suggestion of Mrs. Whelply, wife of the American consul in Barranquilla. The Whelphy's had two daughters who needed instruction, but did not wanted to send them to a Roman Catholic schools. One of the most translucent expressions of the new government was its coalition with the Roman Catholic Church. The Constitution was amended bestowing most of its previous privileges in society. Among them, the educational system was to be directed according to the Catholic religion.[4] As the Whilphy's did not want their daughters to be influenced by Catholic religion, the work of the Barranquilla mission began through the educational system, while providing services to a select group of girls. In only three weeks, Mrs. Candor with the help of a native teacher and the daughter of an English businessman were teaching eighteen girls.[5]

In 1890, Miss Franks was appointed to help in the direction of the girl's school. Franks was a veteran already with some years as headmaster of the school in Bogota. She married Edward H. Ladd, a Christian businessman in the city. As Candor organized the educational work with Ladd (previously Franks), Rev. Candor was securing a place to use as a chapel. He rented a big space in the middle of the city and celebrated Protestant services on Sunday, Wednesday, and Friday with a fluctuating audience between thirty and fifty people. On November 24, 1890 Rev. Theodore Pond were transferred from the Syrian mission to Barranquilla, Colombia. Pond was an old and tired missionary who had been in the field for seventeen years.

---

4   Gabriel De Ibarra, *El Concordato de Colombia: En Algunos Puntos Principales* (Bogota: Editorial Santa Fe, 1941), 21-26. Article 12. In the universities and colleges, in school and other learning centers, the public education and instruction would be organized and directed according to the dogmas and moral of the Roman religion. Religious instruction will be mandatory in those centers, and it will be observe in them the pious practices of the Roman religion.

5   Francisco Ordóñez, *Historia del Cristianismo en Colombia* (Medellin, Colombia: Tipografía Union, 1956), 56.

The fraternal missionary bonds that were supposed to exist among missionaries were not established between Rev. Candor and Rev. Pond because of their theological positions. In a letter to Robert Speer, President of the Board of Foreign Missions in New York City, Rev. Candor complained of the division in the Barranquilla station. He argued, "We are divided in our opinion. I belong to the conservative party in the Presbyterian Church. Pond belongs to the advance party. We are in a delicate position in the face of the enemy."[6] Candor constantly was accusing Pond of not holding to the Presbyterian confessions of sin, the atonement, and the authority of God's Word. In the midst of theological controversy among the missionaries, the first chapel in Barranquilla was formed in 1890 in a rented lot.

In 1895, Rev. and Mrs. David C. Montgomery arrived to the city of Barranquilla. Montgomery was commissioned to work in the chapel of the town. It seems that Rev. Montgomery had real desires to work as a missionary, but was suspicious as to the ability of native members. In a letter to Rev. Benjamin Leberee on September 24, 1896, Montgomery relates part of his ministerial accomplishments:

> Our chapel which is small was filled almost to being uncomfortable last Sunday night. One Hundred-Twenty in the room seated and a large number standing at the doors and windows were present. The congregation has never been so large as now. I am now preaching every Sabbath evening. I began three or four months ago by preaching once in three weeks, then every two weeks and now every Sabbath. The people are not satisfied to listen to one of their own number (as well as Coll and Martinez would do) when there is a minister here. The school miss Hunter had charge of is in a very fair condition considering we have *only native teachers in charge.*[7]

Montgomery was a young minister in his first experience as missionary. Somehow, things were not going well for Rev. Pond in the mission. By 1896, there were four female missionaries in Barranquilla and only two men. Rev. Pond perceived that his power as an ordained minister was diminished by Martha Bell Hunter, headmaster of the girl's school. Rev. Pond believed that Hunter wanted to run the mission according to her ideals. Pond saw in Montgomery an easy ally who could do his dirty work. As expected, Montgomery assumed a hostile attitude against the female missionaries. The female missionaries thought that Montgomery was hostile against them for their different interpretations as the real meaning of evangelization. Hunter complained in a letter to Rev. Laberee dated December 12, 1896, "Sometimes Mr. Montgomery is very hostile when defending his positions about evangelization. He told me that God has appointed preaching as the only method of extending the gospel and it seems clear to him that if we do not "preach," the gospel will not be extended. I understand that we neglect the

6   Rev. Thomas Candor to Rev. Robert Speer, January 5, 1893. The Colombian Mission, 1833-1911. Microfilm Boston University School of Theology Library.
7   David Montgomery to Rev. Benjamin Leberee, September 24, 1896. Philadelphia: The Presbyterian Historical Society.

work of itinerating in may occasions, but our work in the girl's and boy's schools is directed by the evangelical witness of our Lord Jesus Christ and always our aim is to form Christ in our students."[8] The problems in the Barranquilla station increase to the point that the Board of Foreign Mission had to intervene in the matter through an official investigation. The Board decided that both Rev. Pond and Rev. Montgomery were to be retired from the field as soon as possible. The Montgomery's were requested to return to the United States, while the Pond's were reassigned to Caracas, Venezuela. The only missionaries who stayed in Barranquilla were the female missionaries and the Candors.[9]

Rev. Melbone W. Graham, who was transferred from the Bogota Station after the forced retirement of Pond and Montgomery, attributed the lack of results in the Barranquilla station to their evangelistic tactics. The Barranquilla station had shown a small growth by that time: only 300 members, not a single native minister, and only one male evangelistic worker employed. These were facts that worried the Board in New York to the extent that they considered closing the station. According to Rev. Graham,

> The problem is that the majority of the members of the station give the major part of their time and strength to educational work. Mrs. Graham and I have given the greater part of our service to that side of work, and we do not hesitate to affirm our conviction that the results in both stations do not justify that expenditure. As evangelistic agencies the schools cannot be pronounced a success. We should close both schools for three years and dedicate every missionary to evangelistic work.[10]

The arrival of Alfred H. Story in 1897 was a great blessing for the Barranquilla station. Story served in Venezuela as a colporteur and itinerating preacher for the American Bible Society. The Barranquilla station decided to give him an affiliate membership with the usual right to vote in station meetings. Story was in charge of the chapel of the city and itinerating preaching. In his pastoral duties, Story emphasized his work with young people. For him, the youth was the most promising conduit to spread the gospel in Colombia. He organized the youth into a Christian society. The aim of the society was to attract young men under the influence of the gospel and trained them in to be lay workers and evangelists. In 1898, Story was approach by the station to initiate a school for boys. He argued,

> While I do not think that education can in any way take the place of the preaching of the gospel in our work, and I do not advocate the using up of our energies in

8   Martha Bell Hunter to Rev. Benjamin Laberee, December 12, 1896. Philadelphia: The Presbyterian Historical Society.

9   The Board of Foreign Mission to the Barranquilla Station, November 24, 1896. The Colombia Mission Files, 1833-1911.

10   Rev. Melbone W. Graham to Rev. Arthur James Brown, June 10, 1907. The Colombia Mission, 1833-1911.

> any work that is not strictly evangelical, yet I firmly believe, after seventeen years in Roman Catholic countries, that we must take advantage of every means that comes in our way to drive out the false ideas that priest craft tries to instill into the minds of the people, respecting us and our mission; and education is of the powerful means.[11]

In February 1899, the school for boys was opened with a high registration of twenty-three boys. Story was proud of the fact that the school from its very start was self-supporting. He stated, We have open to the public the school for only ten days and in that time we are glad to state that we have started as good as school as can be in Barranquilla, what is more, *paying its own expenses*."[12] Miss Hunter was moved from the girl's school to be in charge of the primary and boarding departments, as well as treasurer. That same year on October 3, Rev. and Mrs. Walter Scott Lee arrived to Barranquilla. He was placed in charge of the boy's school giving more time to Rev. Story for evangelistic work. The boy's school was successful in its first years of operation. Rev. Story resigned from the Presbyterian mission in 1902 and was commissioned by the American Bible Society to Cuba for evangelistic work. The small success of the boy's school was interrupted when the War of the Thousand Days erupted from 1899 to 1902. Nonetheless, when the school reopened in 1903 it had an attendance of one hundred-thirty-five boys and in the girl's school an enrollment of one-hundred-ten.[13]

Bible Women in Mission

Great accomplishments were achieved in the short period of time (1904-1910) that Miss Lena Hastings worked in Barranquilla. She was the first Bible woman in the port city who had a distinctive plan to evangelize native women. Her approach to missions resembles the shift from the missiology of Women's Work for Women to that of World Friendship. Even though Dana Robert argues that a definite missiological shift was clearly seen by 1916 in the study book *World Missions and World Peace* by Caroline Atwater Mason for the Central Committee for the United Study of Missions, the work of Hastings comes very close to the missiology of World Friendship. The missiology of World Friendship fully develop after the First War. Western missions and missionaries were questioned about their claims of moral and ethical superiority in the midst of armed conflict between Christian nations. Robert argues that "World Friendship assumed that western culture no

---

11 Personal Report of Alfred L. Story to the Barranquilla Station, March 8, 1998. The Colombian Mission, 1833-1911.

12 Personal Report of Alfred L. Story to the Barranquilla Station, March 8, 1998. The Colombian Mission, 1833-1911

13 General Report of the Barranquilla Station for the Year 1904. The Colombian Mission, 1833-1911.

longer had a monopoly on virtue, and that women around the world stood poised to lead their own people not to western Christian civilization, but to their own forms of Christian life."[14] Even though Hastings did not construct missions as peace and justice, nor was she promoting theories of indigenization, her evangelistic approach was totally new to the Colombian mission.

For Hastings, native women should be approached in their houses as friends. She argued, "before definite work can be done we must make the woman a friend, for few if any will have any desire to know anything about Christ until that desire is awakened in them through friendship."[15] Hastings recognized that there was a barrier between the missionaries and the natives in their social outlook because Colombian women thought that the missionaries were rich. In response to the social and economic divide, she organized Bible classes for women who attended the local church. After their initial training in Bible lessons, these local women were ready to discuss religious themes with the women they visited.

As early as 1906, a partnership was emerging between the missionary and the missionized. The women who received the teachings of the missionary became themselves Bible women who taught their friends about the gospel. One example of this practice was Hastings' friendship to Isabel Manjarres. She was a graduate of the girl's school and was working there as a math teacher. Both Hastings and Majarres developed a deep friendship bounded by the love of Christ. They founded the *Tabita Society*, a group of females from First Presbyterian. Through the efforts of these single females, the gospel was spread in Barrio Boston. The Society contributed $2,382,60 for the erection of a school and chapel, and after a year the new school was opened.[16] The evidence of how single missionary women uplifted the capabilities of progress in the natives is seeing through the power and vision of Majarres in opening a school in Barrio Boston.

Also, native leaders were taught in the arts of cleanliness in the home, better hygienic conditions, and training children. Hastings also saw the visitation of sick people as one of the greatest opportunities to share the gospel with native families. All these efforts of forming friendships and establishing relationships in the community were part of the evangelistic work of the Bible woman. Apart of being a Bible woman, on Sunday afternoons, Hastings taught the Gospel of Matthew to a group of Jamaican immigrants. After this class, Hastings was in charge of organizing cottage meetings in the neighbor towns of the city. Also, she taught three classes in the boy's school: one Bible and two English classes, and dedicated

---

14 Dana L. Robert, *American Women in Mission*, 272-273.
15 Lena Hastings, "Plan for Developing Evangelistic Work among Women," February 20, 1905. The Colombian Mission, 1833-1911.
16 Barranquilla Evangelistic Report, 1910. The Colombia Mission (Philadelphia: The Presbyterian Historical Society).

three afternoons a week for itinerating work visiting house to house.[17] Once again, the problematic climate of Barranquilla caused serious health conditions to Miss Hastings who returned to the United States in 1910.[18]

The first meeting of the Colombia Mission was held in Barranquilla in September 23, 1910. It was the first time for some of the missionaries to get acquainted with each other. The Barranquilla station was represented by Rev. and Mrs. Lee, Miss Jessica Scott, and Martha Bell Hunter. The representatives from Bogota were the Rev. and Mrs. Charles Spencer Williams, the Rev. Thomas Barber, and Miss Ethel Towle. Some missionaries were not present in the meeting such as Rev. and Mrs. Thomas Candor of Bogota, Miss Leila Quinby of Barranquilla for furlough reasons. As it was expected, the first topic in the agenda was that of evangelistic work.

The Barranquilla station presented their report as one of great opportunities and open doors for the propagation of the gospel. Barranquilla was surrounded by more than one-hundred towns and villages. The station reported three Departments that were waiting for missionaries to implement schools and a chapel: Atlantico (population 104,604), Bolivar (population 287,000), and Magdalena (population 123,548). The town of La Cienega was located eighty miles east of Barranquilla. They manifested to the missionaries their eagerness for schools and a chapel in the town. In the Magdalena River the doors were opened for the gospel. They also wanted a missionary for the erection of schools and a chapel.[19] The missionaries had great enthusiasm while seeing the possibilities of what could be accomplish in such a great field of "lost souls." Nevertheless, there were only three missionaries at that time in the station and the lack of resources prevented them from taking care of the new venture.

Training of Native Leaders: Where are the Women?

One of the biggest obstacles for the establishment of an indigenous Presbyterian Church in Colombia was the lack of ordained native workers. The first step to ordained native workers was in 1916 when the Mission in its business

---

17 Lena Hastings to Dr. Brown, February 24, 1905. The Colombia Mission, 1833-1911. The report shows that Hastings had made one-hundred-thirty-one evangelistic visits that year.

18 The climate of Barranquilla was mortal for many North American missionaries. More than thirty missionaries abandoned the field or died because of sickness. Missionaries or family members who died in the field were Miss Juanita Pratt, Rev. Sharpe, Miss Adeliza Ramsey, and Mr. Willis Findley. Missionaries who abandoned the field due to sickness were Miss Esther Buxton, Miss Johanna Blink, Miss Lena Hastings, Mrs. Ladd, Miss Martha Bell Hunter, Mrs. Caldwell, and Mrs. Graham. The Colombia Mission, 1833-1911.

19 Ibid.

session approved a plan to develop a well prepared national ministry. The program was place in the hands of Rev. Candor, the ultraconservative preacher. Natives seeking ordination were subjected to the same rigorous theological standards as North Americans in confessing the Word of God as inerrant. Missionaries taught as essential the virgin birth of Jesus through a miraculous act of the Holy Spirit in Mary, Jesus' true divinity and humanity, his bodily resurrection, and his return to judge the living and the death. The missionaries taught salvation from sin and eternal punishment was not obtained through good works, nor by the observance of the law; but as a gift of God which the repentant sinner received by faith in the redemptive work of Jesus Christ. The itinerating missionaries spread a form of Christianity that resembled the conservative side of the Presbyterian Church. The same conflicts that were addressed in the United States were transported to the mission field, in this case Colombia.

In 1919, the first Colombians who graduated from the program were Sebastian Berrios, Campo Elias Mayarga, and Juan Libreros Camargo. The second class of students consisted of Julio Hernandez, Humberto Mendez, and Antonio Redondo. The first student who registered from the rural area was Francisco Benitez and two more students registered in 1921: Manuel Manga and Juan Libreros. After three years of experimentation, the small project of training national workers was discontinued by the Mission. The training of national workers in Barranquilla was discontinued for a plan to establish an Industrial and Agricultural Bible Training School. The reasons given for this decision were the following:

1. There seemed to be no more candidates in Barranquilla.

2. The only candidates that seemed to be available for ministerial training were to be found in small rural communities. Men from 18 to 25 years of age who had enjoyed no opportunity for study beyond the fourth grade of primary school.

3. It was thought wise to train these men for the work in the rural areas.[20]

The Industrial and Agricultural Bible Training School opened its doors in February 2, 1925. The first graduate was Gustavo Villa in 1928. The course of studies consisted of four years of scholastic training and one doing practical work as evangelists or local pastors. The new project struggled to survive years with a very low percentage of students registered. The institution did not produce another graduate until 1935 when Julio Orozco finished his studies. The mission constantly failed to provide a solid training for national workers who could take control of the work in the country. The project of establishing a rural school for ministers had little success in producing native leaders who could guide the church.

---

20 Evangelistic Report of the Barranquilla Station for 1923, The Colombia Mission (Philadelphia: The Presbyterian Historical Society).

By 1930, Presbyterian missionaries had opened five stations throughout the country. In 1856, the Bogota station was the first center to spread Protestantism in Colombia under Rev. Pratt. Barranquilla opened as a station in 1888 when Rev. Candor was commissioned by the Bogota station as itinerant preacher to that city. A third station was opened in the Department of Antioquia. Rev. and Mrs. Touzeau were the first Presbyterian missionaries to arrive at Medellin in 1889. In 1912, the fourth station of the Presbyterian mission was organized in Bucaramanga, Department of Santander. The Rev. and Mrs. Charles Williams labored in this field for eight years until in 1920 Rev. and Mrs. Thomas Crocker arrive at the field. The last station that the Presbyterian Mission opened was in the coast. It had as center of operations the city of Cerete, on the Sinu River. Also, the work in the city of Cartagena was attached to this station. The Rev. and Mrs. John Jarrett arrived to the Sinu region in 1913.[21] This last station was integrated to Barranquilla making it the biggest station in Colombia.

The year 1930 witnessed a change in government that will facilitate the work of missionaries in preaching the gospel. In 1930, Dr. Olaya Herrera was elected as the first liberal to occupy the presidential post in the twentieth century. As stated above, the term of Olaya was a transition moment in the life of the country. The new president served as a conciliatory figure uniting a moderate front of Liberals and Conservatives implementing social and economical reform in a time of world crisis. When the missionaries arrived at Barranquilla, the city's population was 45,000. The roads were of dirt with no pavement.[22] The economy was derived from the port were many locals worked. Barranquilla was a cosmopolitan center because of the many nations entering the port to conduct business. Also, the city was one of the most open to other religious traditions because the Roman Church was weak and because the many ethnic groups entering the city for commerce. By 1940, the city has tripled its population to 145,000 inhabitants. Its cosmopolitan character and religious freedom gave missionaries a fertile soil to plant the gospel. The schools of Barranquilla had produced many national workers who established schools of their own following the structure of the missionary schools. The Barranquilla Station Survey of 1940 shows that Miss Ana Carmela opened a small school in Cartagena; Miss Elvira Coll de Mendez and Ana Polo opened a school in the neighborhood of San Carlos; Mrs. Catalina de Orjuelo initiated a school in Cerete; Miss Sornesta Guitierrez opened a school in Sitio Nuevo, and Miss Maria del Real started a school in Cienaga. The schools were at the cutting edge of society been the first ones who approved a coeducational curriculum, and by 1942, the schools for boys and girls constituted one single Colegio Americano de Barranquilla. The itinerating work was also flourishing under national workers. In the Sinu Valley, Rev. Juan Libreros was in charge of the work. He had twenty-

---

21   Reginald W. Wheeler and Webster E. Browning, *Modern Mission in the Spanish Main: Impressions of Protestant Work in Colombia and Venezuela* (Philadelphia: The Westminster Press, 1925): 229-337.

22   Martha Bell Hunter to Rev. Arthur J. Brown, November 14, 1898. The Colombia Mission (Philadelphia: The Presbyterian Historical Society.)

seven preaching points throughout the region and had three churches under his care: Salamina, Nazareth, and San Juan. The three churches of Barranquilla were under national pastors: Rev. Escorcia, Rev. Hernandez, and Rev. Reyes.

Conclusion:

The evangelistic work was accomplished through two different approaches: education and itinerating. Missionaries in educational work were more interested in promoting the gospel to the middle and upper classes through a sound and robust education cemented in the Bible and Protestant doctrines. They were more intimate with their subjects as the case of Miss Hunter who visited every Christmas all the student households; or Miss Manjarees who saw a vision of a better future for children in a poor neighborhood and opened a school there with the help of a woman's society of a local church. Nevertheless, Robert argues, "Many missionary women also shared the crusading optimism and sense of superiority of their fellow citizens during the height of western imperialism from approximately 1885 to the end of the First World War."[23] Thus, single female missionaries transferred those values as conditioned by their cultural, social, and political reality in the United States.

Itinerary preachers emphasized more the results of their adventures in the distant parts of the country than the true vitality of their work after they leave. Many times the itinerary preacher traveled days on horseback to a distant village to spread the gospel through literature and preaching. Most of the time, they were received with open arms by the liberals of the village or city, but the first thing that the Colombians asked was for the erection of a school. Preachers like Rev. Jarrett, Rev. Story, and Rev. Mayorga were constantly traveling and opening new centers of preaching. The only problem was that they stayed for a very short period of time and did not prepare well enough the new members who received the Protestant message of salvation. The theological statements of this group of missionaries resemble those of the rigorous Princeton old school theology. The doctrine of the Word of God was emphasized over all doctrines giving its followers a certificate of membership into the body of Christ. Natives seeking ordination were subjected to the same rigorous theological standards as North Americans in confessing the Word of God as inerrant. Missionaries taught as essential the virgin birth of Jesus through a miraculous act of the Holy Spirit in Mary, Jesus' true divinity and humanity, his bodily resurrection, and his return to judge the living and the death. The missionaries taught salvation from sin and eternal punishment was not obtained through good works, nor by the observance of the law; but as a gift of God which the repentant sinner received by faith in the redemptive work of Jesus Christ. The itinerating missionaries spread a form of Christianity that resembled the conservative side of the Presbyterian Church. The same conflicts that were addressed in the United States were transported to

---

23   Dana L. Robert, *American Women in Mission*, 136.

the mission field, in this case Colombia. One could conclude that the theological development of the first national Colombian leaders was a form of indoctrination to the old conservativism within the Presbyterian Church USA. In this case, the more inclusive, maternal, and holistic missiology of single female missionaries was ignored and a more restrictive mission theory that saw mission as the proclamation of the Word endured for several decades.

Mary McLeod Bethune:

Christ Did Not Designate Any Particular Color to Go

Mary Cloutier

Introduction

Mary McLeod Bethune has a revered place in American history, as an educator, social reformer and political figure. She was born in freedom to a large family that had known the deprivations and injustice of slavery. Her life spanned from 1875 until the mid-1950s, allowing her to speak to, and participate fully in, the social transformation of the twentieth century. Despite her many accomplishments and influence in American history, Mary was prevented from realizing her girlhood dream of becoming a missionary in Africa, when her application to the Presbyterian Board of Mission was denied. Mary would later temper the injustice by suggesting that her missionary calling was based on a selfish desire for travel and excitement. However, hidden in the Presbyterian archives is a handwritten letter from Mary to the Presbyterian Board, which reflects her true perspective on their decision, and reveals that Mary was *certain* of her calling and qualification for mission service— and that the Board's decision was based solely on her ethnicity.

Mary McLeod

Mary McLeod Bethune was the fifteenth of seventeen children, but the first child born in freedom, and the first in her family to receive an education. Her parents recognized that Mary was unusually gifted, and were certain that she would accomplish much in her life. It was during her childhood that the Presbyterian Board opened a school in her hometown of Mayesville, SC. Teachers, both black and white, arrived from the north to offer education to children of color in the former slave states.

Mary's primary education ended when she was twelve. Convinced that she should continue her schooling, Mary prayed that God would make a way for her to go to high school. Her prayers were answered when her teacher came with the good news that a lady in Denver, a Miss Mary Crissman, offered to pay for one African American girl to attend the prestigious Scotia Seminary in a neighboring state. Mary was chosen out of all the eligible children of her school. Her family and friends celebrated this rare opportunity, collecting necessary clothing and materials, and seeing Mary off at the train station.

Miss Mary Crissman

While most biographies describe Mary McLeod's benefactress as a *Quaker and seamstress,*[1] Mary Crissman was, in fact, an educated professional woman, the unmarried daughter of a prominent Presbyterian minister and educator. Her father, the Rev. George T. Crissman had pastored for years in Illinois, but relocated to the western states as a missionary church planter and educator, first in Nebraska, then in Colorado. Mary Crissman always lived with her parents in the minister's manse, though she continued her work as a teacher for decades. She was a mere *eight years older* than Mary McLeod, herself, and would have been in her early twenties when she offered to pay for her tuition at Scotia Seminary. Mary McLeod Bethune, herself, noted that Miss Crissman earned the scholarship money by doing sewing after school hours (Johnson, 1940). Little public information is available on Mary Crissman, but census reports and community directories of the time period invariably list her as a teacher. Her greatest, most lasting kingdom contribution seems to be her support and encouragement of the person who was to become Mary McLeod Bethune. Mrs. Bethune, many years later, thought of Miss Crissman every time she accomplished a new thing or made some contribution (Walworth, 147). Miss Crissman was among a number of godly, single professional women—white and black--who had influenced Mary and served as her models in her own educational ministry.

Scotia Seminary

Mary was likely twelve years old when she transitioned to Scotia Seminary (Walworth, 147), and finished her studies there at the age of nineteen. Mary would note that she was never the brightest scholar, but she was known for her energy, friendliness, hard work and giftedness in practical skills, such as cooking. She was a great favorite among the scholars and teachers. It was during her years at Scotia that Mary became a member of the Presbyterian Church, and eventually sensed God's calling upon her life to serve as a missionary in Africa.[2]

Chartered in 1870, Scotia Seminary prepared African American girls "for usefulness, as teachers and missionaries among their own people in the Southern States and in Africa" (Ladies' Board, 1872b, 135). While many of the pupils worked part-time to help pay for their tuition, Scotia Seminary invited readers of various Presbyterian magazines to contribute to their scholarship at $45 per annum per student (Woman's Executive Committee, 180).

---

1   Sterne, 56; Peare, 49; Hanson, 37. More contemporary biographies (McCluskey and Smith, 42) cite the Johnson interview, and correctly state that Miss Crissman was a teacher, and that she paid for the scholarship through sewing earnings.

2   Card file for Mary McLeod, Moody Bible Institute archives.

Scotia Seminary pupils were encouraged toward missions in Africa as missionary women often visited the seminary, and the pupils took part in mission society activities during their time at the school (PCUSA 1883, 143; 1895, 323). The Women's Presbyterian Board of the North-West supported a number of missionaries, both white and "colored" in Africa, including one well-known to their readers, Miss Mary Harding, a college-educated woman of color who served in Gaboon, Africa, from 1882 to 1889, with the Presbyterian Board of Missions (WPBM-NW, 16). The Women's Board of the Northwest hoped that Miss Harding and one other woman of color would be the first of many missionaries of African descent; they expected that Scotia Seminary would serve as a "feeder" of this supply, preparing missionaries of African descent, "for the education of colored youth of each sex"(WPBM-NW, 16-17).

For years, the Presbyterian Board of Missions affirmed the need for African American missionaries in Africa (BFM 1885, 56; 1886, 296), and offered education and ministerial training to that end. The Board periodically polled their white missionaries in Africa on their willingness to receive "colored brethren" as co-laborers on the field (Reading 1882; 1889; Nassau 1889), and the responses revealed two common concerns: that such candidates might not have the necessary education and qualifications, and that their presence may cause racial tensions among missionaries, and between the mission and the African church (BFM 1895). While the Presbyterian Board was investing in the education and training of African Americans for ministry, their foreign missionaries resisted their appointment to a common mission field. African American missionary applicants were thus given a mixed message: that they were wanted, needed and qualified to serve in mission work in Africa, but that there was no placement opportunities on the field (Nassau 1895; Stewart 1895). While Mary McLeod was still at Scotia Seminary, it appears that Miss Isabella Nassau, of the Gaboon Mission, began a conversation about Mary's coming to work with her on that field. It is not clear whether they had met in person, but Miss Nassau knew "Miss McLeod" by name and reputation, and was in correspondence with Mrs. Satterwhite, of Scotia Seminary, regarding Mary's plans to serve as a missionary in Africa.

Moody Bible Institute

Mary graduated from Scotia the same month that she turned nineteen, in July 1894, and transferred to Moody Bible Institute to further prepare to be a missionary, with the continued financial support of Miss Crissman. Her Moody transcript notes that Mary was recommended by Rev. A. C. Johnson at the Maysville Institute, and Mrs. Satterwhite, of Concord (Scotia) Seminary. In the "Personal Character" section is written "Colored. A bright girl and a good student. A good worker and used in bringing her own people to the Lord. Fine singer and conducts a choir very ably." (MBI, 2016).

While a student at Moody, Mary was involved in practical ministries, singing and preaching at the Pacific Garden Mission, and to the inmates at the police department, and serving in various choir activities. Five months into her studies at Moody, Mary received devastating news from the Presbyterian Board of Mission concerning her application to be a missionary. There is no known record of their letter, but Mary's careful but honest response to the Mission Board gives the reader a sense of what the letter conveyed. Mary waited seven weeks before composing this response to the Presbyterian Board of Missions:

> Dear Friends: —Your letter of Dec. 18ᵗʰ 1894 has been before me for sometime [sic]. I have prayed over that letter time and time again asking the Holy Spirit to give me only out of that letter what you intended me to have. I think I have been rather unfortunate in getting out of it what I have. Indeed, friends and co-workers for the Lord Jesus Christ, I have not been aware of the fact that you have not been sending out Colored Missionaries to Africa or I would not have attempted an exception to your rules. It seems to me that if the Lord Jesus Christ were here on earth in person and wanted someone to go on an errand for Him, He would not discuss the covering He has placed upon the bodies His blood bought people to protect the flesh He has made. As I sit here at my table writing you I can see my Saviour struggling with that heavy cross up Calvary's Mount, I am told that a man attempted to help my blessed Saviour bear the cross! I wonder did the Lord Jesus Christ stop to see whether that man was white or "colored." Dear Friends, I would have looked for almost any other difficulty than the one presented me in your letter. Christ has called me to the work. His command is to "Go." I am so glad He has counted me worthy to lay this Great Command upon my heart. I am so glad he did not designate any particular color to Go. Friends, my plans concerning my stay here in the Bible Institute have been changed and I would like to hear your decision as early as possible so that I may know what to definitely ask the Lord for. May He indeed guide you in your work for Him. Mary J. McLeod. (McLeod 1895, underlining in the original)

Mary may have misremembered these details some five decades later, during her interviews with Mr. Charles S. Johnson and others. She chose to conclude her studies after only one year (MBI, 2016), at which time she transitioned to full-time ministry in the south, with the Presbyterian Freedman's Board. An interview with Mary many years after the event gives the impression that she spent two years at Moody, and then received the letter of rejection. Mary's memoirs give the impression that she received her rejection letter from the Presbyterian Board with great disappointment, and with little question.

Archives of the Moody Bible Institute suggest that D. L. Moody may also have dissuaded Mary from foreign mission work. A broadcast screenplay of her life, aired in early 1958,[3] suggests that Mary had a conversation with Moody in

---

3 The program was aired by the National Broadcasting Company television network on Sunday, February 9, 1858, with the cooperation of the National Council of the Churches of Christ in the US (DeRemer).

his office, during the course of which he suggested to her that her desire to serve overseas was "frivolous" and based on a selfish desire for travel and excitement (Branch, 17). In the script, Moody essentially convinces Mary that serving overseas would be a "false step" and that all of her promise and education would be "gone for naught" (Ibid) while teaching among her own people in the South would be a better use of her giftedness (Branch, 18).

Far away, in Equatorial Africa, the Presbyterian missionaries discussed whether they would receive Miss McLeod as a missionary (or assistant) on their field. While they had no misgivings about Mary or her qualifications, the missionaries openly discussed whether she would be equal to other missionaries in pay, voting rights and social standing, due to her being a person of color. Though many voted in her favor, a majority of those eligible to vote were against her coming. Miss Isabella Nassau wrote a letter to the Presbyterian Board, expressing her conviction that Miss McLeod ought to receive appointment, "on account of her especial call and intelligent consecration" (I. Nassau 1895b). If the Board was willing to go through with the appointment, Miss Nassau would be willing to donate fifty dollars towards Miss McLeod's salary, and offer her room and board, at no charge. Once again, Mary had an advocate and supporter, in the form of a single, educated Christian teacher. By the time Miss Nassau wrote this final appeal, Mary McLeod had long since changed her plans, and had given up the idea that she would serve as a missionary in Africa, and had already begun her teaching ministry in the South, with the Presbyterian Freedmen's Board.

Conclusion

Mary McLeod Bethune used her education and ministry training towards lasting and necessary contributions in education and race relations in America in the twentieth century. She often credited professional Christian women, her teachers in the mission schools, as well as her benefactress, Miss Crissman, as her models and greatest champions.

Few know that Mary McLeod was called and prepared for missionary service in Africa, but was turned away because of her ethnicity. Mrs. Bethune's own biographical history indicates that she was affirmed and encouraged in this calling, while institutional archives offer a deeper glimpse into the attitudes and presumptions of that time period which prevented educated and fully-qualified African Americans like Mary from serving on the predominantly white mission fields in the late nineteenth century Africa.

Works Cited

Board of Foreign Missions of the Presbyterian Church of the United States of America.

    1885. *The Forty-eighth annual report of the Board of Foreign Missions of the Presbyterian Church.* New York: Mission House. http://books. google.com/books?id=bAfPAAAAMAAJ (accessed March 16, 2016).

    _____. 1886. *The forty-ninth annual report of the Board of Missions of the Presbyterian Church in the United States of America.* New York: Mission House. http://books.google.com/ books?id=bAfPAAAAMAAJ (accessed March 16, 2016).

    _____. 1895b. Colored missionaries: Opinions of individual missionaries of the Gaboon and Corisco Mission. Record Group 142, Folder 33. American Negroes: Proposals for appointment to W. Africa Mission: Correspondence; Policy statements; Reports; Background Papers: 1894-1924. Philadelphia: Presbyterian Historical Society.

Branch, William.
    1958. Light in the southern sky: Script written for "Frontiers of Faith," aired February 9, 1958. Bethune file, C-B-B563. Moody Bible Institute Archives.

DeRemer, Bernard R
    Letter to Mr. F. Alton Everest, dated February 6, 1958. Bethune file, C-B-B563. Moody Bible Institute Archives.

Fisk University.
    Catalogue of the officers and students of Fisk University, Nashville, Tennessee, 1905-1906. Nashville: Marshall and Bruce.

Gibson, F. T.
    Two synods among the freedmen. *The Church at Home and Abroad,* 8(1): 51.

Hanson, Joyce Ann.
    2003. *Mary McLeod Bethune and Black Women's Political Activism.* Columbia, MO: University of Missouri Press.

Janosz, Jamie.
    2014. When others shuddered: Eight women who refused to give up. Chicago: Moody Publishers.

Johnson, Charles Spurgeon.
Transcript of Dr. Charles Spurgeon Johnson's interview with Mary McLeod Bethune, circa 1940. https://www.floridamemory.com/onlineclassroom/marybethune lessonplans/sets/interview/?set=4 (accessed 16 March 2016).

Killingray, David.
2003. The black Atlantic missionary movement and Africa, 1780s-1920s *Journal of Religion in Africa* 33(1): 3-31.

Ladies Board of Missions of the Presbyterian Church.
1871. "Our mission field." *The Field is the World* 1(1): 1-3.

_____. 1872a. Home Work. *The Field is the World* 1(3): 82-84.

_____. 1872b. Scotia Seminary. *The Field is the World* 1(5): 135-136.

_____. 1874. Scotia Seminary: From Miss McNeil's letters. *The Field is the World* 3(4): 390-391.

Lake, Marilyn and Henry Reynolds.
2008. Drawing the global color line: White men's countries and the international challenge of racial equality. New York: Cambridge University Press.

McCluskey, Audrey Thomas and Elaine M. Smith, editors.
1999. Mary Mcleod Bethune: Building a better world: Essays and selected documents. Indianapolis: Indiana University Press.

Moody Bible Institute Archives.
File Mary C Bethune [sic]—B—B563. Chicago: Moody Bible Institute Archives. Accessed March 2016.

Nassau, Robert Hamill.
Letter to Dr. Gillespie, dated April 24, 1889, Ogove River. Africa Letters 1883—1886—1887—1888—1889, Gaboon and Corisco Mission, Vol. 18, Reel 78, Microfilm Collection, Letter 44. Philadelphia: Presbyterian Historical Society.

_____. 1895b. Letter to Dr. Gillespie, dated December 25, 1895, from Batanga. Africa Letters: Gaboon and Corisco Mission 1894-1895, Vol. 21, Reel 82, Microfilm Collection, Letter 321. Philadelphia: Presbyterian Historical Society.

Newsome, Clarence G.
   1996.   Mary McLeod Bethune and the Methodist Episcopal Church North: In but out. In *This Far by faith* (Weisenfeld and Newman, eds), 124-139.

Peare, Catherine Owens.
   1951.   Mary McLeod Bethune. New York: The Vanguard Press.

Powell, James.
   1885.   Report of the committee on the Missions in Africa. *The Missionary Herald* 81(12): 508-509.

Presbyterian Church USA.
   1878.   Scotia Seminary report. *Minutes of the General Assembly of the Presbyterian Church in the United States of America, Vol. V.* New York: Presbyterian Board of Publication.

   _____. 1882. Committee on Freedmen: An appeal for a colored girl. *The Presbyterian Monthly Record 33(11)*: 395.

   _____. 1883. Board of missions for freedmen: Scotia Seminary. *The Presbyterian Monthly Record 34(4)*: 141-143.

   _____. 1889. The Southern Whites. *Minutes of the General Assembly of the Presbyterian Church in the United States of America, Vol XII.* Philadelphia: Presbyterian Board of Publication.

   _____. 1895. *Fifty-eighth annual report of the board of foreign missions of the Presbyterian church in the United States of America.* New York: Mission House.

Reading, Joseph Hankinson.
   1882.   Letter to the Corresponding Secretary, dated September 15, 1882. Africa Letters: Gaboon and Corisco Mission 1881-1883, Vol. 13, Reel 75, Microfilm Collection, Letter 213. Philadelphia: Presbyterian Historical SocietySterne, Emma Gelders. 1957. Mary McLeod Bethune. New York: Alfred A. Knopf.

   _____. 1889. Letter to the Corresponding Secretary, dated April 5, 1889. Africa Letters: Gaboon and Corisco Mission, Vol. 18, Reel 78, Microfilm Collection, Letter 43. Philadelphia: Presbyterian Historical Society.

Stewart, Robert L.
   1895b. Letter to Rev. John Gillespie, D. D., dated January 23, 1895. Record Group 142, Folder 33. American Negroes: Proposals for appointment to W. Africa Mission: Correspondence; Policy statements; Reports; Background Papers: 1894-1924. Philadelphia: Presbyterian Historical Society.

Synod of Pennsylvania.
   1882. *Minutes of the first annual session of the synod of Pennsylvania held at Harrisburn, Penna, October 1882, with an appendix.* Harrisburg, PA: Lane S Hart.

Walston, Vaughn J. and Robert J. Stevens, editors.
   2002. African American experience in world mission: A call beyond community. Pasadena: William Carey Library.

Walworth, Dorothy.
   An unforgettable character: Mary Bethune. The Reader's Digest February 1952: 146-151. Bethune file, C-B-B563. Moody Bible Institute Archives.

Warner, Laceye C.
   2007. *Saving women: Retrieving evangelistic theology and practice.* Waco: Baylor University Press.

Weisenfield, Judith and Richard Newman, eds.
   1996. This far by faith: Readings in African-American women's religious biography. New York: Routledge.

Woman's Executive Committee of Home Missions of the Presbyterian Church.
   1887. *Home Mission Monthly* 1(8): 180.

Woman's Presbyterian Board of Missions of the Northwest.
   1883. *Twelfth annual report of the Woman's Presbyterian board of Missions of the Northwest.* Chicago: C. H. Blakely and Co.

Teaching Mission in an Age of World Christianity:

History, Theology, Anthropology, and
Gender in the Classroom

ANGEL SANTIAGO-VENDRELL

Mission and world Christianity are terms that seem to exclude each other. If Christianity is already a world religion, what is the need for mission?[1] The tension between world Christianity and mission also reveals a deeper assumption about the kind of Christianity is referenced in the statement. The assumption is that Christianity is a Western religion and once it has spread throughout the world there is no further need for missionaries to go and evangelize people in distant lands. According to Peter Phan, the myth of Christianity as a Western religion is mostly seen in the way the history of Christianity continues to be taught in contemporary seminaries and colleges by focusing on the Western tradition while ignoring or downplaying the importance of the Eastern expansion of Christianity.[2] This "institutional and parochial" way of teaching the history of Christianity is being rejected in theory by most historians, but unfortunately, mission studies is still taught in the United States as if the Western tradition is universally normative in the spread of Christianity.[3]

By the late 1970s, Andrew Walls drew attention to the fact that Christianity in the twentieth century was spreading and gaining most converts in Africa, Asia, and Latin America while at the same time Europe and North America were experiencing stagnation and decline in numbers and fervor.[4] This demographic shift and the recognition of seeing Christianity as a world religion spread in all six continents has given way to conceiving the study of mission, ecumenics, and interreligious studies under the new nomenclature of world Christianity. The new field of world Christianity studies the Christian faith as expressed in all six continents placing emphasis on the experiences of the poor, women of color, and marginalized communities in the Majority World.[5] These churches were called at one time in missionary circles the 'receiving' or 'younger' churches. Given that the majority of Christians now live in Africa, Asia, Latin America, the Caribbean and the Pacific, and that the gospel was spread mostly through indigenous Christians, how are we teaching mission in North American colleges, universities, and theological seminaries? If the explosion of Christianity in the Majority World was possible because Christianity was already being contextualized by local agency, what role do the European and North American churches play today? Are the experiences of Christians in the Majority World at the center of our teaching of

1 Peter Phan, "World Christianity and Christian Mission: Are They Compatible? Insights from the Asian Churches," *International Bulleting of Missionary Research* 32:4 (October 2008), 193-200.
2 Phan, "World Christianity and Christian Mission," 194.
3 Wilbert R. Shenk, "Toward a Global Church History," *International Bulleting of Missionary Research* (April 1996), 50-57.
4 Andrew F. Walls, *The Missionary Movement in Christian History: Studies in the Transmission of Faith* (Maryknoll, New York: Orbis Books 1997).
5 Dale T. Irvin, "World Christianity: An Introduction," *The Journal of World Christianity* 1:1 (2008), 1-26.

mission in North America? What are the new resources for teaching mission in an age of world Christianity? These questions are of significant importance to mission studies as it faces the new reality of world Christianity.

Andrew Walls in the pioneering essay, "Structural Problems in Mission Studies," argued that what was needed was a complete revamping of the curriculum in order to place the cross-cultural diffusion of Christianity as the lifeblood of the religion.[6] Walls stated, "If culture is the workplace of Christian theology, it follows that the present Christian interaction with the cultures of the South—as intricate and far-reaching in their different ways as the Hellenistic Roman—marks a new creative stage in Christian theology."[7] Justo Gonzalez evaluates the history and legacy of the discipline of Church History by engaging the changing nature and demographic makeup of the shifting center of gravity of the Christian religion as exemplified by Walls calling them "cataclysmic."[8] He argues that the old map is characterized by the centers of power—those of the North Atlantic, Europe and North America. Because Christianity is entering into a new consciousness, this requires a new map, a polycentric map.[9] This polycentric map will reflect the reality that today there are many centers, both in the actual life of the church and in the way the past history of the church is being written. This new map makes it impossible to separate the history of the church from the history of missions or the history of the expansion of the Christianity.

As Christianity has become a truly universal religion, with deep roots in every culture, it is also becoming more and more contextualized, and therefore, out of its many centers of come different readings of the entire history of the church. There is also a changing topography in the study of church history. Geography is not concerned only with the horizontal expanse of the land; it is also concerned with the vertical, with the mountains and the valleys—with the topography of the land. In this topographical changes new voices previously unheard are being heard: people of color, women, children, victims, and vanquished people are the new interlocutors who live different realities and ask new questions.[10] As Walls pointed out, "This is perhaps the first important point to remember about theology: that since it springs out of practical situations, it is therefore *occasional* and *local* in character ... It is

---

6   Walls, "Structural Problems in Mission Studies," in *The Missionary Movement in Christian History*, 143-159. First published in *International Bulletin of Missionary Research* 15 (October 1991), 146-155.

7   Walls, "Structural Problems," 146.

8   Justo L. Gonzalez, *The Changing Shape of Church History* (St. Louis, Missouri: Chalice Press, 2002), 33-46.

9   Gonzalez, *The Changing Shape of Church History*, 12-15.

10   Gonzalez, *The Changing Shape of Church History*, 19-32.

useless for us to determine what we think an African theology ought to be doing: it will concern itself with questions that worry Africans, and will leave blandly alone all sorts of questions which we think absolutely vital."[11]

David Bosch reminded us that theology ceases to be theology if it loses its missionary character. In the first century, theology was not a luxury of the world-conquering church but was generated by the emergency situation in which the missionizing church found itself. In this situation mission became the mother of theology. However, as Europe became Christian and Christianity the establish religion, theology lost its missionary dimension. Therefore, today missiology should reclaim its critical function in theological discourse by helping theology face the concrete world in local situations instead of giving universalizing principles based on the Enlightenment and Greek philosophy. As Bosch claimed, "In this role, missiology acts as a gadfly in the house of theology, creating unrest and resisting complacency, opposing every ecclesiastical impulse to self-preservation, every desire to stay what we are, every inclination toward provincialism and parochialism, every fragmentation of humanity into regional or ideological blocks, every exploitation of some sectors of humanity by the powerful, every religious, ideological, or cultural imperialism, and every exaltation of the self-sufficiency of the individual over other people or over other parts of creation."[12]

The changes in the center of gravity of Christianity must concern missiologists in the West to make an introspection of how their discipline is crafted with "a hegemony postulate" which does not allow for a mutual dialogue, but rather, the conditions for such dialogue to take place are for everybody to agree and abide by the rules imposed by the West.[13] Tite Tiénou argues that the West's self-perception about keeping the gates of scholarship secure by coercing its scientific methodology as the universal validity for real understanding presupposes its superiority over other forms of knowledge and as such is ethnocentric and colonizing.[14]

It appears that David Bosch's description of missiology as an annoying presence in the house of theology pushing it to be creative and not to conform to ideological purity mascaraed in universal categories has come to fruition in *Theology without Borders*.[15] William Dyrness and Oscar García Johnson challenge Eurocentrism in theology and propose a glocal understanding of theology that

11 Walls, *The Missionary Movement in Christian History*, 10-11.
12 David J. Bosch, *Transforming Mission: Paradigm Shifts in Theology of Mission* (Maryknoll, New York: Orbis Books, 1991), 496.
13 Tite Tiénou, "Christian Theology in a Era of World Christianity," in *Globalizing Theology: Belief and Practice in an Era of World Christianity*, Craig Ott and Harold A. Netland, eds., (Grand Rapids, Michigan: Baker Academic, 2006), 37-51.
14 Tiénou, "Christian Theology in an Era of World Christianity," 47-48.
15 William A. Dyrness and Oscar García Johnson, *Theology Without Borders: An Introduction to Global Conversations* (Grand Rapids, Michigan: Baker Academic, 2015).

is multicultural, transnational, and decolonizing. García-Johnson narrates part of his autobiography to illustrate the challenges he faces as a Latin American theologian in the United States on choosing what methodology to follow in constructing theology: the Western encyclopedia or new modalities rooted in his Latino reality? For him, Western theologians should acknowledge the politics of locality in their own theological enterprises as something that has contributed to the epistemological superiority of that tradition over other ways of knowing and relating. He challenges the Western theological establishment by proposing a "transoccidental" methodology of decolonizing theology from its Western epistemological imperialism. Transoccidentalism would be a collaborative, interdisciplinary, and glocal hermeneutics that embraces its own locality while embracing in constructive dialogue other local and global contextual realities.[16]

Doing theology in an era of world Christianity means not only decolonizing the West from its position of power and privilege, but also creating new alternatives to formulate theology. It is at this conjunction that missiology could be a beacon of light by challenging the assumed universals of the Western canon and by introducing new visions and resources to construct theology. In this sense, Phan argues that the contextual realities in which humans find themselves are resources for theology "insofar as they embody and manifest the presence and action of God and his Spirit."[17] Here the resources for doing theology are ordinary people themselves, women and girls sold into slavery, adherents of other religions and their texts and practices, non-Western philosophical traditions, diverse monastic traditions, and non-Western cultures.[18]

The first section of the APM proceeding addresses theological questions such as what theological metaphors or models for excellent teaching and learning are most generative for thinking about teaching mission studies in an age of world Christianity? What are the new resources for teaching mission in an age of world Christianity? How missiology influences theology? In the keynote address, "Teaching Mission in and for World Christianity: Content and Method," Peter Phan presents three theses for a new understanding in the relationship between mission studies and world Christianity. First, missiology is crucial in the formation and articulation of theology in an age of world Christianity. Here missiology is the handmaiden of theology. Second, missiologists must understand that business cannot continue as usual when it comes to teaching mission studies in an age of world Christianity. One of the basic and fundamental questions to be address should be the Western influence in the mission curriculum. Third, there should be a marriage between missiology and the history of Christianity. Phan argues that

---

16 Dyrness and García Johnson, *Theology Without Borders*, 16-22.
17 Peter Phan, "Doing Theology in World Christianity: Different Resources and New Methods," *Journal of World Christianity* 1:1 (2008), 27-53 [37].
18 Phan, "Doing Theology in World Christianity," 39.

"implicit in the subsequent separation between church history and missiology is the colonialist understanding of Christianity/Church as the West and mission as the Rest."[19]

William Gregory's paper "Orthopraxy, Hyper-doxy, and Pope Francis' Missionary Vision," addresses how Pope Francis has shifted missiological attention to orthopraxy while simultaneously criticizing counter-missionary approaches to thinking about doctrine and orthodoxy. This presentation explores the nature and significance of this shift in the Roman Catholic Church. Gregory explains how Francis is reemphasizing Christian identity within the Catholic Church in terms of missionary identity, which focus on the poor, the vulnerable, and the needy.

In "Theological Metaphors of Teaching Mission in An Age of World Christianity in the North American Context," David Thang Moe presents not *what* to teach, but how to teach mission in an age of World Christianity in the context of North American seminaries/theological institutions. In response to the encounter between North American teachers and Global South students, the paper proposes three theological metaphors of teaching mission as the excellent pedagogies in an age of World Christianity. First, a shepherding metaphor of guiding in which teachers as guides should know the needs of their sheep and the models of how to guide them. The second metaphor is a hospitable form of teaching that demands gift exchange between the hosts and the guests. Students have been for many years on the receiving side, but hospitable teachers should reveal their students' gifts and affirm what they have to offer by using their gifts. The third metaphor is a dialogical method of subject-centered teaching where teachers and students are co-learners to discern God's voice anew in the process of interaction. Moe concludes by defining mission as a dialogical discipline, teaching must be both mutually informative and transformative.

The final paper in this section is by Sarita D. Gallagher. "The Elephant in the Room: Towards a Paradigm Shift in Missiological Education" identify the critical need within Western academia to move from an ethnocentric understanding of theology to a global theological framework. Western missiological and theological education is often restricted to solely Western hermeneutics, methodologies, and worldview. While the rich diversity of the global Church is sprinkled throughout traditional Western education, the real vibrancy of global missiology, theology, and ecclesiology has yet to fully impact Western academia. In reflecting on this lack of diversity and inclusivity, Gallagher identify two paradigm shifts that need to take place before Western academia can engage in a true global dialogue. Gallagher

---

19 Peter Phan, "Teaching Missiology in and for World Christianity," APM Plenary Address, June 16, 2016, 9.

argues that by re-determining who has a voice in academia and by listening to global theology in transformative ways, the West can begin to engage meaningfully and humbly as an equal partner in global academic discourse.

The second section is devoted to historical questions such as what historical, biblical, or theological factors seem to be contributing to the changes one observes in mission studies in an age of world Christianity? Who are the new subjects in teaching mission in an age of world Christianity? The plenary session that addressed historical questions at the 2016 APM was "Teaching Christian Mission in an Age of World Christianity: A Reflection on the Centenary of the 1916 Panama Congress" by Philip Wingeier-Rayo. Wingeier-Rayo presents the relationship between mission and world Christianity using the Panama Congress of 1916 as an example. Wingeier-Rayo's argument is that over the last 100 years since the Panama Congress, teaching mission has shifted in its understanding of ecumenism, seen the contribution of indigenous churches and placing more emphasis on what God is doing through the Holy Spirit.

Robert L. Gallagher's essay, "Case Studies Teaching Our Contemporary Age of World Christianity," explores five case studies of educational institutions within early movements of Christian expansion from post-apostolic times to the beginning of modern missions. The movements examined are the Church of the East, Celtic Christianity, the Franciscans, Reformation with Lutheranism and Calvinism, and the modern mission platform of Pietism. Drawing from these findings, this essay will note patterns across movements, including holistic training of students together with the intensity of academics in theology and languages. The paper's historic perspectives of God's past work in mission studies can guide missiologists toward a biblical and insightful future of teaching Christian mission in an age of world Christianity.

The last essay on the historical section is by Matt Friedman. In "How the West Was Won: World Christianity as Historic Reality," Friedman argues that since the end of the previous century, there has been an increasing realization that the Church in the Majority world now forms the "majority" of the Christian population worldwide. To read much of the literature regarding this phenomenon, one would think that the idea of the church being a worldwide community was something that has arisen recently. As one glances back at the history of Christian faith, however, one is struck by the reality that the mission of the Church has *always* been "from everywhere to everywhere," and that the Gospel was brought to the West itself (insofar as the "West" could be understood to have even existed at that time) by people from "colonies" in other parts of the world. Far from mission from outside the West being a "new" thing, the situation can now be understood as a return to the historic norm, in which followers of Jesus from any part of the world can expect to be engaged in God's work among people anywhere else.

The third section deals with anthropological issues on mission and world Christianity in educational settings. Janice Horsager Rasmussen's essay "The World's Christians: Strategies for Teaching International Graduate Students in Kenya's Christian Universities" addresses how globalization influences learning processes in educational institutions and students in Africa. Her research indicates that very little is known about graduate international students "learning experiences" in the United States showing the factors that hindered and facilitated their learning as well as effective teaching strategies.

Aminta Arrington's essay, "Serving and Being Served: The Christian Practice of Hospitality Inside and Outside the Classroom," argues that hospitality as a framework for teaching mission in world Christianity is a valuable strategy whose meaning is understood in most African, Asian, or Latin American cultures better than the West. Hospitality is a practice that cultivates empathy because it requires listening and learning. Hospitality is inherently reciprocal, as all brings gifts to the table. Finally, she sees hospitality engendering transformation because it forces us to leave familiar structures and view life through the eyes of the Other. Through learning about, then practicing hospitality, my students experienced empathy, reciprocity, and transformation, all essential as we transition to the era of World Christianity.

The final section is on gender issues in mission studies and world Christianity. This section addresses questions such as What changes in one's own teaching or in an institution's curriculum are necessary for promoting gender equality in mission studies? What case studies or other instructional methods best promote gender specific mission practices? What would the study of Christianity in Africa, Asia, and Latin America look like if scholars put women into the center of their research? What does putting the experiences of majority world women at the center of our research agendas means for professors in North America? How could this process be achieved? The plenary address delivered for this section was by Mai-Anh LeTran. Mai-Ahn Le Tran's essay, "The Bodies We Teach By: (En)Gendering Mission for Global Christianities" uses critical pedagogy to invite missiologists to ponder the possibilities of a *critical intersectional pedagogical stance* that may be fitting for the teaching of "Christian mission" in an age in which Christianity remains dominant, albeit not in numbers. At this intersectional location, the missiologist is a "teaching body" inasmuch as they are an "interpreting body." Thus, to explore who missiologists are as "teachers of mission" with attention to great commissions and omissions, we ask two guiding questions: what does it mean to take seriously *our* teaching bodies? and what does it mean to take seriously the bodies *with* and *about* whom we teach?

If missiologists take their teaching bodies seriously, they will discover that their bodies are visible, vulnerable, and viable. Also if missiologists take seriously the bodies with and about whom we teach we will discover the "omissions" that many times trap us to legitimize the status quo. For LeTran, "omission" is *not* a problem of those being omitted; rather, it is a problem of those who are fighting hard to maintain their intellectual center and mono-centrism. Thus, the question for the discipline of Christian mission studies is *not* what to do with those whom we've excluded, but rather what to do with those who continue to engage in exclusionary strategies. For her, the teacher of mission may learn to become a "border- crosser" who wields the *trans*gressive power of counter-stories that subtly offer "oppositional" definitions of reality. Some call this a "pedagogy of dissent." This means we submit our own teaching bodies as "oppositional text," just as we strive to interject otherly-marked interpreting bodies as counter-texts to the teaching canon.

Mary Cloutier's essay narrates the life of Mary McLeod Bethune. Bethune was born in freedom to a large family that had known the deprivations and injustice of slavery. Her life spanned from 1875 until the mid-1950s, allowing her to speak to, and participate fully in, the social transformation of the twentieth century. Despite her many accomplishments and influence in American history, Mary was prevented from realizing her girlhood dream of becoming a missionary in Africa, when her application to the Presbyterian Board of Mission was denied. Mary would later temper the injustice by suggesting that her missionary calling was based on a selfish desire for travel and excitement. However, hidden in the Presbyterian archives is a handwritten letter from Mary to the Presbyterian Board, which reflects her true perspective on their decision, and reveals that Mary was *certain* of her calling and qualification for mission service—and that the Board's decision was based solely on her ethnicity and race.

As a conclusion, Angel Santiago Vendrell's essay, "Gendered Mission: Educational Work or Itinerating Preaching? The Mission Practice of the Presbyterian Church USA in Barranquilla, Colombia, 1880-1920," narrates two gendered based evangelistic approaches developed in the Barranquilla mission of the Presbyterian Church USA in the beginning of their missionary work to Colombia in the nineteenth century.[20] One was directed towards the proclamation of the gospel through preaching and the establishment of churches. The missionaries who used this method were more conservative in their theology and worldview. They were interested in the salvation of the soul, but never took care of the daily affairs of life. The other group also thought that they were evangelizing the Colombian people through education. This group of missionaries was theologically more liberal and their agenda of educating the middle and upper classes to influence the elites of the nation was well received by those social sectors. Even though both approaches differ in their methodology, the final goal was the same, to bring them to the blessings of Western civilization through Jesus Christ. The first part of the essay gives a historical overview of missionary work and the formation of the Presbyterian Church in Colombia, especially the missionary work in Barranquilla. In this section,

---

20 This paper was not presented at the 2016 APM meetings, but was written with the purpose of covering any of the presenter's papers in case of any emergency if they could not come to the meeting.

the female missionaries faced great setbacks and attacks against their mission theory by male missionaries. The second part addresses the ministry of Bible women who converted through the missionary efforts of the single female missionaries. The final part presents the missionary efforts to trained national leaders. One of the disparities that the section reveals is that women were not invited to participate in formal theological education while they were fierce educators, evangelists, and pillar of their communities.

APM

Conference
Proceedings

First Fruits Report for the APM

ROBERT DANIELSON, *ADVISORY COMMITTEE MEMBER*

In 2013, First Fruits Press at Asbury Theological Seminary partnered with the APM to produce a digital and print version of the association's proceedings, with the digital version to be shared freely in open access and the print copies to be purchased through an on demand printer for the cost of paper and binding only. This project resulted in the publication of the book, *Social Engagement: The Challenge of the Social in Missiological Education* in October of 2013. This endeavor has proven very successful, even more than originally anticipated. The first copy of the Proceedings has been downloaded some 5,345 times. The second proceedings called *Transforming Teaching for Mission: Educational Theory and Practice* has been downloaded around 2,197 times.

In 2015, the third proceedings were published as *What's in a Name? Assessing Mission Studies Program Titles*. It can be freely downloaded from: http://place.asburyseminary. edu/academicbooks/12/ and print versions can be purchased from this site or from Amazon. Since its January 2016 release it has been downloaded 187 times. While we can't give exact numbers this does include downloads from all over the world.

As with all First Fruit books, we are interested in making academic material available electronically for free (open access) or at a very low cost. The print volumes do cost some money as required by our print-on-demand printer to cover their costs for paper and binding, but even then the 2013 proceedings sells for $13.99 and the 2014 for $13.49. The 2015 proceedings is shorter so it costs $10.50. First Fruits Press does not make any profit off of these items.

This past year, we have been involved in two additional projects. The first is the republishing of the *Past Proceedings of the Association of Professors of Mission* in two volumes (1956-1958 and 1962-1974). Using hard to find mimeographed copies of the originals in the library at Asbury Theological Seminary, we were able to reformat these proceedings and they have been through one round of editing already. After a second round of editing and corrections, we expect these to be available by the fall in 2016.

Last year the APM generously voted to donate $1,000 to the library at Asbury Theological Seminary to be used for the work of First Fruits Press. As a second project this year, I have been working to locate rare materials in our archives related to mission and republishing them. These are materials that are not available anywhere online. In general it costs us about $100 to republish an old book, and so I have aimed to do ten mission related books to honor the donation so generously given to First Fruits Press. To date we have completed four of these books (mostly Wesleyan due to our heritage at Asbury). In each book there is a note stating that the digitization of this book has been made possible through a generous donation from the APM, and once again I would like to thank you for your generous donation. The four books completed so far are:

- *Wesleyan Mission: Their Progress Stated and Their Claims Enforced* (originally published in 1842) by Robert Adler.

- *The Life of Rev. C.F. Swartz: Missionary at Trichinopoy and Tanjore, in India* (originally published around 1830 by the American Tract Society).

- *A Brother's Portrait, or Memoirs of the Late Rev. William Barber: Wesleyan Missionary to the Spaniards at Gibraltar* (originally published in 1830) by Aquila Barber.

- *A Narrative of the Establishment and Progress of the Missions to Ceylon and India* (originally published in 1823) by W. M. Harvard.

As time allows I will continue to search for and publish six more such items to honor your generous gift.

There is one final project, I would like to possibly propose to the APM, which is a republication of Wilbur C. Harr's 1962 book, *Frontiers of the Christian World Mission Since 1938: Essays in Honor of Kenneth Scott Latourette*, which was the publication of the fifth proceedings of the APM from 1960. From my preliminary searching, it appears that the book is now in the public domain and has been reprinted by many others, but since it is a part of our legacy, I would suggest we reprint it as well. I would also like to see all of our resources linked from the website. In addition, I continue to look forward to working with APM this year to produce a fourth volume of the proceedings for the 2016 Conference in St. Paul.

Minutes of 2016 Meeting

1. The APM meeting was held at the University of Northwestern, St. Paul, MN. The meeting was called to order and opened with prayer on Friday, June 17, 2016, 2:30 p.m. by Angel D. Santiago-Vendrell, President.

2. The minutes for the 2015 meeting were submitted by David Fenrick, Secretary-Treasurer, and approved.

3. The Secretary-Treasurer's financial report was submitted and approved.

4. Angel D. Santiago-Vendrell presented the Executive Committee's Report from its meeting with the Advisory Board at Perkins School of Theology, Southern Methodist University, Dallas, TX, February 5-6, 2016. This fourth annual meeting was generously funded by the Grimes Foundation. (A special thank you to Robert Hunt for initiating this funding and partnership.)

    a. Robert Hunt noted the contribution by APM to create an application for smartphones and tablets that will host resources for local churches participating in short-term missions.

    b. The on-going partnership with First Fruits Press at Asbury Theological Seminary was discussed at the meeting. (A full report will follow later in the meeting.)

    c. There was significant discussion and planning for the 2016 APM Annual Meeting.

5.   Other Business and Announcements:

    a.   Dana Robert announced the dates of the Eastern Fellowship of Professors of Mission: October 21-11, 2016, at Maryknoll, NJ.

    b.   Robert Danielson thanked the APM for its generous gift to *First Fruits Press* at Asbury Theological Seminary. He gave a report of the present APM partnership with *First Fruits Press*, including online services and paper publication of the proceedings and papers presented at APM annual meetings. The 2015 APM Annual Meeting reports and paper presentations are available from *First Fruits*. In regards to previous online publications: to date there have been nearly 6,000 downloads of papers, in addition to numerous purchases of printed copies (book) of the papers and proceedings in their entirety. To date there have been 2,197 downloads of papers from the 2015 annual meeting papers, in addition to purchases of printed copies. A significant number of those downloads have come from countries outside the U.S.

    -    Robert Danielson and his library staff at Asbury Theological Seminary have also collected, scanned, and edited all available APM meeting papers and proceeding since 1952.

6.   APM noted the death of the following colleagues this past year, and their unique and enduring contributions to the field of missiology and the proclamation of the Gospel:

- Kenneth E. Bailey, Ecumenical Institute (Tantur), Jerusalem

- Virgilio Elizondo, University of Notre Dame

- Roger S. Greenway, Calvin Theological Seminary

- Marvin Keene Mayers, Biola University

- Roberston McQuilken, Columbia International University

- David Rambo, Asbury Theological Seminary

- Ted W. Ward, Trinity Evangelical Divinity School

- Timothy E. Yates, St. John's College, University of Durham

7.   The report of the Nominating Committee regarding the election of officers was submitted by Larry Caldwell.

    a.   Larry Caldwell, Sioux Falls Seminary, was elected President.

    b.   Linda Whitmer, Johnson University, was elected First Vice-President.

    c.   A. Sue Russell, Asbury Theological Seminary, was elected Second Vice-President.

    d.   David Fenrick, University of Northwestern, was reelected Secretary-Treasurer.

    e.   The new members of the APM Advisory Board were introduced and approved:

- Paul Lewis, Assemblies of God Theological Seminary
- Susan Maros, Fuller Theological Seminary

8.   Angel Santiago-Vendrell thanked the Executive and Advisory Committees, as well as the presenters for their contribution to the annual meeting. He also introduced the new APM President, Larry Caldwell.

9.   Larry Caldwell thanked outgoing President, Angel Santiago-Vendrell, and the Executive Committee for their outstanding work in organizing an excellent conference. He also presented the theme, followed by discussion, of the 2017 Annual Meeting – *"Teaching Mission in the Complex Public Arena: Developing Missiologically Informed Models of Engagement."*

10.   Larry Caldwell closed with prayer at 2:50 pm.

Respectfully Submitted,

David E. Fenrick
Secretary-Treasurer

Secretary-Treasurer's Report

	Credit	Debit	Balance
Opening Balance: June 18, 2015			6,327.06
Receipts			
Membership Dues Received	215.00		
Transfer from ASM (Less Conference Expenses)	1,127.76		
Expenses			
APM 2015 Meeting Honorarium & Expenses		1,477.43	
IAMS – Scholarship Fund		1,000.00	
Asbury Theological Seminary – Donation to First Fruits Press		1,000.00	
Mission Studies Renewal		338.00	
Bank Charge		37.00	
Total	1,342.76	3,852.43	**3,817.39**

Balance at Wells Fargo Bank, Minneapolis, MN, as of June 17, 2016:   **$3,817.39**

Respectfully Submitted,

David E. Fenrick
Secretary-Treasurer

Conference Schedule

APM Association of Professors of Mission
2016 Annual Meeting—University of Northwestern — St. Paul, MN

"Teaching Mission Studies in an Age of World Christianity"

Thursday, June 16

2:00pm   Advisory Committee Meeting

4:00-6:00   Registration

6:00-7:00   Dinner

7:00-7:05   Welcome to the Conference

7:05-7:40   Worship

7:40-8:40	Peter Phan, *Teaching Missiology in and for World Christianity: Content and Pedagogy*
8:40-9:00	Q&A

Friday, June 17

7:30-8:30	Breakfast
8:30-9:00	Worship
9:00-10:00	Plenary Lecture: Mai-Anh LeTran, *The Bodies We Teach By: (En)Gendering Mission for Global Christianities*
10:00-10:30	Coffee Break
10:30-12:00	(4) Parallel Sessions:10:30-11:10; 11:15-11:55

Theology	History	Anthropology	Gender	Other
David Thang Moe: Theological Metaphors of Teaching Mission in an age of World Christianity in the American Context	Robert Gallager: Historical Case Studies of Teaching Mission Studies in an Age of World Christianity	Janice Rasmussen: The World's Christians	Leanne Dzubinski: Gender, Mission, and World Christianity	Amita Arrington: The Christian Practice of Hospitality Inside and Outside the Classroom
11:15-11:55	11:15-11:55	11:15-11:55	11:15-11:55	11:15-11:55
William Gregory: Orthopraxy, Hyper-doxy, and Pope Francis' Missionary Vision	Matt Friedman: How the West was Won?	Christian Dumitrescu: Teaching Mission in Shame and Honor Contexts	Mary Cloutier: Mary McLeod Bethune	Sarita Gallagher: From Ethnotheology to Global Theologizing

12:00-1:00pm   Lunch with Guided Questions

1:15-2:15   Plenary Lecture: Phillip Wingeier-Rayo, *Teaching about Christian Mission in an Age of World Christianity: reflections on the 100th anniversary of the 1916 Panama Congress*

2:30-3:00   Business and Conclusion

* 9 7 8 1 6 2 1 7 1 6 4 0 2 *